INTENSIVE
STRUCTURAL THERAPY

ALSO BY H. CHARLES FISHMAN, M.D.

Family Therapy Techniques
(with Salvador Minuchin)

Evolving Models of Family Change
(with Bernice Rosman)

Treating Troubled Adolescents

INTENSIVE STRUCTURAL THERAPY

*Treating Families in
Their Social Context*

H. CHARLES FISHMAN, M.D.

BasicBooks
A Subsidiary of Perseus Books, L.L.C.

ISBN: 1-4701-1753-3
ISBN-13: 9781470117535

To my family, Tana, Anu, and Zev,
who lovingly make things possible;
and to my parents,
Isadore Fishman, of blessed memory, and Sophie Fishman,
who taught me to love ideas and to abhor injustice.

It takes an entire village to raise a child.
—African proverb

Contents

Acknowledgments   xi

Introduction   1

1   Basic Concepts   13

2   Assessment I: The 4-D Model   33

3   Assessment II: The Homeostatic Maintainer   57

4   The Five-Step Model of Treatment   75

5   Working with Siblings   105

6   Working with Peers   117

7   The Work Context   138

8   The Legal Context   156

9   The School Context   177

10   The Hospital Context   194

11   The Social Service Context   205

12   Epilogue: Altruism   217

References   225

Index   233

Acknowledgments

THIS BOOK is about contexts. By restructuring and recontextualizing family systems, we contextual therapists profoundly change the way families function. In so doing, we transform the selves of the individual family members.

The chapters that follow will discuss a number of broad contexts that impinge on the family and will describe numerous cases in which specific contexts were instrumental in helping to heal dysfunctional families. First, however, I wish to turn to my own personal contexts and acknowledge the people who have been important in the formulation of my ideas and their presentation here.

The demonstration project discussed in the social services chapter was made possible by a number of people. Roberta Knowlton, M.S.W., Director of the School-Based Youth Services Program in New Jersey, was invaluable in the conceptualization and implementation of this project. Much credit for the support of this project goes to the committed professionals in the New Jersey Department of Health: Bruce Segal, M.D., M.P.H., State Commissioner of Health; Terry O'Connor, Division Chief, Division of Drug Abuse and Addiction Services; Edward Tetelman, J.D., Legal and Regulatory Affairs; and Jack Farrell, M.S.W., and Pat Belmont of the Department of Health. I also thank Marcy Kniffen, M.S.W., and Linda Chudoba for providing superb case material.

Gillian Rye helped with some of the early organization of the book. Her husband, Nick Rye, has an almost uncanny ability to transcribe videotapes with "you are there" verisimilitude. I would like to thank Mike Nichols, Ph.D., for his close reading and incisive suggestions on the manuscript.

Jill Silverstein deserves special thanks for helping to coordinate the entire project. Her organizational skills served as an invaluable counterpoint to my bent toward organizational entropy.

I want to thank my friend and editor, Nina Gunzenhauser, who has once again, with this our second book together, demonstrated great skill, insight, and patience. Nina's precision with words and logic was invaluable from the outline to the final draft to the published book.

In the category of most invaluable person falls my dear friend Braulio Montalvo, whose support for this book has been inestimable. We introduced these ideas in two workshops we did together in Saratoga Springs, New York, and Santa Fe, New Mexico. As the book took shape, his incisive comments have been a constant font of wisdom. He is a true midwife of ideas in the Socratic tradition. I would also like to thank Marguerite Montalvo for her support and friendship.

Finally, I thank my family: my daughter, Anu, for being a superb research assistant, able to ferret out resources with skill, organization, and a minimum of family strife; my son, Zev, for always showing me the wonder of young lives and what is important; and my wife, Tana, for her crisp insights, searching questions, patient reading, and belief in me.

Introduction

Turning and turning in the widening gyre
The falcon cannot hear the falconer;
Things fall apart; the center cannot hold.
        —W. B. Yeats, "The Second Coming"

FAMILY THERAPY began essentially as a reform movement pitted against orthodox psychiatry and psychotherapy. Whereas some psychiatrists and psychotherapists insisted on locating problems within the identified patient, seminal thinkers such as Don Jackson (1957), Virginia Satir (1967), and Nathan Ackerman (1962) pointed to the roles families play in supporting problem behavior and led the field in developing ways to treat patients by working within the context of the family. Their new approach represented a generic paradigm shift. The patient's context became as important as his or her personality characteristics, and general systems theory was adopted as a means of conceptualizing the context and the interventions within it.

This paradigm shift proved highly beneficial. Indeed, over the course of 30 years or so, family therapy has been codified and widely taught, and family therapists have become very effective at producing change. Yet increasingly we are encountering cases in which our interventions are less successful than we would like. Many family therapists are becoming frustrated and feeling burned out; they sense that their power is eroding.

One significant reason for this loss of effectiveness is that our psychotherapeutic techniques of intervention have not changed to keep up with the changes in the institution of the family. The major changes in the size and structure of the family unit over the past several decades—increased rates of divorce, single-parent families, teenage parenthood—have been amply documented elsewhere, and there is no need to detail them here. And even in traditional families, family life has been transformed, especially by changes in work life. The participation of women in the work force has increased so dramatically that it is now the norm, rather than the exception, for mothers to work outside the home. In the majority of the families I work with, at least one of the two working parents has a second job. Juliet Schor (1991) estimates that between 1969 and 1987, the number of hours the average employed American spent on the job increased by the equivalent of one whole month a year. It is no wonder that family life has suffered. According to Richard Luov (1990), citing a 1989 report of the Research Council of Washington, D.C., the amount of time parents spend with their children has dropped 40 percent during the last century, and much of that drop has occurred in recent years. Luov goes on to report another alarming finding: "A study conducted by Pittsburgh's Priority Management Co. in 1988 revealed that the average working couple spends four minutes a day in meaningful conversation with each other, and the average working parent spends thirty seconds in meaningful conversation with his or her children" (p. 15).

During the last 20 years there have been profound changes for the worse in the conditions of American families. According to the Children's Defense Fund (1989, p. 16), among children up to 18 years of age, one in four is poor; among infants and toddlers, one in four is poor; and among black children, one out of two is poor (ibid., p. 17). Median earnings have dropped. In families where the heads of households are between 30 and 64, medial earnings have fallen 15 percent from 1973 to 1986; for families headed by someone under 30, the drop has been 30 percent (ibid.).

These profound changes reverberate through all levels of society and ethnic groups. There is a recursive loop between the economy and the social structure of the family. The economic pressures lead to unstabilized marriages, and divorce leads to more economic pressures on the family. In 1987, 34.3 percent of female-headed families were poor, compared with 10.8 percent of all families (ibid.).

The effect is a weak infrastructure supporting these families. With diminished resources, the institutions in the community decay. In a Trenton, New Jersey, high school, there are 2,900 students in a school building designed for 2,000. In the first marking period, 2,000 students received at least one F on their report card.

But as I have said, these pressures visit the middle class as well. I recently saw a couple who had just separated. They had been married a year and a half and had an 8-month-old child who had severe asthma and eczema. Each parent spent 3 hours a day commuting—Mother to her job in the New York financial district and Father to his new business—and their baby-sitter was moving away the next week.

Small wonder their marriage is under siege. Their developmental pressures—a new marriage and a new infant, compounded by the baby's illness (which is compounded by the stress in the home, perhaps)—are only exacerbated by the economic pressure on the family. Further compounding the situation is the absence of a supporting community. While the extended family was not present, neither parent spent enough time at home to create a community that could support their family.

The work force itself has become more mobile as changes in the economic climate have encouraged and sometimes forced workers to move from job to job, often to new communities away from family and other support systems. The resulting erosion of community loyalty is a further loss to the sense of security and stability in family life. At the same time, profound changes in corporations have removed the stabilizing benefit of the workplace as a relatively constant community. The British economist Charles Handy (1989) describes the emerging corporation as a "shamrock" organization, in which one leaf is the core of highly qualified professionals who are long-term employees; another is the contractual fringe of consultants; and a third is the flexible work force, too often "people of whom little is expected and to whom little is given . . . a [labor] market into which employers dip as they like and when they have the need, for as little money as they have to pay" (p. 99). This group is, of course, far larger than the core of professionals who run the organization or the consultants who advise them. (The fourth leaf represents the labor of the public, as when fast-food restaurants get customers to bus their own tables.)

In recent years, the economic insecurity that has resulted from the changes in the workplace has been severely aggravated by the stagnation of the American economy. In fact, the standard of living is declining for many middle-class American families, which have been able to keep up only because, as we have seen, mothers went to work outside the home. At the same time, however, incomes of the privileged few have soared. While the combined wages of all families in the $20,000 to $50,000 annual income bracket grew 44 percent during the 1980s, the aggregate wages of families earning over $1 million increased 2,184 percent. Moreover, the privileged few are increasing in numbers. During this same period, the number of people reporting incomes of over $500,000 a year rose from 16,881 to 183,240. We seem to be becoming a nation of the very rich and the poor, with a shrinking middle class (Bartlett & Steele, 1992).

The 1980s have become known as the decade of greed. By the end of the decade, the country had witnessed a series of scandals in the financial industry, including wrongdoing by some of Wall Street's most prestigious and respected firms. Poor judgment and downright fraud in savings and loan institutions have left the U.S. government responsible for guaranteed loans that may eventually cost taxpayers many billions of dollars. James Lincoln Collier (1991) argues convincingly that America has succumbed to an ethic of selfishness, with the attendant ills of a decline of morality and a triumph of narcissism. I certainly see evidence of such selfishness in my clinical practice as I work with couples in various stages of divorce who persist in fighting over money even when confronted with the fact that their conflict is profoundly damaging to their children. Some divorced fathers are convinced that their child-support money goes only to their former spouses for frills, as though their children have no financial needs.

For most Americans today, the economic future looks bleak. Earlier generations were sustained by the hope that their children would have a better life than they had, but today that hope is compromised by a myriad of factors, not the least of which is the burden of a national debt of such monumental proportions that just servicing it consumes a large portion of the national budget.

All of these changes have added to tensions in families and made people more difficult to live with. Moreover, research has been revealing that the family's ability to manage stress and handle developmental transitions and the attendant crises may well relate to the ways in which the family is connected to the larger social context within which it exists.

One particularly relevant study (Andrews, Tennant, Hewson, & Vaillant, 1978) showed that the availability of support from relatives, friends, and neighbors was associated with higher rates of general well-being and lower rates of physical illness. Moreover, the actual context of families is determined less by kinship, tradition, or geography than by specific social transactions family members have with others. It has been estimated that the average individual in the United States is, over his or her lifetime, embedded in a series of social relationships that include direct or indirect connections with anywhere from 200 to 4,000 people (Pool, 1973).

Thus the picture of the family as the integral and enduring element of society, complete within itself and self-sufficient, has been severely altered in recent decades. The family is fraying at the edges; its members are more stressed, have less money and less time together, and are more dependent on structures in the broader context at a time when the outside structures are themselves being seriously weakened. Family therapists, well aware of these changes, have noted and grieved over them as much as anyone else. Yet they do not seem to have seriously confronted the reality of the broader context of the contemporary family, but have, instead, largely restricted their interventions to the nuclear and extended family. They have chosen to view family distress as internally created and therefore not amenable to change from outside the family, failing to appreciate the extent to which family problems are socially constituted and maintained.

This focus on the immediate family may well have been necessary in the early stages of the development of family therapy, in order to establish a language and a model for the field. Carlos Sluzki (1985) has stated that the first generation of therapists had to observe the family in isolation to establish a theoretical focus and define boundaries with "tight" exclusionary rules. He notes, however, that while this isolationist policy was useful in establishing a model for family therapy, it separated the family from a larger, equally meaningful social context. John Schwartzman (1985) has noted the dangers and cost of this approach, pointing out that problems can often be solved only through changes in the broader system and that "in fact, if clinicians ignore this more inclusive level of organization, the problem can be maintained by the structure created but unperceived by those treating it" (p. 3).

Other consequences of this limited focus have also been pointed out by critics of family therapy, especially by those with a feminist perspective (MacKinnon & Miller, 1987; Goldner 1985; James & McIntyre, 1983; Taggart, 1985). These critics accuse family therapists of forcing families to conform to the traditional image of the nuclear family and failing to address the relationship between dysfunction and the sex roles imposed by society. In their view, therapists thus act as agents of social control, contributing to the transmission of sex-role stereotypes from one generation to another and labeling alternative lifestyles as abnormal.

Whatever the dangers of this limited perspective, the fact remains that the techniques currently being used in family therapy have become inadequate to deal with the problems of the constantly evolving family structure. What is urgently needed is a model that conceptualizes the family as an element of a larger social system, considers that system in any family assessment, and utilizes it for successful family treatment.

John Victor Compher's (1989) "full systems therapeutic approach" provides an excellent model for conceptualizing families embedded in larger systems. He describes four common dysfunctional modes of community intervention: the blind service network, the conflicted service network, the rejecting system, and the underdeveloped system. Compher's ideas have been well received as far as they go, but his book has been faulted for emphasizing organization over process and not providing specific techniques for working with the broader system (Quinn, 1991).

It is that gap this present volume is intended to fill, going beyond organization to address the specific interactional processes by which the clinician can make changes. It will help the clinician to develop a workable, coordinated treatment plan with the family and the broader context and to deal with the boundary entanglements within the network of services that can complicate treatment. It will offer specific techniques for working with individual subsystems and getting around the roadblocks that they sometimes set up.

I call the model I have developed Intensive Structural Therapy, or IST. It is brief but concentrated and forceful therapy in which the therapist works with the relevant contemporary context to bring about immediate, discontinuous change, by transforming the context, adding to that context (recontextualizing), or both. Although it is akin to Ross Speck and Carolyn Attneave's (1973) network therapy, it differs from their approach in significant ways. They described network therapy as a "tribal meeting" in which everyone who has any connection with the client is involved; Speck has told me that the minimum number of people in the room is 40 (personal communication, 1990). IST, by contrast, uses a more refined assessment to determine very precisely the significant people who are maintaining the dysfunctional homeostasis in the family. By means of this assessment, we can bring in those people, and only those people, who are either maintaining the problem or are potentially part of the solution.

Another model that is an important precursor to IST is Multiple Impact Therapy. The work of Robert MacGregor, Agnes Ritchie, and Alberto Serrano (1964) was the first to deal with entire systems to analyze how the parts fit together. They went beyond the idea that the family is an entire system to seeing the family as a set of interlocking systems. In the words of Braulio Montalvo (1986), with this model "you get 'part to whole' understandings and new ways of working for change."

The concept in IST of working through key systems is in many ways based on the concepts of MacGregor, Ritchie, and Serrano (1964). We firmly believe that the system is indeed a mosaic that can, at certain stages, be best treated via the work with key subsystems rather than the entire unit. Although there are instances when the entire system should be addressed, there can be, nevertheless, a power obtained by working with subsystems. I will discuss this issue in more detail in a later chapter.

I first tried this model during a consultation in Sweden a few years ago. I had consulted at this clinic the year before and thought that the work had gone rather well. Now, however, I learned that the staff had, in the meantime, become enamored of another family therapist's approach, quite different from my own. As staff members waxed eloquent on his model, I realized that I had been invited to demonstrate that my system was *inferior*. It was significant, I felt, that they had scheduled just one case for two full days of consultation—perhaps, I suspected, to give me just enough rope to hang myself and prove them right. Nevertheless, the scheduling clearly gave me the time to test the essential tenet of family therapy: that contemporary forces maintain clinical problems.

The single case I was offered was that of Neils, a 36-year-old medical student, married and the father of two children. For 4 or 5 years he had been involved in an obsessive affair with a hospital colleague whom I will call Lillith. During the period when the relationship had been at its most intense, Lillith had terrorized the family. For example, she would call Neils's mother and say, "Your son is dead; I just killed him." She would break into the family's apartment when they were away and smear the walls or be waiting, naked, in the couple's bed when they returned home. The relationship had been broken off about 3 months previous to the consultation, after a cataclysmic battle. Lillith still worked in the hospital, but allegedly she and Neils had little contact. Meanwhile, Neils and his wife had been separated for about a year.

We first saw Neils with his wife and children and then with his wife alone, to get a sense of the interactions within the family. We learned that both his wife and his children were extremely estranged from Neils. We began by attempting to work on some of the patterns in the room in order to allow Neils more access to his children so that the system could begin repairing. We quickly ran into a difficulty, however, that resulted from the complexity of Neils's context. His psychiatrist had told Neils's wife to have no outside contact with her husband. This interdiction obviously blocked any efforts to reunite the family—and without knowing the clinician's concerns we were reluctant to disregard it—but we were unable to get in touch with him. This complication underlines the importance of having all essential members of a system available in therapy.

Because of the estrangement, we were not getting much information from the nuclear family. We therefore brought in Neils's father (his mother had died 2 years before). The father talked about how he was always bailing his son out. According to him, Neils had never been competent or autonomous. At one point the father referred to himself as "Donald Duck's uncle." This session gave us crucial information on why the son continued to act like an adolescent: His father was continuing to treat him as an adolescent.

We also explored the wife's context. We saw her with her best friend, whom we found was extremely influential with her. She and the friend had for years consoled each other about their relationships. Four times in the last 10 years, the friend had abruptly left a man, and she was constantly advising the wife to leave Neils, take the children, and move to another town, leaving no forwarding address. Considering Lillith's threats against the family, her advice was perhaps understandable, but the broader message she was conveying was that the best way to solve problems is not to address them directly but to avoid confronting them. In any relationship, if all conflict is avoided, the system cannot change to accommodate the changing needs of the partners. In this case, the friend's pattern of running away may have influenced Neils's wife not to challenge him in a way that might have allowed them to resolve their difficulties. Of course, her direct experience of Neils (and Lillith) may have given her ample justification for believing that he was beyond rehabilitation and that leaving him was the appropriate response.

The question naturally arose whether we should bring in Lillith. Clearly she would have been an interesting person to include. Neils said that he had broken off with her, however, so following the basic tenet in medicine, "First, do no harm," I did not consider it ethical to bring her in.

What did we learn, then, from the broader system? We learned that Neils's father still rescued his son. We might safely extrapolate that the parents, by repeatedly rescuing their son, had not forced him to experience the existential crisis of aloneness that leads to responsibility. If Neils's mother had still been alive, we would doubtless have learned more.

The wife's friend was also informative. If we borrow from the social scientists the notion that reality is constructed through social consensus (Berger & Luckmann, 1966), then the wife's reality, confirmed by her friend, is that the optimal way to handle differences with a man is avoidance. She chose not to flee the community, but because of Lillith's threats, she necessarily involved the police. The friend continued to be a major source of support, as evidenced by her willingness to take an overnight train to come to the session on one day's notice. Clearly it was important to involve this influential person in the therapy.

There were, however, other important people who would have been informative but whom we could not bring in. In addition to Lillith and Neils's psychiatrist, there were Lillith's two grown sons, with whom she had a very conflicted relationship. There were also the contexts of the wife's family and of Neils's job at a medical lab.

This consultation was a powerful experience for me, bringing together as it did several forces that were functioning to keep this family dysfunctional: the husband's father, who was keeping his son a child; the wife's friend, who was imposing her own example of fleeing from problems; the hospital psychiatrist, whose standing injunction that there be no contact between husband and wife made any reconciliation very difficult. My data on the case were, of course, essentially impressionistic. I knew little about the culture, I never met Lillith, and I was severely limited by language.

Nevertheless, I felt I had demonstrated to the team of therapists at the hospital that the contemporary context was maintaining the problem, that the context was broad and complex, and that they should look even further for people who might be influential and include them in the treatment. The system that had led to the man's initial decompensation was no more; Lillith was no longer in their lives, nor was Neils's mother. The relevant system at this point was made up of those who were impeding Neils's rehabilitation, but it could also have been expanded to bring in people who could help the system transform, in a process of "recontextualization" of the existing system. For example, it might have been possible to find an older physician at the hospital who would act as a mentor to Neils and provide some professional direction (Neils had been a student for seven years).

I was sufficiently intrigued by this experience that I decided to try it again with another very difficult family. Upon returning home, I tried the model on a family during a consultation at the community mental health center in an extremely poor community, with all the social problems of the inner city. The case was that of Luis, a boy of 13, who was in a detention home for stealing a car. In the first session were his mother, his stepfather, his half sister, and his nephew. In addition, I invited his teacher, his school counselor, his pastor, his public defender, and his social service worker, who had custody of him. The next day we had the counselors from the detention center in (they were not available the first day).

The first session, which lasted 3 hours, revealed some valuable things about Luis. First, we learned that the teacher, Mr. DuPont, cared deeply about Luis. No other teacher wanted Luis in class because he was so unruly and disrespectful, but Mr. DuPont had a special way with the boy. A tall Texan, he tolerated no disrespect from Luis, and he got none. His magic potion seemed to be a mixture of humor, clear expectations, and what appeared to be true caring. His hands were both kind and strong when he physically got Luis to obey.

We also found that Luis had learned to use the social service worker to his own advantage. His parents, who were from rural Puerto Rico, were accustomed to very traditional disciplinary measures, such as spanking. When they spanked Luis, he would go to the authorities, who would intervene in his behalf. (During the session, the social service worker told the parents that no matter what their son did, they could not spank him. When the mother asked the worker, "Just what do you do with your kids?" the worker glared back and said, "My children are grown.")

The pastor turned out to be a very influential person with the mother, spending hours each week talking with her about her family. This clergyman had gotten in trouble with his church authorities for giving advice in areas in which he had no expertise. In this case, he had told the mother that her son had a biological problem and that the family should stop family therapy and send the boy away.

What we learned from this session was invaluable—that the broader system had some real positives, such as the teacher, and some very difficult social forces that were making the family's life hell. As therapy proceeded, it became clearer and clearer that having had all the forces, both positive and negative, present at the outset was extremely beneficial. This already-beleaguered family needed the forum and the help of the therapists to martial the positive forces and to negotiate with the negative forces to keep them at least at bay.

I also realized, however, that the resources of the system were not adequate; that is, even if I were successful in transforming this difficult system, it would be necessary to recontextualize it, to patch in another context to help strengthen and stabilize the system and make the transformation permanent. At the time of the first session, summer was approaching and I suggested that Luis try to get a job in the nearby city, to get him away from the social toxicity of his own community and his delinquent friends. Knowing his interest in bicycles, I hoped he might find a job in a bicycle shop. That failed to materialize, but his mother found him a job with a law firm, where he worked as a helper as well as a bike messenger. This new context not only kept Luis away from his delinquent context but also helped to bring out the more positive aspects of his temperament as his supervisors came to like and appreciate him.

I saw these cases more than 2 years ago. At that time, I thought that this broader model of therapy was important; today, I believe it is essential. The country has changed to such an extent, even in this short period of time, that working with the broader context is mandatory in most cases.

The epigraph to this introduction was written in 1921 during reflection on the horrors of the First World War. It was quoted to me recently by a university administrator who had just lost his job; he was the third middle-aged unemployed man I had seen that day. For these men, and for many other people today, Yeats's words apply to their own lives. Our age is experiencing what Charles Handy (1989), borrowing from mathematics, calls "discontinuous change," change that does not fit into a pattern. Our families are increasingly being affected by these changes. We must change our therapeutic technology to fit our new context. It is the purpose of this book to help clinicians do just that.

The first part of the book describes the model and the broad theory on which it is based. Chapter 1 outlines four concepts that are considered basic to the model. Of these, the primary concept is the necessity of working with the contemporary context—not a new idea, of course, but one that in much family therapy seems to have been eclipsed by an increased emphasis on the self.

Closely related to the importance of the broader context is the concept of isomorphism, the idea that certain structural patterns can be carried over from the family to the wider context, and vice versa. An awareness of isomorphism can help the clinician to organize interventions across contexts in a coherent manner. A third pivotal concept is that of the homeostatic maintainer. Homeostasis is a highly controversial theory in the field of family therapy, but its usefulness in guiding treatment and monitoring outcome has been demonstrated to me in many cases, including a number of cases detailed in this book. Finally, this chapter deals with the use of crisis induction as a way of transforming large systems.

Chapter 2 describes a model for assessing the broad system. I call it a four-dimensional model because, in addition to those aspects of the family that can be assessed objectively, it includes the subjective experience of the therapist—a dimension that, to me, is of a different order, as different as the dimension of time, which changes three-dimensional space into a space-time perspective. Chapter 3 describes several approaches to ascertaining who is maintaining the dysfunctional homeostasis in the family and utilizing the concept in therapy. Finally, chapter 4 presents a five-step model for intensive structural therapy.

The second part of the book takes up principles of intervention with specific subsystems of the contemporary context of the family: siblings, peers, schools and other institutions, the workplace, the legal system, social services, and others. Each chapter deals with a different subsystem, discussing how it can be used to aid in transforming the system, as well as the role it may be playing in creating and maintaining the dysfunction in the system. Transcripts of clinical sessions, with the families' identities disguised, are used throughout to demonstrate how the principles of intervention can be applied.

Finally, an epilogue offers a possible explanation for why the IST model works. Recent research suggests the existence of an altruism gene: a tendency, inherent in all human beings, to help others. Many of the people encountered in the pages of this book made major contributions to transforming dysfunctional families, even though they were not themselves members of those families. In some cases their roles in therapy involved considerable cost to themselves. The willingness of such people to participate in therapy is one key—perhaps *the* key—to the success of Intensive Structural Therapy.

CHAPTER 1

Basic Concepts

There are vices and follies incident to whole populations and ages.
Men resemble their contemporaries even more than their progenitors.
—Ralph Waldo Emerson, *The Uses of Great Men*

FOUR CONCEPTS are basic to Intensive Structural Therapy. The first is that powerful therapeutic change is created by working with the contemporary context, the people who are key parts of the identified patient's present social environment and the social forces they represent. The social context that impinges on the nuclear family can, and usually does, include people and forces well beyond the family's bounds. To address fully the needs of the modern family, one must work to transform these outside social forces as well as the forces within the family.

The second basic concept is that certain dysfunctional structural patterns may be isomorphic throughout the patient's various contexts. That is, patterns of behavior within the family can be replicated in the patient's relationships outside the family. Identifying isomorphic structures allows the clinician to organize coherent interventions through the contexts in which the family is embedded.

Closely related to the first two concepts is that of the homeostatic maintainer. In dysfunctional systems, some individuals and social forces, operating in certain interactional patterns, function to maintain the dysfunctional homeostasis of the system. Identification of homeostatic maintainers is key to the incisive treatment that is central to IST. First, it organizes and directs treatment by pointing up where intervention is called for. Second, it allows the clinician to follow the isomorphic patterns of interaction as markers, to determine whether treatment has been effective.

The final concept is that crisis induction can be a powerful therapeutic tool in short-term therapy. It is well known that systems transform in times of crisis (Minuchin & Fishman, 1981). By inducing such implosions, the therapist in IST greatly expedites the process of change. In cases where the implosion is not necessary, then gentler means of employing change are used.

In the remainder of this chapter, we will look more closely at these four basic concepts and how they are reflected in actual therapeutic situations.

Working with the Contemporary Context

The concept on which most family therapy is based is that the problem is maintained by the contemporary context and that therefore the most viable target for our therapeutic interventions is that context. This idea stands in sharp contrast to the psychoanalytic approach of directing treatment to people's hidden motives and assumptions. It does not mean that the clinician in this model is not concerned with the client's inner self; to the contrary, the therapist closely follows the experiences of the individual while working to transform his or her context. The difference is that in family therapy, the therapist assumes that the most powerful context available to transform the present problem and measure change is the contemporary one.

What distinguishes IST is not that it mentions the importance of the broader context; almost all models pay some respect to this aspect of the family's system. What distinguishes structural family therapy is that it offers a clear and useful way to assess and treat organizations in which interactions are embedded. What makes this approach unique is the description of specific interventions for working with the *extended* context. In addition, the concept of recontextualizing the family—admittedly borrowed in no small measure from our social work colleagues—is also different. Finally, the use of the concept of the homeostatic maintainer, which makes it possible to work efficiently with a large system without being paralyzed by sheer numbers or lost when key subsystems are not available, helps to make this a unique model.

The concept of working with the contemporary context is not a new one. George Herbert Mead (1934) and Harry Stack Sullivan (1953) were two of the most influential proponents of this concept. Family therapy's initial adoption of this concept is an area of considerable controversy. Nathan Ackerman's (1958) early work began much of the thinking about families in psychiatry. During a presentation at the Family Therapy Networker Conference in March 1993, Salvador Minuchin noted that the first link among the contemporary context, family interaction, and mental illness was published in the 1956 paper "Towards a Theory of Schizophrenia" by Gregory Bateson, Don Jackson, Jay Haley, and John Weakland. According to Minuchin, this paper marked an important beginning for family therapy since it was the first time clinicians saw an individual's problems as embedded in interactions. After that paper, the works of Nathan Ackerman (1957), Don Jackson (1957), and Virginia Satir (1967) and others began to lay the foundation for the field.

An important early study by Donald G. Langsley and Daniel M. Kaplan (1968) challenged the model of individual therapy that attempted to bring out infantile conflicts so the patient could differentiate them from present problems and begin to work out adult solutions. They advocated intensive outpatient family therapy in lieu of traditional psychiatric inpatient treatment, which, in their view, avoids the reality of the present and ignores the real-life problems of the patient's social field.

Gregory Bateson (1972) has been a major proponent of the use of the contemporary social context as the arena for therapeutic intervention. His concept of the mind as imminent in the social field has been seminal in the development of family therapy theory. In Bateson's view, there is no clear boundary between the individual and the social context:

> If you ask anybody about the localization and boundaries of the self, these confusions are immediately displayed. Or consider a blind man with a stick. Where does the blind man's self begin? At the tip of the stick? At the handle of the stick? Or at some point halfway up the stick? These questions are nonsense, because the stick is a pathway along which differences are transmitted under transformation, so that to draw a delimiting line *across* this pathway is to cut off a part of the systemic circuit which determines the blind man's locomotion. (p. 318)

Carrying this concept further, others believe that a person develops his or her sense of self as a result of interacting with the people and objects in a more or less constant environment (Minuchin & Fishman, 1979). The transactions with significant others bring out those aspects of character and personality that are appropriate to the context. The repertoire of thoughts, feelings, and behavior more or less formulated by the self represent the person's multifaceted self.

The self is thus like a diamond with many facets. If you shine a light on the diamond, certain facets will be seen, depending on the direction, strength, and quality of the light. If you change the light, different facets of the diamond will be reflected. The context of people, systems, and relationships surrounding the multifaceted self is like the light shining on the diamond. It is this context that brings out certain facets of the self and not others; if the context changes, other facets of the self will be expressed. In the clients we family therapists see, some of the facets are problematic. Thus when we want to bring about change in our clients, we must transform their contemporary context such that their more functional facets will be brought out. That is even true in the most encapsulated intrapersonal problems, such as multiple personality disorder or post-traumatic stress disorder.

From this point of view, it is clear why it is essential to bring in all members of the contemporary context who are maintaining the problem. Therapeutic changes can be made—and made longer lasting, if not permanent—only if all members of the context are changing and are maintaining one another in the new position. Members who are not involved in the therapy are far more likely to undermine the changes in the context that have called forth the patient's more functional self.

Of course, as we therapists have been formulating our concepts of the self and its relationship to the context, we have in some ways simply been catching up with fundamental social work principles. For example, Herman Stein (1960) emphasized that social workers must have concern for all the significant figures in the client's family and give more attention to the pressures of the social environment. A significant goal for any clinician, whether therapist or social worker, is to get the organizational structures and other helping institutions to be as responsive as possible to people's needs. Carel Germain and Alex Gitterman (1980) have described what they call the "ecological perspective" of social work, the view that people's problems are based in their transactions with their environment. Germain and Gitterman's approach, in many ways a refinement of classic social work teachings, sees the purpose of social service therapeutic intervention as "the matching of people's adaptive capacities and environmental properties to produce transactions that will maximize growth and development and improve environments" (p. 1).

Much like sophisticated social work, however, the therapeutic model of IST deals not only with the external context of the family but also with the internal structural problems of the system. For example, in dealing with a family that lives in a community where the parents are chronically unemployed, the ecologically sensitive therapist not only looks at the economic problems of the family but searches for dysfunctional patterns within the system, such as a profound split between the parents, with the father overly connected to his mother.

When I consider how essential it is to work with the contemporary context, one family that I saw a number of years ago always comes to mind. Dorothy, 42 years old, had been anorexic for more than 20 years. (I have described her case in detail elsewhere [Fishman, 1988].) She used huge quantities of laxatives ("a box at a time") every day, and as a result she had had at least four episodes of severe metabolic disturbance, during which she would lapse into a coma and have to be rushed to the hospital.

Dorothy's family included her husband, Herb; her parents; and her two teenage children. It was a classic psychosomatic family system, with extreme degrees of enmeshment, conflict avoidance, diffusion of conflict, triadic functioning, overrigidity, and overprotectiveness. Dorothy was deeply involved in mediating between her parents, and her parents were extremely intrusive in her family, especially in Dorothy's personal space.

Treatment involved working with three subsystems. First, in the subsystem of Dorothy and her parents, boundaries had to be created to reduce the intrusiveness. A major source of contention had been the parents' dropping in every Sunday for brunch. They would never announce when they would arrive, and their timing was very unpredictable, yet Dorothy and her family would always wait breakfast for them. With therapeutic help, Dorothy was able to confront her parents with the fact that she and her family felt like hostages every Sunday. New arrangements were worked out that left the nuclear family free to make their own plans. Within two weeks, the parents' pattern of visitation changed.

The second focus of therapy was the subsystem of Dorothy and the children. The children were tethered to their mother by their concern that she would have another metabolic disturbance and that she could die if she were not gotten to the hospital in time. Consequently, they stayed close to home and made sure that one of them was with her at all times. They were so focused on caring for their mother that their adolescent development was being impeded. Therapeutic sessions were therefore held to create an appropriate boundary; the children were encouraged by their parents to go out more with their friends.

This change, of course, put new pressure on the marriage. By urging the children to get out more, Herb was implicitly committing himself to the role of taking care of his wife. Being together more forced them to deal with their problems, including the very severe problem of conflict avoidance that pervaded the entire system and was keeping it paralyzed. By the end of therapy with the couple, Dorothy was able to challenge her husband as well as her parents instead of becoming symptomatic, and Herb, for his part, was able to challenge Dorothy instead of just avoiding conflict.

Thus in this transformed system a new structure had emerged. There was now appropriate distance between the generations. Conflict could be addressed directly; Dorothy no longer had to suppress her righteous indignation and in so doing become symptomatic. In a follow-up session 2¹/₂ years later, it was clear that the changes had been maintained. Dorothy's weight had gone from 70 to 115 pounds, and she no longer had periods of using laxatives. She was teaching calisthenics at a day-care center. Her parents did not drop in unannounced, but at the same time Dorothy had a good relationship with them. According to Dorothy, her parents were, in fact, happier than they had ever been. The children were also doing well and developing normally. More recently I heard that Dorothy and her husband were going into business together. I saw this as extremely positive; the system that for so many years had been organized around Dorothy as patient and "one-down" had now completely transformed into one based on equity. The husband and wife were truly partners, not only at home but also in the workplace.

In the case of Dorothy, therapy was contained within the extended family. The initial assessment indicated that the problem was being maintained by the interactions among the three generations. In many cases, however, social forces beyond the bounds of the family play key roles in keeping the family stuck in its dysfunctional patterns. Ironically, it is often the case that a system that is trying to help the identified patient and the family unwittingly becomes a party to maintaining the problem.

The case to be detailed in the next chapter is illustrative. Michelle was a 13-year-old girl who was out of control. She had run away at least 15 times, had been hospitalized on 3 occasions, and had a court case pending. Social services had been involved for 4 years. Between social workers, Michelle's therapist, the hospital staff, and court personnel, a great many conflicting social forces were impinging on the family, in many cases canceling one another out and, in the end, disempowering the family. The parents felt helpless and had given up trying to retain control, while Michelle had learned to manipulate the various outside agencies to her own ends. The goal of therapy in such a case is to reempower the family, to get the family to take back the responsibility for its members.

Involving the wider context in therapy can, in fact, work in several different ways. It may, as in the case of Dorothy, reveal within the system severe structural problems that can then be addressed in therapy. It may disclose a need for better coordination among outside forces that are trying to help the family. And finally, it may add to the therapeutic process people who are not a part of the problem but are potentially a part of the solution—a procedure I call recontextualization. In the cases described throughout the book, examples of all three functions will be found.

Isomorphic Patterns

Isomorphism is an essential concept for the therapist working with the patient's contemporary context. By bringing out the existence of interactional patterns that have been carried over from one subsystem to another, this concept unifies the therapeutic work with the different contexts of the patient's environment.

Isomorphism means, quite simply, similarity in shape. Two or more complex structures can be mapped onto each other in such a way that for every part of one structure there is a corresponding part in the other structure, a part that plays a similar role in that structure.

The notion of patterns of consequence and the systemic paradigm that underlies this concept has been one of the basic tenets of family therapy. (The major dysfunctional patterns will be discussed in chapter 2.) Much of the emphasis, however, has been on the system as a whole and its homeostasis, not on the fundamental patterns that organize the system. The concept of isomorphism is useful in helping the clinician see the structural similarities between these fundamental patterns in the different contexts in which a given person operates. With this perspective, it can be observed how a pattern of behavior within a family is replicated with others in even the most disparate situations outside the family.

Jay Haley (personal communication, 1975) tells the story of a schizophrenic inpatient in a unit where there was considerable conflict between the head nurse and the psychiatric resident. Just as this young man's symptoms diffused conflict between his parents at home, they did so on the ward. Whenever it became clear, from staff and patients going in and out of a staff meeting, that tension was running high at the meeting, this patient would amble into the conference room, distracting the staff and diffusing the tension.

There has been an almost romantic notion in family therapy that nearly perfect isomorphism exists throughout the system; the pattern with one's parents was thought to be invariably isomorphic with the patterns with one's grandparents, with the other children in school, and eventually with one's boss. That idea has been somewhat modified, and today most people believe the nuclear family can have patterns that are not necessarily replicated in other contexts. Lyman Wynne's (1988) concept of bilaterality, for example, is that multiple patterns exist concurrently in systems and that while some patterns may be isomorphic, there is a great likelihood that others will be nonisomorphic.

Isomorphism is still a powerful concept, however, and a highly useful one, because the more dysfunctional a system is, the more likely it is that isomorphs will pervade in other contexts. It is essential to this model of therapy, for the patterns can be observed in the transactions occurring in the therapy room and then conceptualized and mapped through other contexts.

In the discussion of isomorphic patterns in this chapter and others, we shall be focusing primarily on patterns that are producing and maintaining problematic behavior. It should be noted, however, that isomorphic patterns can be positive as well as negative. Even in dysfunctional families, the patterns that are replicated outside as well as within the family can include productive ones as well as counterproductive ones. In some of the cases to be discussed in chapters 5 through 11, we will see how the therapist can capitalize on the positive isomorphs in therapy with various subsystems.

Isomorphic patterns were clearly present in the case of Tony, a 35-year-old man who since a teenager had been addicted to drugs, most recently cocaine; Tony came to our clinic for treatment after his wife threatened to leave him, "this time for real."

Tony's context was organized in isomorphic patterns of overprotectiveness around him. His long-suffering wife had separated from him twice, but each time she had returned when he promised to reform and stayed on when his resolutions failed. His children, ages 15 and 12, had been rescuing their father for as long as they could remember. If he needed money, they would give him what little they had. When he came home high, they would put him to bed. Even in the therapy room, when the therapist challenged Tony, Joy would lean up against him, as if to shield him.

This pattern of protection was replicated in Tony's contexts outside the family. Even the court extended itself to accommodate him. If he failed to show up at a meeting, his probation officer would call him to reschedule it; there were no consequences for his irresponsibility. During one therapy session, in which the judge was involved by speaker phone, Tony was able to convince the judge that his work responsibilities had prevented him from attending a certain meeting, although he had not called in advance to explain.

Similarly, Tony had been accommodated in several different treatment facilities. He would miss sessions, get excuses from the doctors to get out of work, and use the authority of his therapist to stymie his family's attempts to demand responsibility. When challenged, he would say, "I know I took the car, and I know I have no license, but I have a disease. I'm not responsible."

How are such isomorphic patterns carried from the immediate family context to contexts outside the family? To understand the process, it will be helpful to look first at more functional families. All families have interactional patterns; Salvador Minuchin (personal communication, 1974) speaks of the "family dance." In a functional family, the patterns are relatively flexible. There is considerable latitude that allows new forms appropriate to the needs of the moment to evolve in a constant process of adaptation. In a dysfunctional family, this flexibility and adaptability are lacking. The patterns are simply repeated and become rigidified.

In either case, a family member can be expected to carry over behaviors from family patterns to contexts outside the family. In a family system that is flexible and adaptable, members learn to adapt to change. When a family member enters a new context, the rules of the family system give way; differences between behavior expected within the family and behavior expected in the new context fade. The person is inducted into the rules of the new system and accepted in the new context.

With a dysfunctional family such as Tony's, however, this adaptability does not develop. If the new system is more flexible than the family system, the rules of the new system may give way to those of the family. Within Tony's overprotective family, his irresponsible behavior was congruent with his overprotective and conflict-avoiding context, so that he did not experience the consequences necessary to change his behavior. In the broader context, his behavior was incongruent, yet instead of adapting to it he managed to induce the outside context to accommodate to him.

In many families, as children develop and mature, there is a gradual merging of the rules of the different systems. As the child's context expands into the world outside the family, the child becomes a force for change in the family. The converse is also true: As the the range of behavior available to its members grows, the family encourages the child—and the child encourages the family—to try alternatives. The rules of the various systems do not become identical, but there is sufficient blending so that the child can respond appropriately in other contexts. In dysfunctional systems such as Tony's, however, the contexts rarely merge to allow for the expansion of alternatives. Less blending of rules is allowed. The problem member tends to induct the context, but it is a one-way process; the person does not become inducted into the context.

This process is not to be confused with perceptual distortion, in which the individual misperceives the new context. If that were the case, the new context would only *look like* the family. In contrast to classical notions of transference, what I am suggesting is that the person changes the new system to follow the rules of the family pattern, so that people actually behave according to the family rules. The new context is transformed to mirror the old one.

This reasoning enables us to describe how an individual from a dysfunctional system will behave in other contexts. In fact, thanks to the concept of isomorphism, we can predict how the new context may be inducted by the individual to make it resemble the family system. Of course, new contexts include therapy. Understanding the process of induction allows the therapist to be on the watch for ways in which the rules of the family can induct the clinician. Such induction is an occupational hazard that all therapists constantly need to resist.

The clinical usefulness of the concept of isomorphs should be clear. Considering the possibility that patterns of interaction might be isomorphic and looking for their replication in the patient's various contexts can prove a valuable step in diagnosis; once a pattern is recognized, the therapist can look to see how the patient is inducting this pattern. Clinicians can recognize isomorphic patterns in several ways: by spotting a familiar pattern in another context, by experiencing the pull of being inducted into the system, and by comparing interactional patterns with normality.

In order to define a pattern as deviant, one must have a clear notion of what constitutes normality. Any pattern must be judged against a model of functional structure and developmental appropriateness. One must, for example, have some idea of what constitutes successful parenting or what kind of parenting minimizes high-risk behavior. The contrast with normality also raises the issue of whether isomorphs are culturally bound or whether some are universally considered dysfunctional. A traditional family of Sicilian background, for example, may justify its intrusiveness in a daughter's life by appealing to a cultural pattern of closeness and protectiveness within the family. Braulio Montalvo and Manuel Gutierrez (1983) warn of the dangers in focusing on the specifics of the cultural patterns rather than on the underlying process patterns. The therapist who knows too much about the culture is more easily assimilated and manipulated by a family that is using culture as a defense, they note, and therapists must watch carefully for broader patterns, such as loss of autonomy, which are considered deviant almost everywhere.

Within any culture, the therapist looks for patterns that are not working well: patterns that curtail creativity, personality development, and functioning. Seeing the identified patient in various subsystems, one asks, "How is this group curtailing this person?" and then, "How is this person helping the group to curtail him?" One then looks for patterns of interaction that pervade the different contexts.

An interesting question comes to mind when one considers that the isomorphic patterns I have been discussing tend to be very stable. Clinicians see the same ones over and over again in the families they deal with, and often they appear to be consistent over generations. Indeed, similar ones have been described even in ancient cultures. Could it be that there are interpersonal "deep structures" like the deep structures of the mind described by Claude Lévi-Strauss and Noam Chomsky? Could the psychological "figures" posited by Carl Jung—friend, the shadow, the anima and animus, and so on, representing various levels or depths of psychic experience—be organized into archetypal patterns?

I am suggesting that family constellations manifest similar psychological figures and that these figures pervade the various contexts, so that the skilled therapist can readily recognize the figure as a familiar gestalt. Instead of struggling with identification, the therapist can focus on how the figure and the family can change expeditiously and harmoniously.

How, then, do we break isomorphic patterns? It might be said that the art of therapy is getting people to try to break out of existing patterns. With very rigid systems, this can be difficult because they have higher thresholds for change than less petrified systems. In order to exceed that homeostatic threshold, it helps for the clinician to induce a therapeutic crisis. The induction of such crises will be the topic of the last section of this chapter. First, however, let us look more closely at the concept of homeostasis and who or what maintains the homeostatic threshold.

The Homeostatic Maintainer

The term *homeostasis* was first used in biology to describe the tendency of an organism to maintain itself in a relatively stable state and to return to that or a similar state when it has been disturbed. The classic example of a homeostatic mechanism is the thermotactic system in the human body. This system acts like a regulator to maintain body heat at a constant temperature to maximize efficiency both in cell reproduction and in interaction with the environment. In times of crisis, however, such as infection or injury, the critical function of the thermotactic system is to *raise* body temperature to enhance the production of white blood cells and to destroy infecting agents. The overall goal of the higher temperature is to improve bodily protection, but if this excess heat is maintained for too long a period—if it becomes a new status quo—there can be deleterious side effects. The homeostatic system, then, can prove either a positive or a negative force.

In 1932, Walter Cannon proposed that if homeostatic mechanisms effectively described biological regulation, they might be useful in describing human behavior. Don Jackson (1957) extended the term to *family homeosta-sis*, which he used to describe a relative constancy of the family environment in which therapy for one member of the family can result in change in other members: As the patient improves, for example, another person becomes symptomatic.

Jay Haley (1962) and Virginia Satir (1967) gave further substance to this notion by describing family interactional patterns in detail and demonstrating how they act to preserve intact the family's preset level of behavior. Haley described the family as a "self-corrective system at work" (1962, p. 277). If one family member exceeds the level of behavior tolerated by the others, the others will respond to correct the extreme behavior and restore the family's equilibrium. The range of behavior is determined by a set of private codes or covert rules specific to each family that form an unconscious, collective process of the family (Haley, 1962; Satir, 1967; Jackson, 1965). Adherence to these rules maintains the status quo and protects the family's survival; any threat to them is unacceptable and challenged by family members.

To use the human thermotactic system as an analogy, when the family's survival is threatened by developmental pressures or other stresses, the social temperature of the family rises to deal with the crisis. When the crisis is over, the family's temperature returns to normal, to everyday productive functioning.

Homeostasis as used by these and other theorists does not mean a totally static state, lacking growth and development, but rather a consistent, steady state that all living things must have in order to exist. In the family that is functioning well, the process is fluid and dynamic and by its nature incorporates developmental change even as it lends stability (Ebert, 1978). Like the human body whose temperature returns to normal after a crisis, the family is developing and changing.

It is when the homeostatic mechanisms work to keep the family in a dysfunctional homeostasis that the concept of the homeostatic maintainer becomes important in family therapy. While some forces within the family are striving to adapt to developmental pressures or other stress, one or more other forces are operating to keep it stuck, unable to make the appropriate developmental changes. During therapy with a family in crisis, discovering who or what is functioning to maintain the status quo is key to efficient therapeutic change. Generally the procedure is simple. First, as many of the individuals who are postulated to be maintaining the homeostasis are assembled. The therapist then perturbs the equilibrium of the family system and observes who activates to restore it. Chapter 3 elaborates on the concept and how it is made operational, and examples of its use abound in the cases described throughout the book.

Despite its usefulness as a clinical tool, the concept of family homeostasis is far from being universally accepted by family therapists. Paul Dell (1982) and others (Brodey, 1968; Speer, 1970; Hoffman, 1980; Bogdan, 1984; Wynne, 1988) have found it epistemologically flawed and have offered other concepts, such as coherence (Dell, 1982), in its place. Their arguments are at times well reasoned and persuasive, but in most cases I have not found them to have major implications for clinical practice.

The one criticism that to me has important clinical significance is that the concept obscures the influence of the broader environmental context. Lyman Wynne (1988), in particular, has suggested that in emphasizing homeostasis, family therapists and researchers have neglected the contributions of other, nonfamilial etiological factors to family dysfunction. If this has indeed happened, however, it is not the fault of the concept itself but of a myopic interpretation of it. The idea of homeostasis does not depend on a focus limited to the nuclear family, or even to the nuclear family plus the extended family.

Indeed, Wynne overlooks an extremely important function for therapists—that is, facilitating relationships at the interfaces of the family and its surrounding systems. By using the broader context, the therapist can transform the dysfunctional inner working of the family so that the symptom is dismantled. In normal development, the family organism is not just reacting to outside pressures; it is incorporating the outside. Thus, in the IST model we see effective therapy as replicating nature by helping the family to incorporate the broader context and thereby helping it to develop.

Another area of controversy generated by homeostasis is the accusation that the concept is disrespectful to families because "homeostasis" implies that families are stubborn and resistant and do not change. By the use of this concept of homeostasis, I am not implying anything negative whatsoever about the families.

I find that by examining a system at a cross section of time, one can discover set patterns of organization in families, as within other living systems. And by intervening at this point in a family's life, the clinician can pinpoint the forces that are maintaining the status quo.

Indeed, homeostasis is not just negative. After ascertaining the forces maintaining this status quo, the clinician must determine if these are holding in place maladaptive patterns and to what extent they are holding in place adaptive and positive patterns. Homeostasis is the frame for the clinician—it is the ally of therapeutic forces when it applies to the family's efforts to maintain or protect positive changes in their life or to protect changes that permit the members to function more adequately.

The clinician sees *homeostasis* as a value-free term that can be negative or positive. When the clinician perturbs the homeostasis, he or she is trying to introduce entropy in order to have the system move toward change because change is necessary for the health of the overall system. After the change has been accomplished, after the journey has been traversed, after the reorganization has occurred, then the system relies on homeostasis to protect and stabilize the change. In that sense, the clinician, while working on the maintenance and protection of change, is working more as a friend of homeostasis and perceives homeostasis at the service of and as maintaining a very positive and adaptive pattern.

We always need and require homeostasis in some part. It is part of what maintains stability, but we want that stability to be mastered after the family has accomplished certain patterns or reciprocal respect of conflict management instead of conflict avoidance; after there is an increased openness to the outside rather than rigidity and closedness; after the system fosters life-enhancing patterns rather than blocking the participants or the main path of freedom.

No system can survive in total flux in the middle of entropy. We need a certain beginning of order that stabilizes the system while it remains in flux. That is the mystery of living systems—that they are in flux while they are also stable and contained. What the clinician plays on is the stirring up of those forces, making them more entropic so that there is reorganization. But after the crisis is traversed and the people reorganize and summon their appropriate responses, we all use the help of homeostasis to stabilize things and make the clinician expendable. You do not have to stay there shepherding the change forever because people tend to settle down and accept the new patterns as the previous status quo.

Homeostasis is not just one more feature of families; it is a whole dynamic feature of living systems. A family may be stubborn in defending a daughter from a world of drugs and unbridled sex. Is that stubbornness? That is strength. Anybody who works with biological sciences and studies enzymes realizes that this is not an insult but a characteristic of every system.

Homeostasis can be disturbed sometimes by the clinician, making it the subject of a crisis induction; however, at other points the clinician may use homeostasis to protect accomplished changes that are more adaptive and healthy to the family. The clinician counts on homeostasis at some point to protect the people, and at another point he or she realizes that this could be the same force that does not permit change.

My concept of homeostasis is a broad one that takes into consideration the roles of external systems as reinforcers, sustainers, or modifiers of the internal homeostatic process. In a number of cases in this book, social forces outside the family were indeed found to be homeostatic maintainers—for example, in disempowering parents and preventing them from taking responsibility for their own children. By recognizing the roles that external systems can play, the therapist can develop interventions at the interfaces of the family and the surrounding systems that release the family from dysfunctional homeostasis.

The therapist can use the concept not only to neutralize the negative homeostatic forces in the external context but also to activate the positive influence of outside systems to create change. In a case to be described in chapter 4, therapy for a 7-year-old boy with elective mutism (he would talk at home but not at school) included bringing the parents and the school together to deal with the problem jointly. The school had tried everything in its power to get the child to participate and had considered transferring him to a special school. Doing so would have represented failure for all involved and would simply have reinforced the homeostasis in each distinct sector. Instead, the school authorities were mobilized to allow the parents into the school to be physically present on a daily basis to help the teachers with their son. By establishing this new level of collaboration, the therapy enabled each system—the family and the school—to incorporate the other and to be affected by it.

Thus the concepts of homeostasis and the homeostatic maintainer remain explanatory when one recognizes that the function of maintaining homeostasis is not limited to members of the nuclear family. The homeostatic maintainer may be someone in the extended family, a person or group outside the family, a social agency, an institution, or even a broad social force such as poverty.

As utilized in Intensive Structural Therapy, this concept is the key to many successful interventions, for it grounds our theory in observations. Ross Speck and Carolyn Attneave (1973) accomplished a breakthrough in their network theory by trying to replicate the social system in the room itself in the hope that something would thereby transform. IST goes beyond their method to focus on how the various relationships are articulated and to identify the resulting structures, which can then be changed in the observable system.

Crisis Induction

The Chinese word for *crisis* means "danger and opportunity." At points of crises for systems, each crisis often portends change; the outcome can be either positive or negative.

A family I have been working with recently seemed to be getting nowhere in their therapy. After years of strife in their 30-year marriage, the parents were coming closer to divorce. Their chronically delinquent grown son, whose confusion was the embodiment of their dysfunctional marriage, was showing no sign of mending his ways. Then suddenly the couple came in to the last session transformed. The husband and wife sat side by side, supporting rather than contradicting each other. The tension between them was gone.

I asked what had happened. What had brought about their sudden harmony, when the therapy had been more or less in irons? I learned that one evening the previous week, as the husband was driving home from work, he had come upon a car that had gone off the road and into an embankment. Two men, spaced out on drugs, were asleep in the car. He had no sooner dragged them out when the car exploded. All three men were burned, but not badly.

After this incident, the husband's entire attitude toward his wife and his marriage had changed. Suddenly his resentments of the last 10 years seemed trivial; the only important thing in his life was being with his wife, the mother of their children. Did the crisis transform the system? I believe it did. Will the change last? I am going to wait and see.

In IST, crisis induction is used to open up the system for change. Especially at the onset of therapy, and especially when the salient members of the system are present, creating a therapeutic crisis increases the likelihood of bringing about change. Later in therapy, we all tend to become inducted into the system and find ourselves following its rules. At that point, it is far more difficult to create a crisis. Part of the power of inducing a crisis is that it demonstrates that the therapist has not been inducted in the system and is expecting those rules to change.

A major conceptual basis for crisis-induction therapy lies in work on catastrophe theory. The French mathematician René Thom (Zeeman, 1976) has derived a model for understanding changes in nature that represents a new way of thinking about change. Unlike the continuous change described by the calculus of Newton and Leibniz, by which one can predict gradual change such as in the motion of heavenly bodies and mechanical machines, catastrophe theory describes sudden, discontinuous change produced by the interaction of two or more independent forces—for example, the sudden changes produced in earthquakes. The more forces that are in conflict in any interaction, the more complex the catastrophe and the more unpredictable the outcome.

The concept of catastrophe is predicated on the notion that a system can have more than one state of homeostasis or stable pathway of change. "The catastrophe is the 'jump' from one state or pathway to another. . . .

The transition here is discontinuous not because there are no intervening states or pathways, but because none of them is stable: the passage from the initial state or pathway to the final one is likely to be brief in comparison to the time spent in stable states" (Woodcock & Davis, 1978, p. 32).

In family therapy, the process of change is little understood. We tend to think in terms of comparisons, of conditions before and after change, and we are only now beginning to give serious thought to the process itself. Obviously this gap in our understanding limits our capacity to facilitate change.

Catastrophe theory can be useful to us in two ways. First, it confirms the often-observed phenomenon in family therapy that systems, when perturbed, can manifest discontinuous change and that new organizations can be realized. Second, it provides a model for conceptualizing a dynamic system in terms of the forces at work within that system. Creating conflict between these forces can bring about discontinuous change; the greater the number of forces in conflict in a given context, the greater will be the chances that discontinous change will occur.

Catastrophe theory thus supports the importance of using a broader system of intervention. The more forces that are clashing in the therapy room, the more powerful will be the therapy and the more likely it is that the system will be transformed.

Of course, as we have noted, the more complex the catastrophe, the more difficult it is to predict the outcome. In the physical world, elaborate measurements and mathematical calculations can be developed to reduce the element of unpredictability. In family therapy we do not have the precise quantified data that would allow us to make such predictions or even to chart the progression of change in systems. Yet in many ways, the development of the therapeutic crisis simply telescopes the family's evolution. It brings into the present the crisis that the family may well have in years to come, with the ensuing change in the system. By inducing the crisis in the therapy room, the therapist can monitor the system as the family struggles to regain equilibrium and can work to ensure that the new structures that emerge are positive ones.

Crisis induction proved invaluable in therapy with the family of a 16-year-old girl who had been anorexic for 6 months. The session was a lunch session that included Bonnie, the identified patient; her father, a blue-collar worker in a manufacturing plant; her mother, who, as office manager of a law firm, was considerably more successful vocationally than the father; and Bonnie's sister and maternal grandmother.

Lunch sessions are sometimes criticized as too confrontational and intrusive. The alternatives in severe cases of anorexia, however, are tube feeding and parenteral nutrition, which seem to me equally intrusive interventions. Moreoever, they are administered by strangers rather than by loving family members and have little impact on the system that is maintaining the problem. Lunch sessions, especially when attended by both parents, offer an opportunity to transform the system.

The mother brought lunch for the family. It is illustrative of the way the system accommodated the child's self-starvation that when I asked where Bonnie's sandwich was, the mother replied, "We didn't bring one, because she doesn't eat anyway." She had, however, brought one for the therapist, which was donated to the cause so that Bonnie would have her own sandwich.

As first one and then the other parent pressured Bonnie to eat, the girl stubbornly refused. Two-thirds of the way through the session, an incident occurred that indicated the distance between the parents. The father tried to get Bonnie to drink some *black* coffee, provoking the mother to turn on him and say, "She does not need the coffee, she needs to eat this." At this moment Bonnie's refusal became noticeably more vigorous.

It was clear that the present process of change was sluggish or stuck, and I determined to quicken the pace and create sufficient intensity to provoke discontinuous change. The four converging forces in the room were Bonnie, her mother, her father, and me, and the goal was to create a crisis in which the forces would clash and the system would transform.

At this point in the session, the family members were seated in a widely spaced circle. Bonnie had her legs and arms crossed in the pathognomonic posture of a bored and irritated adolescent. I began to try to create the necessary intensity by delivering an ominous message: "Your daughter is starving herself to death. It is your responsibility as parents to get your daughter to eat. She has defeated both of you. Do whatever you have to do, but don't let your daughter die!" Bonnie continued to argue with her parents, and it was clear that she was skillful at manipulating proximity and distance to paralyze them. Through her patterns of irritability and intimidation, she was maintaining the gulf between the mother and the father. It was essential to get them to pull together and send a clear message to their daughter: "*We* will not tolerate your self-starvation. This behavior must stop!" The goal was to telescope into a few moments the developmental change in the family's life cycle that would make both the girl and the parents autonomous. Only when the mother and father came together and Bonnie was freed from triangulation would change occur.

I therefore changed the seating arrangement, placing the parents closely on either side of Bonnie. With both parents bending over her intently and insisting that she eat, Bonnie began to take bites of her sandwich. At one point, her father lightly held her hands while her mother held the sandwich for her. As her father and mother both leaned over her, each with an arm around her so that all three were touching, she took the last two bites. The discontinuous change had begun. It was no more than a beginning; there was much therapeutic work to be done before the transformation would be complete and lasting. But the problem, which had been seen as an individual problem, one that existed only within the girl, was transformed to a problem in the family interactions.

I saw this family many years ago. Today, I would involve other members of the family and the family's context in the therapy. I never saw some of the children. I never saw Bonnie with her friends; I might have been able to help them support her in her attempts to differentiate. I would work with the sibling relationships to get them to help each other in their developmental tasks. The crisis is only the contextualization of the system; that is, the family members realize that they all play a part. After that, the therapist must work with the different subsystems to stabilize the system in the new status quo.

The crisis induced in IST is not necessarily a strident, unbalancing event, as it was in this example, but it is always intense. There may be a low-key intensity that is still felt as stressful, or the intensity may be created through duration as the therapist sets in motion a new sequence that gradually changes the system. I call the latter the "sunburn crisis": You don't feel it when you're first exposed to it, but its effect shows up later.

However the intensity is generated, the key factor in crisis induction is that the event is decisive. The system is perturbed, the structure is challenged, and new patterns emerge. There is no single technique; the challenge may be carried out through a variety of techniques, such as unbalancing, reframing, or even paradox. What is important is the outcome: The system changes.

Some therapists believe that people cannot reason or communicate when their anxiety is high. They therefore talk to their clients one at a time to calm them down. While this is obviously essential at times, therapists, nevertheless, must not allow themselves to be paralyzed by this occurrence. The IST therapist closely monitors the feedback in the session, moving the system toward transformation. This process was superbly described by a former teacher, Robert Pottash, M.D., many years ago (personal communication, 1973). He said that psychotherapy was a process of alternating between "glue"—talking to people about neutral material—and "solvent"—working to create crisis. The clinician adds "glue" when people disorganize and then adds "solvent," magnifying the intensity to move the system to change.

Crisis induction in the therapy session thus has an advantage that I call the Missouri Factor, for the "show-me" state. When one creates a crisis, one sees the interactional patterns transforming before one's very eyes. There is tangible confirmation that the intervention has been successful—or, conversely, that a change of course has not occurred and that another approach is called for.

As boys, my brother, Loren M. Fishman (a New York physiatrist), and I used to joke about situations where things seemed banal and people seemed so stuck. "They're not going off the deep end," my brother used to say; "they're going off the shallow end."

It is the same with many of the families we work with. They are flirting with forces that are making it very difficult for them to change. I am often struck by how difficult they find it, when they have tried a new pattern of interacting or a new way of being, to maintain the change. Much is dependent on the reinforcement and support from extrafamilial institutions—the teacher, the judge, the friend—as well as from the extended family. The chapters to follow will spell out how the principles described in this chapter can be used to mobilize these outside forces and help families in distress to shed old patterns, maintain change, and avoid not only the deep end but even the more ubiquitous—and at times more insidious—shallow end.

CHAPTER 2

Assessment I:
The 4-D Model

The assumption of being an individual is our greatest limitation.

—Pir Vilayat Khan

THE IST MODEL, as we have seen, draws its power in part from the fact that the therapist deals not only with the nuclear family but also with the broader system. But just who is to be brought in? Where does the therapist draw the line?

The difference between including all those necessary to the therapy and being overwhelmed by sheer numbers lies in refined assessment. An initial goal of therapy is to identify, out of all the people in the patient's broader context, those who are either part of the problem or potentially part of the solution. It is here that the concept of the homeostatic maintainer is particularly useful as a heuristic instrument for determining the dysfunctional isomorphic patterns.

Assessment in Intensive Structural Therapy has been formalized into a four-dimensional model, designed to help the therapist evaluate a family system from a number of different perspectives. The model includes four aspects of the family to be considered in the assessment—contemporary developmental pressures, structure, history, and process—which will be elaborated in later sections of this chapter. The idea of four dimensions goes beyond the simple listing of four considerations, however, to include

This chapter is based on chapter 2 of my earlier book, *Treating Troubled Adolescents* (New York: Basic Books, 1988). Material from that chapter is reproduced by permission of Basic Books, Inc.

the implications of the concept of the fourth dimension, which broadened the traditional three-dimensional measurement of space into a space-time perspective.

The concept of the fourth dimension revolutionized contemporary physics and has had profound effects on non-Euclidean mathematics and other fields, such as the arts. Marcel Duchamps's well-known painting *Nude Descending a Staircase,* for example, depicts not only the three dimensions of physical space but also the fourth dimension of time, since the figure is portrayed in motion from numerous angles.

The processes involved in the fourth dimension of the IST model include both the interactional patterns, such as triadic functioning that the therapist observes in the treatment room, and the therapist's active participation in what is happening. It is therefore more subjective than the first three dimensions, determined in part by the therapist's own feelings in the presence of the family.

The four-dimensional model provides the clinician with a kaleidoscopic view of the subject like that of the Cubist painter. It allows the therapist to look at a moving system from different perspectives. Moreover, it takes into consideration the therapist's own position in the process as he or she moves in and out of the system, now as a neutral observer, now as an involved protagonist, supporting family members or suddenly realizing the family's control. It is this emphasis on process and the therapist's active place in it that helps define family therapy as a therapy of experience, in which the family first enacts its dysfunctional patterns in the therapy room and then replaces them with more functional, corrective ways of interacting. The four-dimensional model can help the clinician guide the family through this transformation. Let us now take a closer look at the individual dimensions of the model.

Assessment of Contemporary
Developmental Pressures

Families, like all living systems, have tendencies toward both equilibrium and evolution. During the course of a family's life, there are destabilizing developmental pressures that disrupt equilibrium and challenge the family to evolve.

That individuals go through regular developmental stages has been axiomatic ever since the theories of Erik Erikson and Jean Piaget were published. Piaget (1950) explored the phases of cognitive development in children, from the sensorimotor stage to the ability to reason abstractly, while Erikson (1950) outlined eight stages of psychosocial development in humans from birth to old age. Families, too, experience regular developmental changes.

Central to family therapy theory is the tenet that families develop. One criticism of Erikson's work is that he described people as developing in isolation—as though they are growing up all alone in the woods. Family therapists see development as superimposed moiré patterns—that the development of the child, the development of the adult (Levinson, 1978) and the development of the family unit itself culminate in the common experience of the family members. The works of Jay Haley (1973) and Elizabeth Carter and Monica McGoldrick (1980) have noted that families develop along regular lines, experiencing change that is discontinuous yet predictable. This is an area in which a great deal has been written, but I will provide here a brief synopsis: To start the circle arbitrarily, the members of a couple get married. Their union represents a developmental passage for them as well as for their parents. This ritual, the wedding, is recognized by the community as their establishing a new family as well as their leaving their families of origin.

The next family developmental crisis is the birth of their first child, when the system recoils and reorganizes. And the system that changes is not only the couple's. Their extended family as well as others in the system are also affected in a discontinuous way—a profound experience after which none of their lives will be the same.

Another passage is the child going off to school—which is less of a stress today since both parents tend to work, making school less representative of a gap in one parent's day. Another is the birth of a second child—which is often profoundly unstabilizing. The emergence of the child into adolescence is a passage that few parents are prepared for; the family witnesses both a profound physical metamorphosis and the transformation of their child due to the increasingly complex world in which he or she is now living. The youngster faces influences as diverse as peers and MTV and a society that *expects* adolescents to be different and difficult and to spend a lot of money. Of course, the child leaving home completes the circle to some extent. But for the parents there is another passage: the experience of changing places with their parents and coming to take care of them.

While this synopsis does not do justice to the excellent literature on this subject, I have always agreed with Jay Haley (personal communication, 1989) that the most profound developmental passages are when people leave and enter the system—by birth, death, or divorce.

These normal developmental changes inevitably destabilize the structure of the family, creating stress that family systems can react to in different ways. As P. Glansdorff and Ilya Prigogine (1971) have said, the fluctuations created by developmental pressures can lead to a dissipative state, which is formed by nonequilibrium conditions and can lead to a new structure. Some systems respond by transforming the rules under which they operate, thereby allowing new behaviors, functionally more appropriate to the new structure, to be expressed. In other systems, the stress on the family is prolonged, and the result is the emergence of medical or psychological symptoms.

Compare, for example, two families that handled the same developmental stress—a child going away to college—in diametrically different ways: one functionally and the other dysfunctionally. In the first family, the parents moved from their large house in the suburbs to an apartment in town so they could go to more concerts together. They both decided that since they had more time, they would take up hobbies that they had put off. The father became an avid fly fisherman, while his wife became active in a music group at the church. They maintained contact with their daughter through weekly calls and frequent "CARE packages." The second family, however, disintegrated when the elder son went off to college. The father announced that he was leaving; he moved to a big city and began training for a marathon race. The younger son began having difficulties in school. The son in college spent the year, in his words, "finding [him]self and partying"; he received only one passing grade and flunked out. The mother gained 30 pounds and went into individual therapy, reporting that she spent most of her time "being angry at the males in [her] life."

In this family, the system did not change to accommodate the developmental change. The family members remained overinvolved with one another to the extent that they did not broaden their interests and expand their lives so that the loss of the son would not be debilitating. The older boy came back home in a developmentally regressed position, and the parents were not able to attend to their own new developmental stage because they were obliged to stay focused on their sons. By contrast, the members of the first family were working on their new developmental stages while maintaining considerable positive contact.

This first dimension of contemporary developmental pressures is extremely important in informing the therapist of the developmental tasks the family must undertake. With this knowledge, the therapist can begin to design and direct the treatment needed to help the family evolve.

Assessment of Structure in the Family

Among the key structural considerations for the family therapist is the demarcation and organization of the family unit, including important relationships outside as well as within the nuclear family. The therapist must decide what, in effect, constitutes "the family," the structure that should be treated. This decision will entail a consideration of the relationship of the defined family system not only with extended family but also with external systems affecting individual family members, such as school, social agencies, and friends.

Within that family unit, the major structural concern is the proximity between the important figures in the system. The therapist must assess whether the distances between various members of the system are appropriate to those members' developmental stages. Even with the developmental stages in mind, however, evaluating distance and proximity is not a simple matter, because appropriate distance is extremely subjective. Some families can tolerate a tremendous amount of intrusiveness without family members' feeling that they are losing autonomy or space, whereas in other families even the most minimal participation by others can create feelings of suffocation. As clinicians, we can best recognize a pathological deviation in distance by its effects; if a relationship appears appropriately close but the patient feels stifled or curtailed, our alarm system should go off and we should explore the distance that must be organized between the participants.

The appropriateness of distance is, in part, dependent on the basis for it. Distance based on reciprocal arrangements and collateral respect, where people decide that they are going to be apart for a particular task, does not lead to pathology. When distance is based on conflict, however, and is used to maintain the integrity and autonomy of the self, it can result in pathology. Thus the parameters of distance are broad, but the concept is useful for the clinician nonetheless.

It is becoming axiomatic in family therapy that the family structure changes with the passage of time and that these changes tend to follow regular developmental patterns (Carter & McGoldrick, 1980). The overlapping development of individual children, individual adults, and the family as a unit results in shifting structural relationships. As we saw earlier in the chapter, the therapist must be able to detect these points of developmental instability, for these represent the "growth buds" of the system and can lead the therapist to conceptualize the new developmental state.

I recently saw a family that clearly illustrates a structure that is developmentally askew. George was 40 years old and had been divorced after a brief marriage. Although he lived alone, he spent most of his time with his family (he worked with his father). When asked about his friends, he said, "I have none—except my father. He is my best friend, and my only friend." George did, however, have a woman friend whom he supported. She visited a few times a week, and every weekend they used a large amount of cocaine together.

George was more conscientious as a son than as an employee. Although he was well paid, he was extremely casual about going to work, yet his father never called him on the carpet for it, much to his mother's chagrin. The mother was infuriated that the father never said no to his son—"My husband has not allowed anyone to discipline our son since George was eight years old"—and the parents were talking about separating.

When this family was referred to me, the exasperated therapist described them as one of the mental health industry's best supporters. This upper-middle-class family seemed to have handled stress, developmental and otherwise, by going into therapy. My referral source related that they had been in and out of therapy for 20 years. My sense was that this family diffused their marital difficulties by focusing on their son and by involving a therapist. As I met with the parents, it was clear to me that their marriage had died long ago, in terms of passion for each other; ironically, they were kept apart by their "seconds" in their lifelong duel, a fight they never allowed themselves to have.

This system was developmentally stuck. George was not achieving his developmental goal of having his own life, and his parents had no expectations for him to live up to the responsibilities appropriate to his age. Furthermore, his parents were not achieving their goal of successfully launching their son and reorganizing themselves as a couple without a child living at home. The mother was contributing to the problem through her omissions (she had not threatened to leave her husband, for example) and was thus implicitly supporting the dysfunctional structure.

Structure, then, is the patterns of relationships in the system. There is no shortage of useful material on how to read and assess structure, and it need not be repeated here. What is essential for the purposes of this book is to understand that structure must be determined not just among family members but at the interface of the family and its influential broader context.

Assessment of the History of the System

The third dimension in the assessment involves the history of the system: elements in the background of the patient and the family that may be contributing to the present identified problem. The therapist must take a history of the important family events, such as deaths of parents, loss of children, divorces, illnesses, and financial reversals.

The work of Thomas Holmes and Richard Rahe (1967) confirming the association between stressful life events and illness that leads to hospitalization supports the clinical observation that patients who present with medical or psychological problems are living in a system in which some destabilizing factor has increased the stress on the family. The destabilizing event may be positive or negative (a new baby or the death of a parent); it may be predicted or unpredicted (a move to another city or the accidental death of a child). Whatever the nature of the precipitating factor, these symptomatic families have become stuck and are unable to resolve the resulting stress. In such families, the symptoms that emerge help to maintain the system's status quo, thus acting to stabilize the situation.

In addition to taking the general history of the family and its stressful life events, the therapist must learn the history of the problem presented, the steps the family has taken in the attempt to resolve it, and the involvement of any other therapists and agencies, past and present. Of particular importance is any history of psychiatric illness, such as schizophrenia, that may be treatable by medication. Other medical diseases should also be considered if the patient has been experiencing severe memory problems or has newly emergent physical complaints. I am not suggesting that the family therapist should be an internist, but I am suggesting that we should be aware of the individual physiology as a total system. We do not want our therapy to mirror the age-old mind-body split.

In assessing the index patient, it is useful to search for any isomorphic patterns in the history that are being manifested in the present. The patient can be asked whether there are persistent patterns of dreams, traumatic events, or memories that intrude frequently. One woman, for example, reported that she was still very troubled by an experience she had had following surgery. As she was waking from the general anesthesia, she had been unable to speak and had flailed her arms. The medical personnel in attendance thought she was having a psychotic reaction and sedated her. She had been extremely traumatized by this experience of being speechless and, in essence, a hostage. It recalled to her the similar experience of having her tonsils out in childhood and of being without a voice and feeling totally powerless. Her present situation was isomorphic in that her husband was a workaholic businessman who was unsympathetic to her indignation that he was not a truly participatory member of the family. She felt trapped in this situation in which, again, she felt she had no voice. Identifying such patterns can be helpful in establishing empathy with the patient. More important, it can help motivate the patient to change the present situation, because it is an opportunity to redress the earlier wrongs.

The history dimension is essential in providing information about the chronicity and severity of the system's dysfunction. It also gives the therapist vital information about the current concerns of the family, for the history a family reports reflects only a partial reality. It is a selective chronicle edited according to what is concerning them at present. Even when families scan their reflections collectively, they remember and retell events that are congruent with their present problems. The resulting narrative, while it does not represent a complete history, is of value in telling the therapist a great deal about the present state of the family.

The family history is therefore taken at several points, with differing objectives. Before the first session, the therapist obtains as much information as possible over the telephone, in order to identify members of the system who will be significant to the therapy. During the first session or sessions, the therapist elicits the history again in order to draw out the concerns of the various participants and to observe their reactions to each other's accounts.

The history dimension, as we have seen, encompasses the family system as a whole, but it would not be complete without an assessment of the history of individual family members. In particular, I consider it essential to explore, not only for the index person but also for other key family members, their experience as makers of choices in the system in which they are living. As we have seen, individuals within the system are multifaceted and responsive to the context, but no one is completely at the mercy of external forces. As human beings, we all have some leeway in manipulating these forces and buffering their impact on us, as well as the innate ability to create outside forces that will propel us forward. Indeed, a great deal of pathology is related to restriction of choice. Of course, the ability to make choices within a given context is, in part, a structural consideration, but it is also a personal one, involving beliefs about the self. Thus, as transformation of the system takes place in therapy, an important facet for the therapist to monitor is how the changes in the system are affecting the basic premises of the self held by the various individual members. In a sense, we as clinicians must have binocular vision, looking at both the individual and the context. To the extent that we follow both, our therapy is richer and more powerful.

Assessment of Process

In assessing the family, it is helpful to keep in mind that descriptions of a system by family therapists are different from those by anthropologists or

novelists. Unlike our colleagues in these other fields, we as family clinicians do not maintain a fixed distance from the family. At times, we may
in fact become part of the system and, through techniques such as unbalancing, act as protagonists in the family drama. The therapist must therefore be aware of, and be able to describe, the various processes at work in
the system, both those that can be observed among the family members in
the treatment room and those of which the therapist becomes a part, acting
and being acted upon.

The latter type of interaction involves the difficult area of the therapist's
own subjective responses. As therapists who also have lives of our own,
we bring into the treatment room a number of subjective factors that can
affect our reactions and assessments. To some extent, our own family
background, current family system, and professional context all influence
how we perceive and respond to what is happening in the therapy room.
For example, a therapist treating a family that presents with an unruly
adolescent may be dealing with a similar situation at home. In such a case,
a yellow light of caution should go off, warning the therapist to be wary of
first reactions. It is important to recognize and, if necessary, to resist the
pressure of one's own context and to take account of one's own part in this
fourth dimension of assessment in evaluating the information received
from and about the family.

When assessing the process dimension within the family system, the
therapist focuses on two primary tasks: identifying who or what is acting
to maintain the homeostasis in the system, and identifying the dysfunctional transactional patterns at work.

IDENTIFYING THE HOMEOSTATIC MAINTAINER

As we saw in chapter 1, a family system remains stuck in dysfunctional
homeostasis when some person or force is keeping the family from adapting to developmental pressures. We have called this person or force the
homeostatic maintainer. The system cannot heal and begin to operate in a
more functional manner until the operation of the homeostatic maintainer
has been identified and changed to permit the system to change.

In some cases, the identity of the homeostatic maintainer is quite clear
without any therapeutic intervention. Some years ago, the newspapers reported the story of a 19-year-old man who had committed an armed rob-
bery in a rural community. When his court-appointed attorney went to see
him, the man pulled a knife and held the young woman prisoner for 3
days. Finally, the man was apprehended and had his day in court. When,
just before sentencing, the judge asked, "Is there anything you would like
to say in your own behalf?" the man remained silent but gestured to his

mother. The mother then stood, pointed to the judge, and said, "How dare you treat my son like this! It's not fair. He's done nothing wrong."

With just this brief story to go on, one can only guess about the true nature of the forces in the young man's life that had buffered him from facing the consequences of his actions. But it is clear that even at this 11th hour, in the face of overwhelming evidence of culpability, the mother refused to hold her son responsible and instead acted to maintain the status quo.

In most cases, the homeostatic maintaining process is less blatant, and the therapist must delve into the context to discover how it is operating. Most commonly, the therapist perturbs the system and observes who reacts to return the system to its status quo, and by what processes. In doing so, the therapist becomes a kind of foreign body in the system, an irritation that must be accommodated in order to restore the smooth functioning of the system. These homeostatic forces that emerge allow the clinician to ascertain with a high level of reliability, patterns that have kept the system from changing.

This perturbation of the system is, in fact, like a kind of homeopathic poison that will lead the system to transformation. As therapy proceeds, the clinician will continue to challenge the rules of the system in order to provoke the emergence of new patterns. These patterns will be used to provide the family a new perspective in which the forces of homeostasis can be seen for what they are—roadblocks to adaptive change. The therapist will then work with the family to remove those barriers by helping them transform individual behaviors or social forces that are acting to maintain stability and thus prolong the problems keeping the family in crisis.

IDENTIFYING THE TRANSACTIONAL PATTERNS

Once the therapist has determined who or what is maintaining the problem, the next step is to identify the patterns at work in the system that are contributing to dysfunction. The therapist's goal here is to make use of these patterns to map out a strategy for brief therapy, a treatment that will produce the fastest possible change.

There are a number of key patterns that the therapist looks for. One is *conflict avoidance*. Dysfunctional systems often take steps to detour confrontation and avoid acknowledging conflict. For example, if the therapist brings up a difficult issue and asks the parents to discuss it, their pattern of avoiding confronting each other may be evident as they persistently direct their responses to the therapist or to their children and retreat to safe ground whenever possible.

For example, in one therapy session, a couple was being urged to discuss their disagreement about whether to let their daughter return home with her 2-year-old child. The mother began talking to the father about how little money they had. Although they were in their 50s, they had no savings, because all their lives they had spent everything they had on their children. As she became more and more exercised, her husband only looked down or glanced nervously at the therapist; at no time did he respond to his wife.

Another pattern common in dysfunctional families is *schizmogenesis*. Bateson (1972) coined this term to refer to escalating sequences of interaction, which he described as occurring in two forms, complementary and symmetrical. In its complementary form, the pattern can be observed as a series of reciprocal behaviors. For example, a family may include a wife who is angry and a husband who complains of stomach aches. When the pattern escalates, the wife becomes angrier and the husband's symptoms exacerbate. In the symmetrical form of the pattern, the participants act in concert. They may get into a heated argument, for instance, in which neither can back down. When this pattern escalates, violence may erupt.

There are additional patterns that may be observed in certain special families, such as psychosomatic families (Minuchin, Rosman, & Baker, 1978). As we saw in the case of Dorothy, discussed in chapter 1, psychosomatic families are frequently characterized by *enmeshment*, an extreme form of proximity and intensity in family interactions that results in poorly differentiated boundaries. Family members fail to make the proper distinctions in their perceptions of one another and of themselves. A videotape of Minuchin working with a psychosomatic family contains a very graphic demonstration of the lack of boundaries in an enmeshed family. In the therapy room are the father, the mother, and a 12-year-old diabetic daughter. Minuchin walks into the room and squeezes the girl's arm, asking the father, "Can you feel that?" The father replies, "You know, it's odd, I *can* feel that!" Minuchin then asks the mother the same question. She answers, "I can't feel that, but I have poor circulation."

Another pattern often encountered in psychosomatic families is *rigidity*, the inability to depart from accustomed patterns of behavior when circumstances would seem to necessitate change. This is an especially problematic pattern for families with adolescents, in which issues of autonomy are apt to stress the usual rules of family interaction. Rigid families frequently make fixed demands on the child; their message is, "You are valued for what you *do*, not for being *you*." Another frequently seen pattern is a rigid stance that communicates to the adolescent, "No matter how hard you try, the family does not want you."

Overprotectiveness is yet another pattern that may be found in psychosomatic families and other dysfunctional systems. Here, the degree of concern that family members have for one another is exaggerated, often to the point that a member is hindered from developing autonomy and competence. In an interesting case of overprotectiveness, a mildly retarded 19-year-old woman was living in a system that was organized to provide for her every need. The society provided an abundance of helping services, and between the family and the outside helpers the young woman was prevented from becoming more independent. After a cautious suicide attempt, she confided to a therapist that she desperately wanted to try to get a job in a horticultural nursery, make a life away from home, and manage her own money. These seemed like simple and attainable goals, but the overprotective system was not allowing her to try to attain them.

Many families that exhibit patterns of enmeshment, rigidity, and overprotectiveness also demonstrate an inability to cope with conflict directly. When the existence of problems is not denied outright in professed harmony or consensus, the avoidance of conflict is often manifested in a pattern of *conflict diffusion*, in which another family member not directly involved acts to distract attention from the conflict and thus diffuse it, a pattern frequently observed in therapy sessions. During one session, for example, when the father and the eldest son began to argue, the next eldest son chimed in and complained that he wanted to be heard. What identified this as a clear case of conflict diffusion by the system and not of the boy's spontaneous need to be heard was the fact that at virtually every point in the session when conflict seemed about to emerge, one or another family member would act to diffuse the tension, with the net effect that the conflict would be forgotten.

Some or all of these aspects of psychosomatic family organization—enmeshment, rigidity, overprotectiveness, and conflict avoidance and diffusion—may be seen in families that present problems other than psychosomatic ones. When they are present, they must all be addressed for the therapy to be brief. These and other pivotal process patterns can be not only observed but changed in the therapy room. When therapy is directed at them, the treatment can move forward rapidly. Conversely, if these patterns are not being altered in the therapy sessions, the clinician should conclude that it is time to change course.

The model of assessment described in this chapter is well illustrated by the following case.

CASE EXAMPLE: MICHELLE

One definition of a difficult family is a family in which there are so many conflicting social forces that everybody's best efforts are neutralized.

This was true of an extremely difficult family with which I consulted. A number of mental health and social service professionals had been working with the family, but in each case the work had been with a part of the system and not with the system as a whole. The result was a disempowered family in terms of parental authority and an out-of-control teenager. The case serves to demonstrate how the system can be moved to change when the lens is broadened and all the essential people are brought in.

The identified patient in this case was Michelle, a 13-year-old who had been hospitalized for 6 weeks. This was done at the request of the day treatment center where she had been enrolled after she had thrown a flower pot at her sister's head and run away. She had also threatened her sister with a knife, and a court hearing was pending on that incident.

This was Michelle's third hospitalization. After the second hospitalization, she had been discharged to a group home from which she had run away. She had a long history of truancy—she had run away from home at least 15 times—and was now 4 months pregnant. The Department of Social Services had been involved with her case for 4 years.

Neither the family nor the staff at the small rural hospital where she was an inpatient had been successful in changing the girl's behavior, and she was scheduled to be sent to a state psychiatric hospital on the day following my consultation with the family. This was a step that I felt should be avoided if at all possible. Not only was I concerned with what awaited this vulnerable youngster at a state psychiatric institution, but I knew that it would give the parents even less control over Michelle than they now had. The hospitalizations had let the family off the hook. My goal as a therapist was to empower the family so that they would take responsibility for Michelle and take their daughter home.

Michelle had other ideas, however. She had been having a good time in her present placement, where she liked the group therapy and had gotten close to a young male psychiatric aide. She apparently assumed that the state hospital would be much the same, and she had made up her mind that she wanted to go there.

As the session progressed, it became clear how the focus on Michelle and her problems was diffusing the conflict between the parents. Present at the session were Michelle; her mother; her stepfather; her 17-year-old sister, Tiffany; a staff psychiatrist in the hospital where Michelle was now an inpatient; Michelle's therapist from the hospital; and a social service worker who had been working with the family for 10 or 12 years. Notably missing from the session were the girls' maternal grandmother, who was a highly relevant figure, and a therapist who had worked with Michelle for 4 or 5 years and on whom the parents relied greatly.

Michelle's appearance seemed calculated to express rebellion. She wore a punk hairdo and earrings with dangling crosses, and she had an obvious tattoo on the back of her hand. Tiffany, by contrast, was neatly dressed in collegiate attire. The mother, whose hair was close-cropped, wore a plaid hunting shirt. The stepfather was a short, heavy man with a full red beard. He had been part of the family for about 8 years.

Several of the developmental pressures on this family were obvious. In addition to the presence of two adolescents in the family, there was a stepparent relationship. Moreover, the parents were experiencing some occupational pressures. The stepfather was in a new, lower-paying job, and the mother was having trouble with people at work.

The history dimension was clearly significant. From the long-term involvement of social services, it was clear that the problems in the family were chronic. In fact, during the first 4 or 5 years of Michelle's life, the mother, a biker, had left the girls with her mother and taken off. She had had several boyfriends before the present stepfather, and one of the earlier boyfriends had sexually abused Michelle.

Thus the major elements in two of the dimensions of the 4-D assessment were fairly well established by the time we met in the therapy room. What remained to be determined were the structures and the isomorphic patterns of relationships in the system and the forces that were maintaining the dysfunctional homeostasis. I began the session by asking individual members of the family what needed to change.

TIFFANY: Somehow we don't get along, and I think we need to change how we feel about one another and learn to make more compromises. We always want to change while we stay the same sometimes.
FISHMAN: Like what kind of compromises?
TIFFANY: Well, like with curfews. Mom says be home at ten and we say twelve, so we need to make a compromise, and none of us are willing to compromise.
FISHMAN: So what time do you come home?
MOTHER: Eleven.
TIFFANY: (laughing) Twelve. No, eleven.
MOTHER: It took a long time to get to that eleven o'clock curfew, and she still stretches it.
FISHMAN: How about you, Michelle? What do you think needs to change?
MICHELLE: I just think our family needs to learn to talk to each other instead of blaming each other for everybody else's problems. And I think that's the problem.
FISHMAN: Do you feel blamed?
MICHELLE: Yeah, and I think everybody else in this family does too.
FISHMAN: When you're blamed, it's a bad rap? You're unfairly blamed?

MICHELLE: Yeah.

FISHMAN: For what?

MICHELLE: It's a lot of things. I think me and Tiffany both are blamed a lot for what happens between Mom and Dad. I can't speak for Tiffany, but that's how I feel.

TIFFANY: I think that every time something goes wrong, like when Michelle used to run away a lot, she would blame Dad or she'd blame Mom, saying, "She's doing that to me," but actually it's her own free will to go, but she's blaming everybody else.

Michelle's sister is clearly not supporting her—she's on her parents' side.

FISHMAN: (*To mother*) So what do you think?

MOTHER: Michelle does blame a lot of things on everybody else. She is not responsible a lot of times for her actions—"Well, I can't help it if I did that." (*After a pause*) I can't begin to tell you how many times she's said, "Oh, I won't do this again" and turns around two days later and does the same thing. And running away, her past of running away—

FISHMAN: What do you do when she runs away?

MOTHER: Call the police. We've been involved with social services for so long, that you call the police, you call social services.

The family's dependence on outside forces thus emerged early in the session. The family could not handle Michelle by itself; whenever she ran away, social services became involved.

FISHMAN: What happens when she comes home?

MOTHER: She comes home again and we start all over at ground one again, constantly. (*Michelle is shaking her head.*)

FISHMAN: And what is ground one?

MOTHER: Ground one? First of all, abide by the rules. Stay home and go to school. When you come home from school, there are some chores you need to do. After that, your evening is usually free, but since you've run away fifteen hundred times I don't want you leaving the house. (*Looking first at husband, then at Michelle*) Anything else?

MICHELLE: I don't think so. But are you saying that it's just me that has to change?

MOTHER: No, this is my opinion—

TIFFANY: She's talking about the blaming.

MICHELLE: Okay, because it's not only me that needs to change. It's the whole family.

TIFFANY: We're talking about you right now.

MOTHER: This is just my opinion. I'm entitled to an opinion. I didn't say you were the only one.

MICHELLE: (*Rolling her eyes in exasperation*) I didn't say you weren't entitled to an opinion.

FISHMAN: (*to Michelle*) Okay, so who supports you? Your sister supports your mom. Who supports you?

MICHELLE: Myself.

FISHMAN: Does your dad support you?

MICHELLE: I think most of the time I support myself. What do you mean by support?

FISHMAN: In arguments and so forth.

MICHELLE: I think I support myself. Sometimes my mom supports me, but most of the time I do it myself.

FISHMAN: (*To stepfather*) What do you think about this, sir?

STEPFATHER: Just what we've been talking about. You know, she doesn't respect others, she doesn't respect herself. And its everybody's fault but hers. She always says everybody's picking on her, but really they're not. She brings it all on herself.

FISHMAN: And what do you think needs to change in this family?

STEPFATHER: Well, we'd like to try to sit down and talk it over, but she doesn't give you the chance to sit and talk things over. She blows up so fast and we don't gain anything. It just makes her madder and she goes off to her room and we don't see her again for a while, but then she comes in and tries to blame it on everybody else, 'cause she doesn't want to sit and talk it out.

FISHMAN: It sounds like you've all been trying.

STEPFATHER: We've tried it all ways. I've been nice to her, I've been mean to her, but no way works. So I don't know what to say or do.

FISHMAN: I understand there are some new things on the scene. What else is happening?

MOTHER: (*laughing ironically*) She's pregnant, on top of everything else.

This first segment of the session with this extremely unsuccessful system revealed several isomorphic splits. The girl was out of control because the lack of coherence among the adults surrounding her was allowing her to do whatever she wanted to do. The ineffectiveness of the parents in controlling her indicated that there had to be a split between them. In fact, Michelle's statement that her parents blamed the girls for what happened between the parents themselves indicated that she had become wise to therapy lingo and was using it on the professionals in the room. A statement like that is irresistible to therapists; we are immediately drawn to focus on the parents and leave the girl alone, and another split is created in the system, between the parents and the therapist.

There were also splits with the family's broader context. The fact that the police were of no help suggests that they and the parents were not working together. More overt splits had developed with the social service system. As the session progressed, the role that the social services played in the family became clearer. Not only had the family become dependent on them, but also Michelle had learned to induct them as allies against her parents, even to the point of using deceit.

FISHMAN: What do you do when she comes home from running away?

MOTHER: We go over rules, we tell her what's expected of her. We have asked no different of her than we asked of Tiffany at that age. When Tiffany was fourteen, there were certain things that had to be done. But Michelle would be upset and think she should be able to stay out as late as Tiffany, and she hadn't got the age and she hadn't done anything to earn the privilege.

FISHMAN: What do you do? Do you punish her when she comes home?

MOTHER: We gave up doing that, too, because no matter what we did, it didn't work.

FISHMAN: You don't punish her?

MOTHER: What do you do? Ground her? We ground her, it don't make no difference; she runs away. Spank her?

The members of the family all responded with talk of child abuse.

TIFFANY: One time my dad was accused of child abuse, and it was found, you know, he didn't do it. So then we went to a therapist, and the therapist said that my parents cannot spank Michelle, so they don't spank her.

SS WORKER: Well, you can't leave a mark on your child.

MOTHER: You can spank her with your hand, but when I spank her she breaks the blood vessels in my hand and I end up with big blood blisters, and I ain't gonna do it. And when you're this age, what good is spanking going to do, anyway?

MICHELLE: It doesn't hurt.

FISHMAN: Spanking is a personal, moral, and legal issue, but you guys shouldn't feel that you're trapped. (*Mother and stepfather agree that they're trapped.*)

STEPFATHER: We have no authority.

MOTHER: She has even admitted to bruising herself and accusing us of child abuse.

Michelle had caught on to the workings of the larger system and was making it work for her. She would pinch herself to create bruises and then run to the authorities and claim her parents had hit her. The authorities would intervene, in the process disempowering the parents of control over the girl. She had them over a barrel.

MOTHER: We don't have just one problem, honey, we've got zillions of them. We started when she was in first or second grade, started taking her to Bonnie Wright, and then we had this calm period for a while, and then we hit puberty, and then everything fell apart. She didn't get along in school, she didn't get along with her sister, she didn't get along with her mom, she didn't get along with her dad, she didn't like her grandma—I mean she didn't like anybody, not a soul. So we tried Tai Kwan Do, because that's supposed to give you self-confidence and teach you self-control. So she turned around and tried to kick her dad. So we didn't do that any more. So we took her for gymnastics—

FISHMAN: What did you do when she kicked you?

STEPFATHER: Socked her.

FISHMAN: And then what happened?

STEPFATHER: The cops came over to my house and accused me of child abuse.

MOTHER: That was the beginning.

STEPFATHER: That's when all hell broke loose.

FISHMAN: You guys have been disempowered as parents. You have all this help, and we as helpers are trying to do our best. And the more we do, the less help you get. Now we're dealing with the escalation—the pregnancy, going to the state hospital. Meanwhile, if you hadn't had so much help, chances are you'd handle it. (*Parents laugh.*) She's a very bright girl. (*To Michelle*) What do you want to be? I'll bet you could be very successful.

TIFFANY: (*Slapping Michelle on the knee*) Why don't you be a psychiatrist?

FISHMAN: She could do better than that. (*Laughter*)

TIFFANY: How about a lawyer?

FISHMAN: (*Turning serious*) You've become completely disempowered. And she knows it. It's interesting, the power that the authorities give her. She knows the system.

MICHELLE: (*Smiling to stepfather*) That's what you get for putting me in places like that.

STEPFATHER: You did it before I ever slapped you. You just did it so you could get that power.

MICHELLE: What did I ever do to you? I don't understand. I'm always the one that's doing something. It's always me. What did I do? What could I possibly have done to make your whole world crumble? (*As stepfather tries to respond*) I'm just a kid. You're an adult. You could do whatever you wanted to with me. You're like a god, okay?

STEPFATHER: It doesn't work that way. You remember the social services were on your side that day when you'd been talking with all those so-called foster kids across the street about what's the law and what's not the law. You finally got me to slap you and you went around the house for two days pinching yourself black and blue and then you went to your teacher and said I'd slapped you. Two days later they finally got ahold of me.

MICHELLE: It didn't happen that way. It was the very next day, and I had a bruise up here. How I could possibly get a bruise up there above my eye when there's no bone there is beyond me.

STEPFATHER: I slapped her on that side and the bruise was on this side.

MICHELLE: How could I make you hit me?

FISHMAN: You guys are no match for her.

MICHELLE: I can't make you do anything.

STEPFATHER: But the law sure did.

We can see here a series of coalitions with forces outside the family. The girl had been able to create a coalition with the social worker that led to getting the stepfather in trouble with the law. There was also an isomorphic coalition between the girl and her friends in the scheme to pit the authorities against the parents. Finally, Michelle had inducted the hospital staff into an alliance, moving them to send her to the state hospital, which would increase the distance between her and her parents and further immobilize the parental hierarchy.

As we saw in chapter 1, isomorphism is a useful clinical tool in helping to identify interactional patterns within the family. When a dysfunction pattern is detected in the broader system, the concept of isomorphism alerts the clinician to look for the pattern within the family.

To bring out the interactional patterns that were maintaining the homeostasis within the family, it would be necessary to unbalance the system to see who would return it to the status quo. In some families, this might be done by referring to the authorities—for example, suggesting that someone who has always been bailed out be forced to face the consequences of his or her actions within the court system. In this case, however, the opposite approach was called for. Whenever Michelle misbehaved, the outside authorities were immediately involved, and the family was immobilized. I therefore suggested an approach that would keep the response within the family and take the attention off Michelle, instead of focusing attention on her when she misbehaved.

FISHMAN: You tell your daughter that if she wants to live with you, she follows these rules. If she doesn't, you do what you have to do, regardless. If she visits you, if she comes home, if she doesn't follow the rules, you do what the Amish do: You shun her. She just stops existing.

At this suggestion, a kind of shudder went through the room. The girl's eyes started to well up. The mother's face flushed and she, too, started to cry.

STEPFATHER: (*Pointing to mother with his thumb, as though quoting her*) "I'm not going to abandon my child." I've tried to talk to her.
FISHMAN: Talk to her. She's got to change.
MOTHER: I can't do that.
TIFFANY: You can't abandon a child. You can't do that.
MOTHER: (*Crying*) You don't know what it took me to get over the guilt feelings the first time.
STEPFATHER: We went through all this.

The seemingly innocuous suggestion of shunning was apparently experienced as a powerful imperative. The mother was activated as homeostatic maintainer in her tearful rejection of the idea of "abandoning" her daughter. Of course, that was not what I was advocating. My suggestion, however, ran exactly counter to the prevailing isomorph of overprotectiveness and enmeshment in the system. I was suggesting distance in place of the very dysfunctional closeness between the mother and daughter that had kept the mother from joining with the stepfather and maintaining a hierarchy that could appropriately discipline the girl.

This pattern had undoubtedly occurred many times in the past. Whenever the mother was challenged to distance from her child by making Michelle suffer the consequences of her behavior, she refused and instead opted to bail the girl out. The mother's response occurred in the context of her husband's antipathy to her daughter—when she would refuse to challenge the girl, he would throw up his hands in anger and frustration—as well as in the context of a number of other isomorphic splits: between the family and social service, between the family and the hospital, and within the hospital between the doctors and the nursing staff. With all the adults split over what to do with the girl, the mother was continuously driven to the extreme position of supporting her daughter against the warring adults.

Years later, I learned that the mother had been having an affair, creating yet another split in the system. Her immorality mirrored her daughter's, and perhaps her guilt made it all the more difficult to discipline her daughter. Indeed, her sensitivity about not "abandoning" her daughter might have come from the fact that in a very real way, by her behavior, she *was* abandoning her daughter (and her family).

FISHMAN: (*To mother*) A little while ago, your daughter accused you of being a codependent of an alcoholic. (*To stepfather*) If your wife is addicted to her daughter—can't say no to her daughter—you are the coaddictive one.

MOTHER: We put up a united front. We talk a lot about what we've got to do.

STEPFATHER: Yeah, and we end up battling, too. It usually comes down to this one line: "She's my daughter, and I'm not going to abandon her." So everything I've said to do, before we take this action, it's always nipped in the bud right there. Rather than break up the marriage with this, I just go right along with what's going on.

MOTHER: But we've discussed it. You know, we've talked about this pregnancy, that we will not support it, we can't support it.

STEPFATHER: But I never did get a straight answer to this. I've asked it a couple of times.

MOTHER: What?

STEPFATHER: What if she comes home and she wants to keep the child, what are we going to do? And I didn't get no answers. So what will happen? I'll end up keeping her and the baby and we'll all get real attached to the baby and there's no way she'll ever get rid of the child.

FISHMAN: There are two things you have to be clear about and put up a united front. One, what you're going to do about the baby, and the other, the consequences to your daughter of this behavior—shunning, or whatever. Otherwise she's a lost cause.

As I tried to get the parents to discuss the situation between themselves and come to some decisions on which they could hold a united front, Michelle persistently tried to derail my efforts. In her experiences with social services, she had absorbed concepts that she could exploit in manipulating her parents and trying to control the course of the session.

MICHELLE: (*Raising her hand*) Could I say something? Because I'm here, you know.

FISHMAN: Sure. I was telling this to your parents because it's relevant to them.

MICHELLE: God. Just because I'm pregnant does not mean I'm a bad person, okay?

FISHMAN: Nobody's saying that.

MICHELLE: But you are saying that I should be shunned for being pregnant, and if I keep it I'm going to get wholly ignored. You know, that really messes somebody up. I have had friends whose parents didn't give them any kind of love, and them kids are crazy, they're really crazy.

FISHMAN: (*to parents*) Is that what happens? (*Shaking head sympathetically*)

She's so good [at getting around people]. (*To Michelle*) I'm talking with your parents because they have some decisions to make.

MICHELLE: But it's my baby, it's my baby!

FISHMAN: That's not what we're talking about. Nobody's disregarding that. It's your decision. Your parents have two other things they need to decide.

MICHELLE: Then how come you're telling them to shun me if I keep it? Isn't that what you're saying?

FISHMAN: (*Shaking his head no*) We're talking about two different things. One has to do with keeping your baby. That is your decision. The other has to do with running away. (*To parents*) Why don't you talk about that?

STEPFATHER: Talk about what?

FISHMAN: What you're going to do the next time she runs away. Is she going to be there for lunch, or will she stay home, or what?

MOTHER: (*Looking at husband, resignedly*) First we'll lock the door . . .

MICHELLE: (*As Tiffany tries to interrupt*) You know, my sister has the right to say what she needs to say.

STEPFATHER: Just lock her up. Then what?

MICHELLE: Say it, Tiff.

MOTHER: You mean when she runs away?

STEPFATHER: Yeah, when she finally decides to quit running and it's time to come home again.

MOTHER: Then she has to live by the rules, and then she—God, then we're right back in the same boat again.

MICHELLE: Uh huh.

When Michelle's efforts to get the floor were unsuccessful, she tried to make an opening for her sister to speak. That failing, she began agitating to leave. Meanwhile, her parents were struggling to come to some decisions.

MICHELLE: How long are we going to stay here?

STEPFATHER: (*To Fishman*) There's nothing we can do.

FISHMAN: You don't realize your power, your power in terms of your emotions. Withdrawing—just do what they do in the Amish country. If she disrespects you to such an extent, then the two of you shun her, and when she respects you and follows the rules—and you can negotiate the rules, I'm not saying this should be a police state—then you start speaking again.

Everyone began talking at once. The parents seemed to like the idea, but the girls continued to object. As the girls demanded attention, Fishman insisted on talking with the parents, telling them there were some decisions they had to make. When they seemed inclined to adopt the shunning tactic, Michelle tried a new tactic: declaring that it was unfair to Tiffany.

FISHMAN: Do you think it will work?

STEPFATHER: It'll work. Let 'em know we mean business.

MICHELLE: Tiffany has never done anything wrong to you guys.

STEPFATHER: Then why should Tiffany be worried about it?

MICHELLE: Because she doesn't feel it's right for any parent to do that to their kid. She's never done anything wrong to you, ever! She's been a good kid.

MOTHER: Parents have a moral responsibility to raise their children to have respect, to treat everybody fairly.

MICHELLE: Tiffany does!

MOTHER: Well, then, if she treats everybody fairly then she'll be treated fairly, won't she?

MICHELLE: I guess so. But you guys aren't even acknowledging that she's here.

FISHMAN: Do you think you could get your kids to allow you to have a conversation? Why don't you go ahead and do that? (*Laughter*)

MICHELLE: Are we almost done?

MOTHER: Shall we try it?

STEPFATHER: Sure, I'll try anything once. But it's got to be the two of us together.

MOTHER: Oh, yes.

STEPFATHER: No giving in—one saying go and the other saying no. We'll have to draw up some new rules and regs. (*Mother agrees and they laugh.*)

FISHMAN: (*To stepfather*) So you're the codependent here, what do you think?

STEPFATHER: We'll shun 'em. If they don't behave themselves, we'll shun 'em.

MOTHER: We'll try anything once.

FISHMAN: Once is not enough.

MICHELLE: Why do you say "them"? You have no reason to do whatever you're going to do to me to Tiffany. She has never done anything that bad, ever!

MOTHER: And when you say "once is not enough," how many times do we try?

FISHMAN: Until you see some changes. You don't stop until she changes. I've seen it work many times. It'll work. It would only be sometimes, only when she runs away, when she misbehaves. Otherwise, you'll welcome her into your home as your loving daughter. It's up to her.

MICHELLE: (*After a long pause*) Can we go?

FISHMAN: It's up to your parents.

STAFF PSYCHIATRIST: (*To parents*) Do you think they understand that that's the way the rules are going to be?

STEPFATHER: Michelle's trying to change the subject, so she's letting it sink in a little bit.

MICHELLE: No, I just want to go.

STEPFATHER: She wants to go; she thinks we're done. She wants to do it her way.

MICHELLE: (*nods*) Uh-huh. I'm afraid so. Can we please go? I want someone to take me home. I might as well call it home, anyway.

The consultation in this case was done for the hospital staff. Apparently there had been one more manifestation of the isomorphic split among the professionals at the hospital; the psychiatrist had wanted to send Michelle home with outpatient therapy, whereas Michelle's therapist wanted to send her to the state hospital. The psychiatrist had capitulated, but after this interview, in which they witnessed the parents' reaction to the "shunning" intervention, they agreed that the parents were strong enough and that the girl did not have to be placed in the state hospital. Michelle went home, had her baby, and put it up for adoption.

As I mentioned, the therapeutic team subsequently learned that during this period the mother had been having an affair with someone at her workplace. Every lunch hour she and her lover would take off on a motorcycle for their trysting spot. After Michelle's baby was born, the mother left her husband and she and her lover took Michelle and moved out of the state. Tiffany stayed with her stepfather for a year and then joined her mother. I have been told that once the mother and stepfather had separated, Michelle's runaways stopped.

This family typifies the troubled family of today. It is not just that there is an organizational lock on the family. These systems are double-, triple-, and quadruple-locked. To move them, we have to have the keys to all these locks—that is, to include them in the therapy.

CHAPTER 3

Assessment II:
The Homeostatic Maintainer

A S WE SAW in the last chapter, dysfunction in the family is maintained through transactional patterns, such as conflict avoidance, overprotectiveness, and enmeshment. It is by helping the system to change these patterns that the therapist brings about a healing transformation in the system.

A key to identifying the dysfunctional patterns is to identify the homeostatic maintainer(s). When a sequence of interactions is perceived to be acting to return the system to homeostasis after it has been perturbed, the pattern of the transaction becomes clear. The process can often be elicited in a simple and straightforward procedure in the therapy room: The therapist disturbs the balance of the system and watches to see who acts to return the system to homeostasis. The behavior of the homeostatic maintainer reveals not only who is maintaining the dysfunctional homeostasis in the system but also how it is being maintained. The clinician can then map out a strategy for therapy in which changes in the dysfunctional patterns serve as measures of outcome.

One problem that has limited the effectiveness of traditional family therapy is that the family's dysfunctional interactional patterns are often isomorphic, with patterns in the broader context. Outside forces may be reinforcing the dysfunctional homeostasis through the same patterns at work within the family unit. The therapist must therefore be aware of how the larger context is impinging on the family. Is it trespassing over the boundaries of the family? How is it responding to changes internal to the family? Is there someone or something at the interface with the outside world that is reinforcing the dysfunctional homeostasis? Or is there someone there who is undermining the dysfunction and could serve as an ally in the therapy?

For example, in one family the index person was a 32-year-old man who had been using drugs since he was 16. His family not only supported him but also tolerated his irresponsibility and violence toward them. Similarly, whenever he became involved with the legal authorities, the court system always gave him a second chance (and a third, and a fourth, and on and on). Over the years a number of social agencies had been involved with this family, but at no point had anyone ever insisted on job counseling. This family strikes me as part of the cadre of victims of urban blight. In the inner city in which they live, there are no more jobs of the sort that their parents had. Tired and defeated-looking, the couple and even their adolescent children seem weary. Part of their fatigue may be combating the father's drug abuse; they nonetheless have a spark that makes them very likable. They laugh together, commiserate, and exhibit a good-natured weariness of helpers like us, who have failed them over the years.

A pattern of failing to hold this man responsible for his livelihood and his behavior was thus operating within his family and outside of it, in the compelling social system of the drug culture as well as in the legal system. Identifying the pattern made clear that the therapy should involve not only the family but also the judge (who was brought into several sessions via speakerphone) and a job counselor. In addition, it provided the treatment markers: (1) no drug use, which would remove him from the toxic drug culture and increase the likelihood of changing other problematic aspects of his life; (2) employment that would make him self-sufficient, which would be an obvious indication that the system was no longer providing for him and protecting him; and (3) changed family interactions, as monitored in the therapy sessions.

This chapter describes in more detail several cases in which the concept of the homeostatic maintainer proved invaluable in revealing the process patterns underlying the dysfunction and planning treatment that would make possible a rapid transformation of the system.

Perturbing the System to Draw Out the Homeostatic Maintainer

The technique of perturbing the system to determine who is maintaining the homeostasis is illustrated by a case involving two children who were having difficulties in school. The family consisted of the mother; her 11-year-old daughter, Heather; her 7-year-old son, Joshua; and Ralph, the stepfather, who had been living with the family for 5 years and was an established member of the family (although they were not married). One stress on the system was the fact that the man worked in a city 2 hours away and was out of the home every evening. The couple was biracial and lived in the mother's lower-middle-class white community, in close proximity to her parents.

The family came in for therapy because of Joshua's difficulties at school. He was experiencing learning problems, and his behavioral problems were so severe that the school considered him uncontrollable and wanted to expel him. At the same time, Heather was manifesting numerous psychosomatic symptoms at school, frequently going to the nurse's office and complaining. The session included the mother, the stepfather, the two children, the therapist (a trainee), and me (as supervisor). At the outset, I was observing from behind a one-way mirror.

STEPFATHER: We're here because of Joshua, but I think the problem is with everyone. We're here because of Joshua's symptom. It's a symptom we all have to deal with. He's the first one to come out with a symptom to deal with.

MOTHER: I think I've been trying to deal with it for a long time.

STEPFATHER: I think you've been trying to deal with it, but you haven't been dealing with it.

MOTHER: It's not the first time it arose, just the first time it's been given a name.

STEPFATHER: I'm not talking about that. I'm talking about this is the first time we have had to deal with it.

From behind the one-way mirror, I observed two things. First, it was apparent that these people were schooled in the ways of therapy: "He was the first to come out with a symptom to deal with." This couple had had a lot of treatment; in fact, they had met at a methadone treatment program. Second, and more interesting, the girl was clearly being triangulated. I noted that as the adults began to disagree, the girl became psychosomatic; she began to cry, saying, "My tummy hurts."

HEATHER: (*Crying*) I don't want to be here.

MOTHER: (*To Heather*) Come on over here.

STEPFATHER: This is what's been happening. Just let her sit there and cry. You're doing exactly what that sign says—you're not facing the problem. By bringing her over and comforting her, you're not dealing with the problem.

The youngster became increasingly distraught as she was further triangulated. What was she to do? Sit on her mother's lap and upset the other adult or sit in another chair and upset her mother?

MOTHER: She's crying miserably, and you're telling me everything I'm doing is wrong. You're not helping.

STEPFATHER: I wouldn't be helping if I just let her sit over there and cry with you.

MOTHER: I wish you could help.

STEPFATHER: I'm not allowed to. Only in certain instances.

THERAPIST: I'm not sure that we have a specific thing that Joshua does that you disagree about.

STEPFATHER: That's the thing. I don't feel there's something specific with Joshua. He is the place where it's coming out, where it's visible. The actual thing is not just with Joshua. I feel that what we're seeing in Joshua is not a result of a direct relationship between his mother and Joshua or me and Joshua but is a result of the whole interaction of me and Heather, and Heather and her mother, and me and her mother. I think the actual source of the problem is more here (*Pointing out a triangle between Heather and her mother and himself*) and here (*Gesturing between Heather and himself and the mother and himself*) than here (*Pointing to Joshua and the mother*).

MOTHER: And Joshua pays for it.

STEPFATHER: What he's doing, he pays for it.

THERAPIST: So I guess Joshua's just a scapegoat, and Heather's the source of the tension. What can you do with her now?

MOTHER: Nothing.

STEPFATHER: Nothing.

THERAPIST: You're the mother and you can't do anything?

STEPFATHER: Right, and that's part of the problem.

THERAPIST: I guess it's time to start. (*To mother*) Why don't you take care of her?

From behind the mirror, I began to pace. I felt like the pitcher in the bull pen who sees the game going sour and starts to warm up. The therapist was beginning to develop the same challenging, confrontational relationship with the mother that the father had. I suspected he would need help shortly (or, more likely, the mother would need help, to keep her from experiencing the same disrespect she gets from her man).

MOTHER: I did. I said come over here, and he thought that was pandering to false needs or something. She's upset, she's just had diarrhea, her stomach's upset, and she's uncomfortable. I think it's not [pandering].

THERAPIST: Well, I want the two of you to somehow control her.

HEATHER: He [the stepfather] doesn't want it.

MOTHER: Come on, Heather, help me. Let me help you. Come on. (*Heather goes to her.*) It's hard to go through this.

STEPFATHER: (*To Joshua*) What's happening, Joshua? What's happening inside, what are you thinking?

JOSHUA: My stomach hurts a little bit.

STEPFATHER: Do you know why?

JOSHUA: Why?

STEPFATHER: I'm asking if you know why. (*Joshua shakes his head.*) It bothers you to see Heather like that? (*Joshua again shakes his head.*) It doesn't? It bothers me. Doesn't it bother you, too?

JOSHUA: A little bit. I'm tired.

FATHER: (*To therapist*) This is also typical.

This was a telling exchange. In assessing a system, I diagnosed not only pathological processes but also positive resources in the family. It was a sign of family strength that when the mother became occupied with one child, the other adult engaged the other child. Joshua responded by talking about how he had a belly ache and was tired; what he really meant was that he was depressed and triangulated.

THERAPIST: (*To stepfather*) So what do you think of this?

STEPFATHER: It's out of balance.

THERAPIST: How should the balance be?

STEPFATHER: I don't think it should be separated by sex, and I think it ends up that way.

At this moment, Joshua reached out and grabbed his sister's hand. I interpreted this to mean "We are not separated, we are united. He is an outsider."

THERAPIST: How do you think we should have it arranged now to break it up?

STEPFATHER: It isn't a matter of how we arrange it, it's a matter of how we do it. When Heather has tension and problems, she runs to her mother. Her mother's the only one who can do anything. And what she does is protect Heather from it, so Heather never actually deals with it herself.

THERAPIST: I think I know how you feel a little. She just said something, little secrets between them (*Pointing to Heather and the mother*). They said something about me, about my interpretation.

MOTHER: No, she said she does take care of herself, especially at school, and I said that's Ralph's interpretation.

THERAPIST: I see. (*To stepfather*) But that can kind of bug you, that they're so close like that. It makes you suspicious.

STEPFATHER: No, it doesn't make me suspicious.

THERAPIST: Well, it made me, then, I'm sorry.

The therapist was becoming paranoid! In a way, he was experiencing the stepfather's position in the family. His paranoia was a reflection of what had happened to the stepfather's displacement; the stepfather's experience had been captured in the system. Moreover, that experience was isomorphic in the family's role in the community as a biracial family in a lower-middle-class white neighborhood.

MOTHER: I feel very torn between both of them. When she comes close to me and I accept her and he gets angry, it's very hard to deal with both of them.

The mother was describing her agony, caught between her daughter and her friend—two of the three most important people in her life. Seeing how much pain she was in and how the therapist was struggling, I decided to enter the room.

FISHMAN: (*To mother*) I wanted to come in and support you.

At this, the mother started to cry, and Heather went over to comfort her.

FISHMAN: (*To stepfather, indicating Heather*) She's taking your job.

STEPFATHER: She's taking my job. She's always had it, from the beginning of the relationship.

FISHMAN: Don't let her take it!

STEPFATHER: I fought for a long while to take it. But I never got support back from her.

FISHMAN: Try now.

MOTHER: Do it!

STEPFATHER: I'm not allowed to.

MOTHER: I wish you would help me.

STEPFATHER: I'm only allowed to help you in certain instances.

The stepfather got up and went to hug the mother, at which the daughter angrily went into the corner. The last exchange gave a clear sense of stalemate. As in many blended families, the stepparent would have liked to enter the child-rearing turf but was prohibited by the biological parent from doing so. The ambiguity and paralysis of the system were highlighted in her saying "I wish you would help me" and his responding "You don't let me."

The perturbation to the system was my going into the room and supporting the mother. What then emerged was the homeostatic-maintaining pattern of the little girl activating in her role of her mother's protector. The stepfather, meanwhile, was stopped by his wife's silent command and his own inability to feel enough of the pull to break through this barrier.

The stepfather was like a coiled spring; he wanted to act but did not dare to because he did not have permission. The power of my therapeutic intervention was in releasing that spring. In forcefully urging him to step in, I enabled her to give him permission and broke the directive that was holding him back. It was an important moment. At that point, she had both hands over her ears, in a posture of being overwhelmed, conveying extreme distress. Her daughter was standing with her arms wrapped around her, staring at the adults, and she seemed to be beginning to say to herself (and to her mother), "The wrong person is here." It was a courageous act, at this painful moment, to displace the inappropriately responding daughter and allow the proper person to go to her. Through her "Do it!" the mother introduced discontinuous change; the old homeostatic pattern was broken.

FISHMAN: (*To Heather*) This is the way it should be: the little girl should be playing. What kind of games do you play?

My intervention with the girl was designed to reinforce a boundary between her and the adults, to strengthen the adult subsystem and to help free the child from being in the middle between them. In retrospect, while I respect the adults' private moment, I think I might have encouraged the adults, after they had hugged each other for a while, to include the children, especially the daughter. That would have been a powerful intervention, because on a process level, the prevailing isomorphic pattern had been triadic dysfunction: Each dyad was being stabilized by excluding the third person. To have encouraged the adults to reach out and include the girl after they had been close would have introduced a new, more functional pattern.

We can say, on the one hand, that the girl was maintaining the homeostasis—the split between the couple and the involvement of the children in the adult relationship. But what is more relevant here is the isomorphic-process pattern of a third person intervening to diffuse the conflict between two tense people. This was a system of overlapping triangles, in which both youngsters displayed dysfunctional behavior in response to the stressful conflict between the adults. It was not just the girl who was psychosomatic; the boy was tired and depressed and had headaches. The school perceived him as hyperactive. In more functional systems, there is often a flip-flopping: When one child regains health, the other becomes symptomatic. The symptoms shared by the children in this case suggested that the conflict and turmoil in this family were very severe.

The exposure of the homeostasis-maintaining process provided a guide for planning treatment. It was clear that there was a triangular structure in the family. The little girl activated when conflict emerged; therefore, one clear goal was to establish a new behavioral pattern in which conflict was resolved by the dyad.

If Heather's role as homeostatic maintainer was enacted only in the home, freeing her from triangulation in that context should theoretically ameliorate her problem and she would no longer have to keep going to the nurse's station. And that's indeed what happened. But if she were functioning in the same capacity in other contexts, the same goal of detriangulation would have to be met. If the girl had taken on the job of overseeing her mother's welfare, there would be a problem not only for the dyad but also for her own development.

There were several areas in the family's broader context where we might expect to find an isomorphic pattern. One was the tension between this interracial couple and the neighbors in the lower-middle-class area in which the family lived. This unacknowledged conflict was further unstabilizing the family, and making it explicit as a step toward resolving it became a goal that would help to detriangulate the children. Another potential arena for triangulation in the outside context was the mother's parents. They were very unhappy with their daughter's choice of mate, and Heather might well be found to be supporting her mother here as well.

One context in which homeostatic-maintaining processes are often found is the school. In this case, however, the school was functioning as an antihomeostatic force. In refusing to accept the behavior of the children and threatening to expel Joshua, the school personnel challenged the isomorphic processes of the family and forced them to be attended to. As we will see in a number of the cases in this book, institutions often foster family pathology, but here the institution responded adequately to the need to end the pathology.

A final question in this case would be how to strengthen the new system, once the little girl had been severed from the triangle. Do you simply leave her out in the cold? Obviously the answer is no, you move to her and restore her to an age-appropriate level. I played with her to distract her from the conflict of the adults. It is important to emphasize that the goal was not just to break up the dysfunctional pattern but to build a more stable and equitable system.

Using "Hunchiology" to Expand the System

In some cases, such as the one just described, perturbing the system in the therapy room will disclose the identity of the homeostatic maintainer. In other cases, that technique will fail to produce evidence that the homeostasis is being maintained by anyone in the room, and the therapist must look elsewhere for answers. Here, the history of the family and what I call "hunchiology" are useful guides. The therapist considers the family's history in light of his or her past clinical experience and develops hunches about whom to include in an expanded therapeutic system.

This technique worked successfully in the case of Mary Lou, a 15-year-old who had run away from home many times. Out of desperation, her mother and stepfather had sent her to live with the mother's parents in the Midwest. She was now in a psychiatric hospital and, after 4 weeks there, was about to be discharged. I was a consultant to the hospital staff, who were deciding how to proceed with her treatment and where she was to go after discharge. The grandparents wanted her to live with them, but the grandfather demanded obedience from her. The mother also wanted her, but she was afraid of the prospect. Mary Lou herself wanted to go to Florida with her boyfriend.

The family's history did not offer many clues about why this girl was out of control. There was very little extended family and no ex-spouses where they now lived; they had fled the Midwest and moved to California. It was only recently that Mary Lou's behavior had involved them with the courts and the social services.

One interesting fact was that the mother and stepfather had been in trouble with the law for most of their marriage. In the last year they had straightened out their lives, however, and it was at that point that Mary Lou's behavior problems began. I speculated that Mary Lou's misbehavior might be serving to stabilize the marriage, pulling them together as their problems with the courts had given them a common cause in the past. Of course, Mary Lou's adolescence might have been enough of a developmental pressure for the family to create a symptom; my hunch was that it was a confluence of pressures, as is often the case.

The participants in the first session were Mary Lou; her mother, Wynne; her biological father; both grandparents; and a cousin.

GRANDFATHER: I don't understand why she would want to have antisocial behavior . . . we'll put it that way. It looks like she would want to please somebody, if even herself.
FISHMAN: (*To Mary Lou*) So you're an antisocial kid?

MARY LOU: No, not me.

FISHMAN: (*To grandfather*) Mary Lou is a puzzle to you?

GRANDFATHER: Yes.

MOTHER: To everybody. In June we said, Okay, quit being a pain and go to Nebraska. You know, she loves my mom and dad and they get along real well. So I wanted her to finish the school year and she did, and she came up here and started getting into trouble, which I kind of antici-pated. And then she wanted to come back home, and we talked to her about getting some outpatient counseling, which she didn't want to do at first. So we decided to try this [inpatient hospitalization] and see what would happen. So she's actually lived with me and my husband until May or June.

FISHMAN: (*To Mary Lou*) How do you get along with your stepfather?

MARY LOU: Not too well. I mean, he's arguing most of the time.

GRANDFATHER: (*A few minutes later*) Do you have a problem with obeying your mother or your . . . Lee [the stepfather]? I noticed that when I asked you to obey me you would not. I mean, how do you feel about that? I mean, I had a reason for having you go with me and you refused and I made you, and you still feel mad at me about that?

MARY LOU: I am pissed.

GRANDFATHER: Well, that's fine, but you are going to obey me whether you want to or not.

MARY LOU: I don't have to any more, though.

GRANDFATHER: No, not unless you get under my roof you don't. Of course, that's . . . I don't have much to say for it right now . . . about it . . . but if you want it, I would be happy, just really tickled, to have you live with us. But there's going to be some rules. One of them is that you will obey.

MARY LOU: But one of them isn't having me . . . making me . . . take a walk.

GRANDFATHER: (*Chuckling*) You've got a surprise coming.

MARY LOU: Well, I don't have to worry about it, because I'm not going to live with you.

GRANDFATHER: Is that the reason? Because I made you obey me? I mean, if I would have let you do every little thing you wanted to do, you'd have been happy, huh?

GRANDMOTHER: Well, I think people have to sit down and talk things over frankly, like everything else.

GRANDFATHER: But when a kid looks you right in the eye and says, "I'm not going to walk with you and you can't make me," well, what do you do? Say, "Well, I'm gonna send you back to California, or give you a ticket to New York"? (*Chuckling*) We don't have any brave relatives in New York.

GRANDMOTHER: (*To Mary Lou*) Do you want to go back home?

MOTHER: (*Crying*) I miss having a bratty little kid around the house.

GRANDMOTHER: (*Talking at same time as the mother*) We'd love to have you do that.

MOTHER: The house isn't quite the same thing.

FISHMAN: (*To grandmother*) What did you say?

GRANDMOTHER: I said we'd like to have her at our house, too.

I was not sure I had heard the grandmother. Was she really telling the granddaughter that she wanted her to live with them? This was not supportive of her daughter's position of wanting to have Mary Lou come home, if she would behave. I asked myself if this was a significant rift between the two women. If so, would the split allow the youngster to continue to be uncontrollable?

A little later, the father joined in.

FATHER: The problem is supervision. Her mom and dad both work and they're gone a lot.

FISHMAN: (*To mother*) So you're guilty again.

MOTHER: People have to work, but . . . I go to work at eight and come home about six.

Another rift was emerging: The mother's former husband was blaming Mary Lou's problems on his ex-wife and her current husband, whom he accused of favoring the son born of that marriage over Mary Lou. But he was such a peripheral figure in Mary Lou's life that I doubted he could be the homeostatic maintainer. His attacks on the mother and her husband were only the relics of a war fought long ago; they had been apart for years.

Thus, as the session unfolded, a number of conflicts were becoming evident. The parents apparently were not in agreement on the grandfather's demands for obedience, and the grandmother seemed to be vying with her daughter for Mary Lou's attention. But Mary Lou brashly rejected the authority of her grandparents, and they had no ultimate sway over her. I did not see the interaction of any of these people as sufficient to explain Mary Lou's running away. There remained just one potentially significant figure—the stepfather. I felt hampered by his absence.

FISHMAN: (*To mother*) Can your husband come down here? I mean, can you invite him down for. . . ?

MOTHER: What, for a day?

FISHMAN: To work some of this out. Because, as you said, he's very significant.

MOTHER: I know he's important . . . but he's not here to speak for himself, poor thing. He's got the mean stepfather image, and he's really a nice guy.

I encouraged the stepfather to fly down for the next day's session. He could not leave his business to do so, but he agreed to participate by speakerphone. The next day, then, we began with Lee, the stepfather, on the phone. I asked him if he had had a report of the previous day's session.

STEPFATHER: No, I really didn't hear that much about what y'all talked about.

FISHMAN: Okay, maybe your wife can fill you in a little bit on what was the upshot of the session.

MOTHER: Well, we concluded that unfortunately you couldn't be here to say a whole lot about everything, but it's . . . everybody said a little bit about . . . gave their little tidbit about Mary Lou.

STEPFATHER: (*Mishearing what she had said*) We're talking totally different things. We're talking when she ran away for a week straight. And Wynne and I were on the road day and night trying to find her, worried sick.

GRANDMOTHER: (*Smiling*) Yes, and Wynne never did run away from home, either.

STEPFATHER: Yes. I wanted to beat her butt, but I didn't because I wanted to show her that I didn't have to spank her or anything. I would treat her like a young adult if she would try to treat us better. So when she ran away for a week, when she came back she was expecting to be killed, and instead we just sat in the middle of the living room and started crying because we love each other a lot and we have to deal with this stepparent thing, too, and it makes it real, real, real hard on me. And I know it's hard on her, too.

FISHMAN: So right now, then, there's a discipline problem. How do you handle it?

STEPFATHER: Well, we just try to restrict her.

FISHMAN: But does Wynne support you? Or is that like ganging up on Mary Lou when that happens?

STEPFATHER: Well, one of us usually lets her slide. That's for sure. We're not very strict on her punishment.

FISHMAN: You know, Wynne just had a big smile at that.

MOTHER: Lee, we usually . . . we used to go around and around in fights if I was trying to back up Mary Lou. If he set punishment for her, then I had to back it up, but he's usually the one to let her slide.

STEPFATHER: That's honest.

MOTHER: I think if Lee sets a punishment where she can't go anywhere for a week, two or three days later it shouldn't be null and void.

STEPFATHER: The thing is, she would jump into this ball of depression or something, where I couldn't stand to see her act like that, or feel like that.

FISHMAN: She had your number, but good.

STEPFATHER: Yes. But you'd just have to see the way she is.

FISHMAN: It's not that you don't love her. You love her too much.

STEPFATHER: I love her a lot, that's for sure.

GRANDMOTHER: Lee, you all have gave her too much, in my estimation.

STEPFATHER: Well, maybe that's trying to overcompensate for the past.

GRANDMOTHER: Yes.

MOTHER: Yes. When she ran away—you're going to find this really strange—when she ran away for a week, we got her back, right. When she gets off the plane, dumbass goes and buys her about two hundred dollars worth of clothes. I wouldn't have bought her nothing. I don't know why you did that, Lee. That was very stupid, and . . .

STEPFATHER: Just to let her know that I loved her.

MOTHER: Yes, well, she didn't need the clothes. (*To Mary Lou*) I don't know how you talked him into it.

MARY LOU: I didn't. (*Chuckling*) He asked me to [buy the clothes].

FISHMAN: Listen, if you run away to Hawaii, maybe he'll buy you a car.

The mystery was solved. The stepfather was unmasked as the homeostatic maintainer. Broadening the system via speakerphone allowed us to ferret out the person most clearly responsible for maintaining the pattern of overprotectiveness in the system. That pattern was apparent in the overinvolvement and alliance between the man and his stepdaughter; the stepfather was in fact rewarding the girl for running away.

We could now plan treatment to address this homeostatic-maintenance mechanism. The isomorph that needed to be addressed was triangulation leading to the undermining of the mother. In spite of the mother's outrage at Mary Lou's running away and the weeks of misery the family suffered as they searched for the girl, the stepfather was not subtly but overtly undermining the mother by giving the girl gifts. The grandmother, in turn, was undermining the mother by implying that she could do a better job of raising the girl. The biological father, for his part, was complaining about the immorality of the couple (referring to their earlier legal problems) and suggesting that the stepfather favored his own son over Mary Lou. The end result of all this sabotage was that there was no effective hierarchy controlling Mary Lou, so that she was not only more powerful than she should be but also in danger.

Another, more subtle isomorph was rigidity and the fear of ultimate rejection and banishment. The stepfather was so concerned that the girl would reject him that he almost pandered to court her favor, in spite of her behavior. This, of course, was isomorphic with a fear of rejection between husband and wife, which would make the stepfather all the more vulnerable to rejection by Mary Lou. In fact, the isomorphic pattern of fear of rejection and rigidity was exhibited by the entire system—the mother, her parents, the biological father, and even the hospital staff—when they all seriously entertained the girl's suggestion that she leave home (at 16) and live with her boyfriend. Nobody seemed willing to confront her. The sense I had in the room was that the rigidity of the system and the subtly warring forces around the girl were disastrously powerful.

It is important to add, however, that because this was only a single consultation, another issue was weighing heavily on my mind: Exactly what did go on between the stepfather and the girl? That would be virtually impossible to ascertain through the speakerphone, but the girl's almost compulsive running away made me wonder if there were something toxic and dangerous at home. That question would have to be addressed and treatment planned accordingly.

Ascertaining the Homeostatic Maintainer by Report

There are times when the identity of the homeostatic maintainer can be obvious simply from reports in the therapy session. When one can assume that people are essentially competent and not organically deranged, then the question can be asked in plain behavioral terms: Why are people acting as they are? What are the reinforcers in the contemporary context that are keeping things from changing for the better? The feedback we get from the participants in the session often provides the clue.

Ray, a single man, was the adoptive father of three boys: James, 16; Bob, 13; and Sam, 3. He was a schoolteacher and had always been very involved with helping children. He was now HIV-positive, coping very well physically with the disease—he had had no serious medical illnesses—but his immune competence was gradually diminishing.

I saw the family as part of a research project with HIV-positive families. They had volunteered to participate in a pilot study designed to determine whether decreasing social stress would enhance a patient's quality of life and strengthen the patient's immune status. Ray had gladly volunteered when he heard that there could be help with his boys, who were of great concern to him.

The boys, who had come to him over the past 4 years, had given him numerous difficulties. Currently, the older boy was getting very poor grades at school. The middle boy had had such constant behavior problems that his father was called by the school almost every day. This child had also sexually abused a fourth boy in the home, who had then been removed by the social service authorities.

The session included Ray, the three boys, and Jean, a friend of Ray's, a single woman in her 60s who helped him with the children.

FATHER: I told the teacher at Bob's school she should just tell him to sit down, that he was just a great big ball of wind. I've been at this school several times for these problems, but finally they just put him on home instruction. Because it finally got to the point that they just didn't want to deal with him any more. He stayed on home instruction until he got into trouble in January.

FISHMAN: What happened in January?

FATHER: Well, he started terrorizing the neighborhood. When I was at work, he started breaking into people's houses, eating their food, watching dirty videos, and leaving sexual notes on the floor. Not taking anything.

FISHMAN: What did the police say?

FATHER: The police wouldn't do anything, because no one would press charges.

FISHMAN: Why not?

FATHER: Because he would only break into people's houses that I knew.

FISHMAN: Your friends, right?

FATHER: Yes. But one particular day, a friend stayed home to see who was breaking into her home. She wasn't going to work, she was waiting there for him. Sure enough, he came in—that's how they found out what was happening.

FISHMAN: What happens if this happens this year?

FATHER: If it happens again, he's going away. I'm not going to deal with this anymore. But nobody was giving me any assistance, no one would press charges. So he couldn't get into any of these programs, because he had to do something, and nobody would press charges.

The father's demeanor was one of hopelessness. Clearly, his friends thought they were helping him by not pressing charges, but they were only compounding the problem. They were helping to maintain a situation that was adding to the stress he was under.

We then went to work to examine the interior of the family—what was happening between these boys to make them all so troubled.

FATHER: James appears to be afraid of Bob. It's like Bob has something over him, so he just does not tell when Bob's bad. We thought we had uncovered what Bob had over him.

FISHMAN: What might that be?

FATHER: Last June, I had to work kind of late. The school was getting ready for graduation, and I was in charge of it. I went to the school, but something told me to come back. When I got in the door I heard this screaming. You see, I had another little boy that I was taking care of at the time, who was five years old. So I ran upstairs, and I found Bob trying to molest him. I went off. James was in the house, but conveniently he was in his room with the Walkman on. So supposedly he didn't know anything about it. Anyway, I lost control and started beating Bob. I told James to call the police before I hurt him. So they took Bob down to the police station, and the police told me that we had problems at home: Bob had told the police that James had molested Bob. I took a lot of criticism from social service. They criticized me for jumping on him.

The father had an incredulous look on his face as he described how, in spite of his problems and the enormity of the boy's behavior, he was blamed and told that he should not discipline his son.

FISHMAN: What were you supposed to do?

FATHER: Yeah, what was I supposed to do? I walked into a rape in progress. Because if I had not gotten there, my son would have raped the boy. Nobody can say what their reaction would have been unless they had been placed in that situation. I accepted a lot of criticism, but I stood my ground. I asked social service, "What would your reaction have been?"

FISHMAN: I think one of the ways things would change would be if there were real consequences. Your friends' not wanting to press charges is really unfair to him.

FATHER: Exactly. I thought it was pretty ignorant of them that they thought they were helping Bob when really they were hurting him. And I said, these are not little boys and they should not be treated as such. But the neighbors actually thought they were helping him, when they were hurting him. The other issue is that he's required by social service to go to counseling, but he doesn't go. He thinks it's a joke.

FISHMAN: Why don't you call the police?

FATHER: Well, the social service worker is involved, and she won't do anything.

FISHMAN: Is it that social service is somehow holding your hands behind your back?

FATHER: Exactly. Social service shouldn't even be in there.

FISHMAN: Well, maybe it would help if we had a session with social service. Because in some ways it puts you in a tough position. You have all the responsibility and none of the authority.

FATHER: Exactly.

FISHMAN: Sometimes I see children who actually call social service on purpose.

FATHER: He did something like that one time. When I was about to spank him, my son said that he was going to call social service. He did call. When I got home from work, the school called and told me a social service worker had checked him out for marks and even my little boy as well. As if I was totally abusing them! So they both know how to play the system. I've just given the boys the social service number and told them if they want to call go ahead, because I'm not going to stand for this anymore. I should have a number where I can call, because they abuse me sometimes. So now I just try to keep my hands off them. But I'm just tired of it. I told them they can call and social service can take them away, because I'm not going to have social service put my head in a noose anymore.

FISHMAN: I think it will be very useful to have a conference with social service next time we meet.

Clearly the social service system was at odds with the father. As a result of their involvement, the father was left powerless and the adolescent boy was empowered and hopelessly undirected. The broader system was thus maintaining the dysfunctional homeostasis. The next stage of therapy would therefore need to include the social service worker and the friends who were refusing to cooperate with the father in disciplining the boy.

Of course, there are many other dynamics in a troubled family like this. The epilogue presents more of the issues in this family, especially the altruism that the boys demonstrated toward their adoptive father.

Blame Allocation and Personal Choice

One of the criticisms that I have been confronted with when teaching is that the concept of the homeostatic maintainer implies the allocation of blame: One person is held responsible for the maintenance of a dysfunctional pattern. And in fact a beginning therapist might look for the most obvious person to identify as the homeostatic maintainer and allocate blame strictly, excluding other considerations. The more seasoned therapist, however, would examine how that person's behavior is being controlled by larger processes. Through the concept of isomorphism, we can go beyond blame allocation to see how the homeostatic maintainer is embedded in a larger homeostatic process and direct the therapy to that process. The critic can say that this is just another version of blame allocation, because it is difficult to address the process without addressing the person. And, indeed, many people feel that the larger philosophical base of homeostatic process means that the therapist should not confront people. They begin to suggest that therapy is a process of not blaming anyone for anything.

Therapy in IST involves both the process and the people, recursively driven by the system to maintain the dysfunctional homeostasis. The theory advocated here does not attempt to avoid selecting key participants to hold responsible for certain modifications of behavior. People's choices may be limited by larger forces, but they still have some freedom of choice in how they will react. They do not have to be totally at the mercy of the homeostatic maintaining process. In fact, that is why change is possible.

CHAPTER 4

The Five-Step Model of Treatment

Keep the explanations clean, simple and economic.... [T]he best explanation is one which makes the fewest assumptions. "Multiplying one's hypotheses" beyond the minimum is forbidden.

—Sir William of Occam

THE FIRST THREE chapters of this book have described the basic concepts and tools used in Intensive Structural Therapy. In this chapter, we will see how these concepts and tools are applied step by step in treatment, with special reference to the extrafamilial systems that are impinging on the family.

When therapy involves working at the interfaces of the family and one or more extrafamilial contexts, the key issue is whether there is isomorphism in the patterns operating within the family and in the external context. Is the outside structure sustaining the homeostatic patterns within the family and hindering the family from making the necessary changes? If that is the case, the therapist must work to disrupt the balance between the demands of the outside and those of the family. Or is the external system maintaining its own integrity and not being inducted into the family patterns? If the extrafamilial structure is not supporting the dysfunctional patterns in the family system, it can be mobilized as an agent of change. In the case excerpted at the end of the last chapter, an unusual collaboration with an extrafamilial context—in this case, the school—was worked out to force a change in the patterns that had been maintaining the problem.

Step 1: Gathering the Members of the System

The process of putting together the group that is to constitute the therapeutic system has two parts. First, the therapist must decide who should be included initially (and who should not) and motivate those people to come. Then, when these people are assembled, the therapist looks for clues to people who are missing. If key family members are cooperative and willing to come to therapy, their help can be enlisted in bringing in other important members of the system. If, on the other hand, the family will not or cannot attend, other germane people in the system must be called in to serve in their place, to the extent that it is possible for them to do so.

The key to motivating the family is to reflect the concerns and values of the family. Being sensitive to the family's concerns and values enables the therapist to employ the technique of "joining" (discussed in depth in Minuchin & Fishman, 1981), which is based on the notion that the good leader is a good follower. When there are cultural differences, the clinician must operate from what Montalvo (personal communication, 1990) calls a stance of "informed one-down," meeting the family without preconceived notions about their culture and in effect saying, "I am an expert about families, but you are experts about your culture; teach me about it (and I'll help you)."

The initial phone call is crucial in the motivation of family members. It is important to adopt the right tone by emphasizing the gravity of the situation. For example, the mother of a 21-year-old woman with an eating disorder was reluctant to begin treatment, saying the she was "not sure it was the right thing to do at this point." The disorder had been going on for a number of years and she was at this point taking 10 to 20 laxatives a day. We told the mother that the daughter's health was seriously compromised. She could have a severe metabolic problem that could prove fatal if left unchecked. In a situation such as this, it is easy to generate intensity, because one can dwell on the medical threat. Admittedly, these are scare tactics, but scare tactics are sometimes warranted.

Even when a condition is not life threatening, the clinician can emphasize its seriousness. If the problem has existed for some years, the therapist can point out that it may have serious social ramifications and that it is essential the family members commit themselves to a course of therapy immediately.

A useful tool in motivating people to attend is the "power of the third"—the strength of the argument that a third person or agency has mandated participation. Given that triangles are so much a part of problematic systems, it seems only fair that we should tap this same power in motivating members to attend therapy sessions. One way of using the power of the third is by appealing to authority: "The director of the agency says it is essential that all members of the family be present." A more subtle use is to bring in the specter of what a third party might say: "We'd like to hear your side" ("How would you defend yourself?") or "You might have a different perspective" ("You know a lot more about the situation and could be more helpful"). This technique has long been known to bureaucrats.

Part of the beauty of the power of the third is that it takes the therapist off the hook. People are coming in not because you have insisted that they be there (and must therefore prove the need for their participation) but because someone else wants them brought in.

Another wisdom known by seasoned therapists is that the therapist's intentions regarding the importance of full family participation can be extremely influential. The therapist's comfort and insistence convey this to the family. Many young therapists and trainees convey to the family their own anxiety with a large group of family members. A corollary to this is in the area of videotaping. Legion are the families who have declined being videotaped when the inexperienced clinician asked them, "You don't want to be videotaped, do you?"

Ideally, the family will be motivated not only to come in themselves but to bring others in. Moreover, their participation in the recruitment process is important to the therapy itself. In dealing with a dysfunctional family, there is always the potential for making the family more dependent on outside forces. Making them central to the process of bringing in others is one form of empowerment.

A helpful device in deciding who to bring in is the process of imaging. The therapist asks one or more family members to imagine what someone else would say about a situation or how that person would react to a specific question. For example, the wife might be asked, "Does your best friend think your husband is wrong?" The wife's response might suggest that there is an alliance between the woman and her best friend against the husband and that the therapist might want to consider including the friend in the therapy. Asking family members how another person feels often triggers either strong expressions of feeling on the part of the family members or indications that the other person has strong feelings. Either response would suggest to the therapist that that person be brought in, because it indicates a position at odds with that of others in the system. It is the search for these dissonant voices that enables the therapist to map the relational structure of the system.

At the first contact with a family to be seen, I attempt to create what I call the "hit list." I try to identify anyone who has any connection whatsoever with the family. Obviously, this list is very useful in getting people to the first session, but it is also useful for later sessions, when it may not be possible to bring in some of the people who were present initially. One can then go down the list and bring in others and still be working with an authentic part of the system. Since the ultimate goal is to create coherence in the entire social network, this later inclusion can be extremely important.

There are, however, situations when bringing everyone in would be counterproductive. For example, there are times when certain subsystems need to work things out for themselves, without the involvement of other family members. A young couple for whom the intrusiveness of in-laws has been problematic may need to be allowed to settle their own differences. In other situations, the presence of too many people in the therapy room can interfere with the intensity needed to transform certain transactional patterns. In still other cases, particularly cases of sexual abuse and violence, it is important to exclude certain people whose involvement could be dangerous.

The therapist must assess the surrounding orders with some mindfulness that not everyone is an invaluable resource. The possibilities exist that one may capture into the network somebody who is a nefarious influence. For example, in the chapter on using peers, I made it clear in my early directives that we wanted the people who cared for the patient. We did not want the contemporary friends who were leading Beth into heroin and influencing her to go to New York and/or her 27-year-old boyfriend, with whom she was having sex. We picked friends from her more stable, mainstream life. For example, her 21-year-old friend Kate cared for who she used to be—the caring, responsible girl. We created a supportive network as well as incorporated the homeostatic forces that were maintaining the problem. However, it was not a matter of de facto getting the full network.

The therapist must look for nurturing resources, for guidance, for people who are close to mainstream values. I do not think I can escape saying that the therapist makes a value judgment. He or she makes a preliminary value judgment and asks the family members to bring the significant people in their lives, the people who care for them and would like to see them. Yet we do not want just people who are ultraclean, either. Indeed, we are especially interested in bringing in people who are in conflict with the system. The concern is not in bringing "good guys" only, but it is definitely important to have a preference among the peers who want to rescue the patient from a delinquent life.

In certain systems, the therapist may want to bring in the patient's toxic friends. In the case of children, it is best, when possible, to bring in the parents of the child's friends as well. In so doing, you can create an umbrella system—around all the kids.

Determining which people not to bring into the therapy means you must walk a fine line. When introduced into therapy, some people cause such unproductive sequences to emerge that therapy goes backward and the therapist has to retrench. For example, if a therapist prematurely introduces into a session two former spouses who have been embattled for many years, this will only make work with their child (who is already suffering for being triangulated by them) more difficult. What is advisable is to do an ample number of preparation sessions with each spouse so that when they meet they can lay down their weapons for the good of their child.

Later in therapy, there are always decisions of when to ask people not to return. If sequences emerge that paralyze the therapeutic process, the therapist must retrench. Another way of retrenching without literally asking someone not to return is to broaden the system, which can dampen the person's affect on the process and open new possibilities for change.

Indeed, this kind of network intervention creates new ethical demands and new problems in terms of the definition of who is the patient. The therapist must emphasize to people that he or she is viewing them not as patients but as resources—that they can help. Chapter 6 discusses this matter in more detail.

A final point about the inclusion of key members of a system: Thanks to modern technology, distance is no obstacle. I have found the speakerphone to be an extremely helpful way of getting input from people who cannot be present; at times it has been invaluable. The case of Mary Lou, described in the previous chapter, is a good example of its effective use. During the first session, we struggled for the better part of a day to figure out how this system was being maintained. It was not until the next day, when we included the girl's stepfather by speakerphone, that it became clear that the person who was not present, the stepfather, was indeed central to the homeostatic process. Had we not used the speakerphone, it might never have come out that he was playing that role.

Step 2: Generating Goals and Planning Treatment

The tone of the first session is one of respect and concern. It should never be forgotten that people come to therapy, as to any healer, because they are hurting. They are also coming for nurturance. My rule has always been to confirm the individual and challenge the system—the former at all times, and the latter as needed, sometimes with intensity.

After I have asked each person present about himself or herself, I go around the room asking each one to describe his or her concerns. It is important to get everyone to talk at least once. It is the same as at a party: If there is someone you have not talked to, as the evening wears on it becomes more and more difficult to open up a conversation. An unspoken rule seems to prevail: We should not talk.

The main work of the first session is the assessment described in chapter 2. As we have seen, the objective is to uncover the dysfunctional structural patterns in the broad system and determine who or what is maintaining them. This process makes considerable use of what I like to call the "science" of hunchiology. On the basis of clinical experience, the therapist will begin to develop hunches that can be pursued to reveal the dysfunctional patterns. If a father is very childlike, for example, the therapist can begin to generate ideas about what in the broader system might be keeping him a child: What is his relationship with his own parents?

When examining the transactions among family members, the therapist looks for complementarity in the system. People in general tend to see cause and effect as linear; as we proceed through life, one event tends to follow another as a consequence of that earlier event. From a systems perspective, however, cause and effect are also circular. As individuals, we are profoundly influenced and even directed by others, whom we in turn influence. For families in therapy, the transformation of their thinking from linear causality to complementarity—from "He or she is the symptom bearer" to "We are all involved"—is a profound change. They must learn a new way of experiencing themselves in relation to others in order to understand the part they are playing in the problem and how they must change so that the symptomatic member will improve.

The therapist also looks for the absence of complementarity. In that situation, people are not being given appropriate feedback on dysfunctional behavior, and the behavior therefore continues. For example, a father may be excessively punitive with an adolescent, yet the mother does not intervene to try to modify his behavior. In some situations, friends can really be enemies because they fail to give corrective feedback. This is often true in cases of symmetrical escalation of conflict between spouses, when "best friends" side with the feuding spouses, fueling the flames instead of pointing out the dysfunctional pattern of escalation.

An important part of the assessment at this first session is to identify those participants who might be resources to the family. Do any of those present appear to be resisting the family's efforts to avoid conflict but instead are pushing the others toward conflict resolution? Are there members of the broader system who have strong relationships with members of the family and might serve as a bridge to the outside? Does anyone present show an inclination toward acting as cotherapist, supporting the therapist's interventions with members of the family?

The use of the informal cotherapist taps another tradition—the role of altruism and the generosity of bystanders. Good Samaritans, people who contribute to others without any expectation of reward, are a tradition in most religions. From the point of view of the family therapist, there are certain concerns that must be kept in mind.

The informal cotherapist from the client's natural network should be not only a bully who adds his or her two cents but also somebody who shows some willingness to shoulder some responsibility. The goal is that the cotherapist become part of the person's support system in an ongoing way. Since the cotherapist shoulders some responsibility for promoting change, therapy can be greatly facilitated.

Of course, in this utilization we counter the hubris of the clinicians, who must realize that, increasingly, with families so stressed by infrastructure problems both within and without, a visit to our office, even if the family is present, may well not cut enough of a swath to make significant change. The goal is to have the naturalistic cotherapist go home with the family—that thereby further maintain the changes begun in the session.

In a sense, during our therapy we are a conduit for the processes of other people to reach others. And if the clinician is to center upon himself or herself, he or she cannot facilitate this process. The goal is for people to stretch out intensely for others, and they often do it at a sacrifice of themselves; the clinician has to get out of the way and facilitate that. The real intercession is by the friend or the other person. The therapy can capitalize on this process.

The therapist must bring in people with the willingness to participate in a heart-felt intercession. If those invited are not of this mind and heart, the therapist cannot make it happen. If they show up, the therapy can facilitate things.

At the other extreme, the therapist must not fall into the classic mistake of overburdening people who are friends; people who are friends should not be made into therapists. The clinician is to be extremely respectful of whatever people can do and not overtax them. A danger of this model is that people might come to feel that they are being entrapped or exploited as informal therapists for their friend. You can have people in too much—they have difficulties in their own lives. As professionals, we must be fully aware that we cannot extract too much from people.

Another pitfall is that this way of working attracts people who lose boundaries very easily. The therapist must be vigilant to protect against loss of confidentiality and autonomy. Consequently, the parameters for the therapist are very strong and clear: You assemble a group to accomplish certain goals, then you dismantle it after that. Good timing is essential here—use the moment where people are highly motivated and willing, manifest the dynamics of change, and let them go. One must not let them feel that they have frozen into a new role, a role that can lend itself to grandiosity and gross manipulation.

As the session progresses, the therapist uses hunchiology to speculate on likely outcomes. Certain problems tend to resolve in certain ways; for example, parents tend not to throw grown children out of the house. If there is a problem with an adolescent, there is a split somewhere in the parental system. If there is a critical mass of helpers (two or more), chances are the helpers are part of the problem. Incompetence is a systemic phenomenon; look for the person(s) maintaining the incompetence. There are many more of these "systemic therapist aphorisms." Like all clichés, they are often true, but they are also irritating. They frustrate the quest for discovery and take some of the mystery out of therapy. Ideally, by the end of the first session, the homeostatic-maintaining mechanism will have become clear and the therapist, together with the family, can generate the goals of therapy and plan treatment toward those goals.

The process of generating goals and a treatment plan can perhaps be conveyed more clearly by example than by description. Following are descriptions of initial sessions (or in one case, a renewed contact) with five cases I encountered in a single day last year. They are thumbnail sketches, mapping out the outstanding processes the therapist may need to address. These are tentative goals.

CASE EXAMPLE 1: PAULA

Paula was referred to me because of extreme anxiety and depression that had lasted for several months. She was 33 and had been married for 5 years. She and her husband, both teachers at a local school, had a 16-month-old son. She had no history of psychiatric problems and felt that she had been a happy person up until the last few months, but now she was very tense and preoccupied and felt that in many ways she was failing.

During the course of the interview, Paula presented a lively demeanor but expressed concern and puzzlement about her sadness and anxiety. Where were these feelings coming from? Why did she feel that she was doing something very wrong with her life? As she spoke, her husband, Jim, looked at her lovingly.

I began to explore the couple's wider context. Their jobs were under control and did not generate much stress. Paula's parents, who lived nearby, were extremely supportive. Jim's mother was dead; they had an amicable relationship with his father. The exploration of the extended family did reveal problems, however. Jim's brother's wife was extremely hostile to Paula. She had expressed strong disapproval of Paula for putting their son into day care instead of staying at home. When the other 35 members of the family came to their home for Thanksgiving, she refused to come. Jim suggested that one of the problems was that his father often spoke glowingly of Paula to his other daughter-in-law, with whom he had a less-than-warm relationship.

These preliminary bits of information suggested that Paula's depression was stemming from the rivalry and antagonism between her sister-in-law and herself. The homeostatic maintainer might well be Jim's father, whose praise for Paula seemed to be designed, in part, to hurt his other daughter-in-law. There appeared to be an isomorphic pattern of conflict avoidance; the two women never talked about their relationship, and the father-in-law never said directly what he did not like about his daughter-in-law. There might also be another isomorph of triadic diffusion of conflict, with everyone participating in keeping people apart by rerouting conflict. The dyads never worked things out between themselves by dealing with each other directly, but instead said unkind things behind each other's backs, only exacerbating the tension, which had led to Paula's depression.

On the basis of these ideas, I drew up a preliminary plan for treatment. First, the marriage should be investigated. Specifically, why was the wife so vulnerable to her sister-in-law? Was her husband not being supportive of her? Was he, in fact, in alliance with his family against her? The second area of concern should be the dysfunctional structure of Jim's family. The goals here would be the resolution of the conflicts between the sisters-in-law, and between the father-in-law and his other daughter-in-law.

Another relationship that in the best of all possible worlds would be assessed and treated was Jim's brother's marriage. There seemed a likelihood that it was unstable and that the brother was fighting with his wife through his father. In my experience, however, the opportunity to work with all the dysfunctional relationships in a given system are few and far between.

CASE EXAMPLE 2: MELISSA

Melissa, age 24, called in the night before Labor Day, suicidal. She had just broken up with her boyfriend of 1 year, the first significant relationship of her life, and was profoundly depressed. The breaking up of a relationship is a deeply upsetting event that happens to almost everyone. What had made Melissa so vulnerable to this developmental passage that she would react suicidally?

Melissa was a brilliant scientist, a former Fulbright scholar, who worked at a major university. Examining her system, one saw a very talented woman with very few friends, living in a family with an alcoholic father, a mother who was a successful businesswoman, and a number of very needy siblings. Her role in the family had always been that of helper and giver; there was very little nurturance and emotional support for her. She was a very hard worker, sometimes working 70 hours a week.

Two patterns emerged: isolation and an isomorphic pattern of rigidity that pervaded her family, her social relationships, and her work context. Her work context was the most upsetting for her. She was the youngest, by almost 10 years, of all the scientists in the laboratory. The other female scientists were all Asian and constituted a support group for each other. Her only support had been the male colleague with whom she had the recently severed relationship. In her discussions of the problems of her career, she described missed opportunities and rejection by colleagues. In fact, one felt that the recursive rigidity between her and her contexts prevented her from responding flexibly to the feedback of people her context presented, so opportunities passed her by.

Several forces seemed to be possible candidates as homeostatic maintainers. For a time, her boyfriend had ironically maintained the pattern of social isolation because of her insistence they spend so much time alone together. Her work context was also functioning in that capacity. Another possibility was her family. As the best-functioning child, did she need to be closely connected to the family (and the parental marriage), and vice versa? Her family could also be seen to be maintaining the pattern of rigidity to some degree. The dysfunctional relationship between her parents, which had not changed for a generation, was serving to keep Melissa caught in a system in which she was triangulated. It also served to reinforce the metarule that things do not change—hence the rigidity.

One focus of intervention, therefore, would be Melissa's dysfunctional family. The goal would be to develop it as a source of nurturance to her but without Melissa having to pay the price by allowing herself to be triangulated. The other would be Melissa herself—to help her develop a broader context that would give her immediate support—so she would be less vulnerable to losses. School, church, or groups such as Mensa could help ease her social isolation. When the latter was suggested, however, her reaction was, "I hate Mensa. They are people who think too much of themselves." Her summary dismissal of a large organization of people whose motives for being members doubtless varied, suggests that underlying her rigidity is a kind of defensive reaction to her own low self-esteem, which stemmed from her social isolation. Indeed, if reality is confirmation by significant others, low self-esteem (in this case) is the absence of people who confirm her as a valuable person.

Because of her extraordinary rigidity, it would be necessary to help her at the interface with such contexts. Working as a volunteer with children or becoming a Big Sister would help to mitigate that pattern.

CASE EXAMPLE 3: DARRYL

Darryl, 37 years old, had been using crack and cocaine for 20 years. He had been referred for evaluation by his employer, who was threatening to fire him. Six months earlier he had been referred for treatment, at his insistence, and had been placed in a detox program. One week after discharge, he began using drugs again.

Darryl's family system included his mother, with whom he lived; his three children, aged 20, 18, and 13; an aunt and uncle; another aunt, who lived in a different part of the country; two girlfriends; and two former wives. He came into the session with his mother, who was clearly disgusted with him. She had done everything for him since he was a little boy, she said, and now all he did was abuse drugs. It was a classic story of overindulgence. Born in poverty, she was now a woman of considerable wealth, "for a poor person." She controlled his money, even his paycheck, and gave him money beyond his salary (2 days earlier she had given him $200 to buy drugs). The isomorphic pattern of overindulgence extended to her grandchildren, on whom she lavished gifts. When she bought the 18-year-old a Honda, he said, "No, I don't want a Honda, I want a Mercedes." Darryl was very proud of his 20-year-old son, who was making $6,000 a week selling drugs.

The mother was despondent, holding little hope that her son would change. Yet she said she was constantly surprised that he would continue to steal from her. "Everything in the house is locked up, or it has been stolen." Most recently, her son stole her VCR and two TV sets.

The prevailing isomorph in this sytem was overprotectiveness. The question would be how to change the homeostatic maintainer, who clearly was Darryl's mother. She said she would never throw him out on the street, because she could not stand the thought that her son would become a street person. Therapy would therefore involve an intensive session and would include his three children, his aunts, his uncle, and friends who had given up drugs and turned their lives around. Also signficant in the therapy would be his girlfriends and possibly his former wives. Another sub-system to be included would be his boss, if that could be done without jeopardizing his job.

The goal would be to create a context that would nudge and support the mother away from supporting her son. Involving the children might put social pressure on him to change his ways. (I knew that bringing these kids in would be no mean feat!) Treatment markers would be the following:

1. A cessation of drug abuse, confirmed by urine testing, if possible
2. A changed relationship with his mother, in which she stops bailing him out
3. A change in the mother's context, in which her system becomes broadened and transformed so that her son is no longer the center of her life
4. Creation of an active interpersonal network with his friends who have given up drugs
5. A better relationship with his children, in which the children become an important part of the fabric of his life
6. Improved performance at work

CASE EXAMPLE 4: THE OLSON FAMILY

Over the last year and a half, the Olsons had first separated and then divorced. During that period, they had been in court many times regarding custody and visitation of their 4 1/2-year-old son. The family had been referred to therapy because the child was having problems in preschool.

The parents entered the room seething with anger at one another. As they told their story, it appeared that their separation had started out amicably. When they moved on to divorce, however, each of them hired an attorney, and their dealings became more complex and eventually embattled. Then each of them became involved in a new relationship.

On the basis of this history and past experience, hunchiology told me that the homeostatic maintainer in this system was in the broader system. Lawyers and the adversarial legal system can keep embattled spouses fighting, and having them dragged into court over and over again could only aggravate the hostility. The new relationships of the ex-spouses would make their encounters even more rancorous.

The first goal of therapy here would be damage control. The fighting was clearly hurting the child, and it would be essential to get the parents to put the boy's welfare ahead of all other considerations and to lower the level of hostilities. To that end, it would also be necessary for the parents to get their seconds in the duel—whether they be lawyers, friends, or significant others—to back off as well. Finally, the extended family would be examined to see if they might be supporting the problem. Was the pattern of triangulation isomorphic in the relationships of the parents with their families of origin, for example?

CASE EXAMPLE 5: JOE

During the course of that day, I received a phone call from a former client, a doctor, who had been referred when he began acting irresponsibly at work. In the time I had worked with him, he had made considerable improvement, but now he had become very depressed. He was still facing legal charges for prescribing drugs improperly, and his prospects looked poor. He was threatened with losing his license to practice medicine. His marriage, which had been embattled for 25 years, continued to be a problem as well.

The prevailing isomorph here was the rigidity of the systems in which Joe was embedded. The longstanding dysfunction in his marriage, the complexity and immobility of the courts and the state licensing authority, and the impediments to professional survival were daunting at best. At age 50 he would have to deal with the midlife issue of an alternative career if he were to lose his license. A second isomorph was a triangular structure: The man was torn between his family and his work; the woman was torn between the family and her family of origin (her parents were chronically ill); and the couple were divided by their 11-year-old daughter, who was closer to her father.

At the end of the day, I went over my notes, focusing on the concrete parameters to be addressed in each case. I had some confidence that the parameters I was looking at for treatment were, for the most part, treatable. As I addressed the dysfunctional patterns in the next step, I would be prepared to change the parameters as I got feedback from the system. After all, one thing that makes contextual therapy so powerful is the fact that we are always reading and responding to the context.

Step 3: Addressing the Dysfunctional Patterns

In effect, the goal of addressing the dysfunctional patterns is to destabilize the organization by creating discontinuous change. As we have seen, one way in which the organization can be destabilized is by creating a therapeutic crisis. The therapist first uses this procedure to expose the homeostatic maintainer by perturbing the system and observing who activates to return it to the status quo. Subsequently, therapeutic crises are created to provoke the members of the system to different interactions; when the system is challenged, it is not permitted to return to the status quo but is forced to reorganize. Note, however, that it is the system that is challenged, not the individual. Even better is having one of the members of the family do the challenging. Ideally, the family members themselves will continue to challenge the old patterns as they struggle to maintain a new organization.

When and where does the therapist intervene to create a therapeutic crisis? First, the intervention clearly must include the homeostatic maintainer. If the forces maintaining the problem are not involved, the system cannot be transformed. Once the homeostatic maintaining mechanisms have become clear, the therapist looks for a point of instability in the system, a crack in the armor, at which to intervene. Such a point is often marked by an incongruity of affect; what is spoken or expressed in body language may not fit with the situation. For example, in one of the cases described in chapter 6, the father of a teenaged boy was describing his son's out-of-control behavior, but his face, instead of registering outrage or concern, displayed a big smile. I created a crisis in the session by rendering explicit the covert alliance of the father with the boy and siding with the mother against them.

An important component of the therapeutic crisis is what I call the immovable therapist. As the crisis builds intensity, the therapist doggedly refuses to budge; any movement, therefore, has to come from the system. The therapeutic immovability generates even greater intensity, which empowers the therapist to catapult the system into a new organization.

This focus requires a kind of tunnel vision. Recently I came out of a session in which I was creating a crisis between a mother and daughter regarding the daughter's bulimia. A trainee asked me, "Don't you think the daughter is following the pattern her mother followed?" I replied that, while that might be a correct observation, it was not germane to what I was attempting to do. One must remain intently focused on the change that one is trying to bring about; anything else is a distraction.

Obviously, in order to be immovable, the therapist must be free of institutional pressure, or at the very least must be aware of organizational forces trying to direct the therapeutic efforts. The therapist must have the freedom to change the system, just as the system must have the freedom to change.

One of the most frequently used techniques of crisis induction is unbalancing. As in the case just described, the therapist sides with one member of the system over another. This approach, of course, flies in the face of what many of us were once taught: that one must maintain a position of complete fairness at all times. Unbalancing, however, is an extremely powerful intervention in shifting people's realities. In a session with an embattled couple, for example, the husband is obliged to see his wife through different eyes if the prestigious person in the system—the therapist—is supporting her. Of course, unbalancing is a short-term tactic. In fact, it is not really a violation of the principle of fairness, because it is an intervention, not a stance, and soon afterward I might be siding with someone else.

At times, it may not be necessary to create a new crisis but merely to amplify the present one. In the case of Bonnie, mentioned in chapter 1, what I did was to exacerbate a crisis that was already present in the system. The therapist is always searching the system for "indigenous" crises to exaggerate therapeutically. For example, in a family where the 15-year-old daughter brings home a report card with two Fs, the therapist can accentuate the poor performance by relating it to the worsening employment situation in the United States: "It will not be as easy for today's kids as it was for us. We are a country of diminishing opportunities." Either way, each unbalancing of the system offers the therapist an opportunity to call for a new, more functional interaction as the system struggles to regain equilibrium.

In some cases, an organization is best made discontinuous by creating a "soft" crisis, one induced by gentler means. A fragile system, for example, may require support rather than challenge. The therapist then must work to build a network of people who are coherent in their support of the family and who can work cooperatively in helping to strengthen the family system in the new organization. In so doing, the therapist creates a crisis in the literal sense—a drastic reorganization—but without the usual pyrotechnics. For example, an elderly woman who lived alone had been very depressed. Despite medication, her depression persisted until, at a relative's suggestion, she found a woman in the same situation to share her apartment with her. The sudden reorganization of her context created a transformed system, which, in therapeutic terms, constituted a crisis.

Step 4: Establishing and Maintaining a New Organization

The key to lasting success in Intensive Structural Therapy is change in the family's context. As we have seen, subsystems within the nuclear family,

within the extended family, and at the interface of the family and the outside world may be functioning to maintain the problem. From the first session on, the therapist is involved in dealing with the various subsystems,
such as siblings, peers, and the school system, working to resolve conflicts
and change dysfunctional structures. Conversely, any of these subsystems
may prove to be sources of support as therapy proceeds. Much of the
work of the fourth step in the model, therefore, consists of working with
these individual subsystems. Each of the chapters that follow deals with a
particular subsystem, providing specific principles for working with that
context and describing one or more cases in which it was crucial to the
therapy.

In many cases, changing the existing broad system is sufficient to stabilize the new organization. New patterns of behavior within that system
replace the dysfunctional patterns that were supporting the problem. In
some cases, however, it has proved extremely useful to bring in new contexts as forces for change. I call this process recontextualization. It is a kind
of "contextual engineering," designed to create a new context in which the
new behavior patterns can be consolidated and strengthened.

The idea of recontextualization is not new, of course. Alcoholics Anonymous and other such groups represent new contexts in which changes in
patterns of addictive behavior are encouraged and supported. In addition
to AA and other groups that rely on the support of people who share a
problem, however, there are other new contexts to which families have
been introduced with highly successful results.

Sometimes the context is not actually a new one but an old connection
that has lapsed. Reconnecting a family with its religious roots, for example, can be a powerful recontextualization. The family's religious network
can provide strong support, encouraging and helping to stabilize the system. The ritual itself can be important, especially at a time of crisis. I frequently ask Jewish families who have had a recent death in the family if
they have sat *shivah*, the Jewish ritual of mourning, which gives people the
opportunity to join a community of mourners.

The variety of contexts that can be considered in the process of recontextualization is theoretically limited only by the specific needs of the system, logistical constraints, and the imagination of the clinician. As examples, I will mention just two, both of which have been very beneficial in a
number of cases of eating disorders in women.

Women's eating disorders are generally an expression of conflict avoidance. Specifically, there is conflict between what our culture tells them
they should be and their own views of who they are or what they want to
be. In our society, the message some women receive is that to be loved

they must be sweet, quiet, and unassertive. In situations that call for indignation and confrontation, if a woman is unable to take action on her own behalf because of the internalized rule that she must be sweet and submissive, the unsatisfactory resolution of the conflict may be manifested in an eating disorder: bulimia, anorexia, or compulsive overeating.

We have found that introducing such women to feminist groups can be an empowering process that gives them greater control over their eating disorder as it makes them more powerful in their lives in general. They overcome their feelings of paralysis, learning to act to change things by directly confronting the people who are making them unhappy. By adding this dimension in the treatment of the eating disorder, we are able to address not only the symptomatology but also the embedded individual phenomenology that has led to the expression of the sense of weakness and helplessness in the eating disorder.

In a similar fashion, the use of the martial arts has proved to be an extremely powerful adjunct to therapy for eating disorders. If the essential issue in eating disorders is fear of conflict, then the martial arts, which provide a context in which people learn to deal with conflict, can clearly be very valuable. The goal is not to give people a skill with which they can go out on the street and commit mayhem; to the contrary, the skill gives them the self-confidence they need to address conflict and resolve issues. The mayhem, which had existed in the system as personal angst, disappears.

One patient in a program for compulsive overeaters weighed 365 pounds when she entered the program. Now 40 years old, she had been severely overweight since she was 10. When it was suggested that she might benefit from martial arts, she was at first surprised and fearful, afraid of exposing herself and the extent of her obesity and wondering if she could physically handle an arduous martial arts program. After a go-ahead from her internist, however, she began the course. What follows is her description of the program and how she feels she benefited from it.

FISHMAN: How has the martial arts been helpful?
BETSY: When I found out I had to do martial arts, I didn't think I could do it, to begin to accomplish something like that. I was mortified and terrified, and miserable. Within four weeks I began to love it.

There's been four major things that have happened. One was that I did not know that I was afraid I couldn't take care of myself in certain situations. I thought, I'm so independent, I can sit on people. Who's going to threaten a woman of three hundred fifty pounds? I didn't know that the knowledge I could defend myself in a clinch would be so important to my own self-esteem. Second, I was sure that he [the martial arts instructor] had never worked with overweight people before, and he'd make fun, but he was so understanding. He helped me. Rather than demand what a person of eighty-five pounds would do, he would demand I'd do the best I can do. Third, the active exercises—he paced it. The fourth thing was being able to work with other people in the program at martial arts. All of us had misgivings about our abilities. The others would offer encouragement.

FISHMAN: How do you think it's affected your relationships in your life outside the program?

BETSY: A couple of major ways. Like, the date I had that didn't go real well, and I realized at one point that I was grateful that I knew martial arts, and I actually said to this man, "Are you aware I've been taking martial arts?" And he said, "Why do you think you'd have to do that?" And I said, "It comes in pretty useful." And in five minutes he was gone. Unconsciously, it just sprang to the fore that I knew I was in a tight position, probably a dangerous position. I would have done what he wanted to do, and it was clearly not what I wanted to do, and I had a means to tell him no. The other thing is, when I tell people I do martial arts, they want to do it, too. They've noticed the difference in me; they want that, too. It's a very important program. Looking back at it now, I can't believe I dreaded it.

The power of the martial arts created a context that gave Betsy renewed self-confidence, not only in situations where she was physically threatened but in many difficult situations that came up in her life. Because of her physical self-confidence, she was able to stand up to people instead of avoiding conflict.

In the feminist view, being fat is often a woman's expression of rebellion against her powerlessness and against the pressure to conform to an ideal image. By taking up as much physical space as a man, she indicates her need to be taken as seriously as a man and to be accepted for herself (Orbach, 1978). It is against these feelings of powerlessness and ontological insecurity that the martial arts and feminist groups have been so powerful.

Step 5: Ending Therapy

Ideally, therapy will end when the presenting symptom is ameliorated and the dysfunctional organization of the system has been transformed. New interactional patterns have resulted in a changed structure within all of the subsystems in which the family is involved.

Such ideal results do not always occur, however, and a good therapist does not go on working infertile ground. If there is no true change, if no progress is being made, the family should be informed that therapy will end on a specified date. The end of therapy should be presented as an unfinished work—an "unresolved chord"—or as a lost opportunity. The act of ending therapy can, in fact, be a challenge and produce a crisis in the system that can be exploited therapeutically.

At the end of therapy, the therapist should be positioned within the system with the door open, like a general practitioner. Even when therapy has been successful, we cannot assume that the changes will be self-sustained, given the vagaries of life. The forces that are supposed to maintain the change cannot be taken for granted, and the continued presence of the therapist is needed to watch for any attempt to dismantle the change. The clinician also continues to look for new resources to recontextualize and stabilize the change. This continued emphasis on recontextualization is crucial to avoid excessive involvement and enmeshment between the therapist and the family. It is the family members, not the therapist, who must own the change; if they do not, they have been swindled.

Whatever the outcome of the therapy has been, the door should be left open. Whether or not the family feels the need for further consultation, periodic follow-ups help to reassure the family that they are not in a no-exit situation, that someone is available to them who understands that in the course of the family's life cycle, they may need someone to intervene.

Tracking a Sample Case Through the Five-Step Model

When working with the family's broader context, the therapist is constantly assessing the relationship between the family and the extrafamilial systems. At every interface the therapist examines whether family patterns are mirrored in the external system. In the case about to be described, there was no isomorphism between the external system (the school) and the family. What was happening at home was not happening at school. The school had the correct pattern, while the family did not.

The intervention was therefore designed to create a coherent system between the family and the school whereby the school's more appropriate pattern would prevail. A collaboration was set up between the parents and the school staff in which special arrangements and allowances were made for the parents to work with their child in school.

Jason was a 7-year-old boy with a diagnosis of elective mutism, a condition in which the patient speaks in some contexts and not in others. Jason behaved normally at home, but at school he was both mute and inactive. He would not take off his coat, would not go to lunch, and would not even go to the bathroom. He would do no written work in school, although at home, with an instructor, he would do minimal work. Various kinds of psychotherapy had proved futile. At the time the family was referred to me, there had been talk of hospitalizing the child in an inpatient unit for a comprehensive series of tests. Also under consideration was a course of treatment with Mellaril, a major tranquilizer with potentially permanent side effects.

At issue now was where to place Jason in school. At the end of first grade, he had been put in a special class and a teacher had been sent into his home. Jason had not responded to this approach either, however, so several months into the school year, the school decided to return him to regular classes. They wanted to place him in second grade, where he would be with his peers, but in fact no one had any idea what his academic level was, because no one had ever gotten him to take a test.

One interesting point should be noted: In the car on the way to the first session, Jason said to his mother, "If I speak in school, who will be there with you?" This question could be interpreted as indicating that Jason was extremely overinvolved with his mother—a classic school avoidance where the child stays home with a depressed parent. I saw it as such, but his mother did not seem depressed, and the marriage appeared to be without severe conflict.

STEP 1: GATHERING THE MEMBERS OF THE SYSTEM

When the parents made contact with the clinic, I used the various rallying cries mentioned earlier in the chapter. I talked about the seriousness of the problem: Not only was Jason's learning being compromised, but also his ability to socialize was being severely inhibited. This dearth of socialization could lead to social developmental lags for their son.

I asked the parents to identify the relevant people within their system. Who in particular was giving them support? Who were they in conflict with? The father stated that he had "no use for [his] family." He had no contact with them and no desire to include them in the therapy or in his life. The mother had a better relationship with her family, warm and close. The people with whom they had the most problems, and even hostility, were the school authorities. Over the years, everyone involved with Jason had tried to come up with a creative way to get Jason to speak and participate in school, and all had failed. As a result, the family and school were at each other's throats, with each side blaming the other.

In this case, it was quite easy to bring in the whole system. The seriousness of the problem and the frustration of the parents made them ready allies in the recruitment process. Since the ultimate goal is to empower the parents, I asked them to bring in the necessary people, and they suggested the school principal, Jason's teacher from last year, and his present teacher. The two teachers were eager to participate, and I was glad to have them bring in the principal as well; the higher up in the hierarchy you go, the more executive power there is to implement change.

Within the extended family, imaging procedures revealed areas of conflict but no immediate resources open to the family. Later on in the therapy, I felt, it might be necessary to work with the father's estranged family, but at this point, bringing up that issue would distract us from the goal of rendering Jason a functioning student at school. Pressuring the father on this issue might even have sent the parents off in a huff.

STEP 2: GENERATING GOALS AND PLANNING TREATMENT

Present at the first session were Jason, his parents, his teacher from last year (Teacher 1), this year's teacher (Teacher 2), the principal, and the therapist (me). The principal described the history of the case from the school's perspective.

PRINCIPAL: This is one situation we've never dealt with before. Certainly not in this way. We have sought the input of our school psychologists and independent family counselors. Originally, the advice was that this was a separation conflict and that we should just back off and let it take its course. But that's very difficult to do as you approach the completion of one full year of school and have absolutely no indication whatsoever whether any progress is being made, or whether any learning has taken place, because our attempts to evaluate have been a total failure, with the exception of the Peabody picture test on one occasion. That is the only subjective analysis of achievement.

FISHMAN: You mean objective.

PRINCIPAL: Objective, rather.

FISHMAN: He does no homework at all? I mean, I'm not being negative. Kids don't like to do homework anyway.

FATHER: He does his homework.

MOTHER: We have recordings of him reading. They found out that . . .

PRINCIPAL: But we have no way . . .

FISHMAN: Jason has been participating in Homebound?

MOTHER: Right.

FISHMAN: And he is now?

MOTHER: No, we stopped it.

TEACHER 2: When a Homebound instructor went into the home, Jason did not participate. We went on sending homework home. Yes, it came back finished. And I have every confidence that Jason was able to do that homework, but that was only at home. We have never seen any work produced in school. He has not lifted a pencil in school.

PRINCIPAL: We don't doubt that Jason has learned in his two years. The parents have advised us that he reads. He reads to them. He does activities at home. However, I can't . . .

FISHMAN: People can still be smart and not educated.

PRINCIPAL: Right. But we have no way, in a traditional school environment, to make a judgment as to what his levels are, what his progress is, what his achievement is—for that matter, his intelligence, his IQ, if you want to look at that. Or even a standard psychological evaluation. We haven't done any of that, because we've never been able to . . .

TEACHER 1: The reading that Jason did into the recorder at home was *not* on the second-grade level.

FISHMAN: What level was it?

TEACHER 2: It was around a primer.

FISHMAN: A primer is what?

TEACHER 2: Beginning first grade.

FISHMAN: So really what you're talking about is the beginning of a profound educational deficit. And is the system asking Jason to do work of a certain grade that he really can't do? I don't know, and apparently nobody knows. Are we putting Jason in a completely untenable situation? The first thing is, I wonder if the two of you (*To parents*) could get Jason to do an achievement test, whatever achievement test you (*To school personnel*) would want.

PRINCIPAL: We talked about that.

FISHMAN: Is there such an instrument that you have?

TEACHER 1: Yes, we have those kinds of achievement tests. And in special ed, in order to generate an individual plan, we have many instruments that could be used.

FISHMAN: So, an instrument of your choosing. And the other thing that has to happen is that there have to be some consequences, such as the Nintendo game. It seems to me that he should not be rewarded, assuming that this is voluntary behavior—and obviously there is nothing biological if he's a normal kid with his friends, right? So this is a voluntary kind of behavior, part of a pattern. So there need to be some significant consequences, such things like games, going out, and things like that.

MOTHER: Punishment, right?

FISHMAN: Yes, to coin a phrase. Instituted especially by Father.

MOTHER: We've tried lots of things, but have really never stuck to it.

FISHMAN: You've got to stick to it. The reason is that this is the beginning of real problems. We are talking about a life of illiteracy. You don't realize how many people can't get driver's licenses because they can't read. You sometimes see them in public agencies or in public places. They are afraid that they have to sign something, they have to fill out a form.

PRINCIPAL: I taught nonreading adults for fifteen years . . .

FISHMAN: And this is the beginning. His world is going to be a lot different from ours.

MOTHER: Right.

PRINCIPAL: This is urgent, because he has been in regular kindergarten, first grade, special class, and now is returning to regular. We have no more settings that I know of to try to resolve this, so we are now up against a wall.

FISHMAN: Well, everybody has obviously been bending over backwards. It's time for him to start acting his age. I mean, this is two-year-old behavior. This is intentional behavior that is on the level of a temper tantrum, and you've got to succeed. You have all the cards. He can have everything he wants, including Christmas presents. It's already Christmas this year. You have some presents for this guy? (*Mother and father nod.*) It seems to me you have to have one of those achievement tests before Christmas. If Jason completes the achievement test, he gets his Christmas presents. I mean, if you're not going to be tough, what you're going to have is . . . (*To father*) How tall are you?

FATHER: Six foot.

FISHMAN: You're going to have . . . You know how the next generation gets taller . . . You're going to have a six-foot-four kid who doesn't talk, who's twelve years old . . .

TEACHER 1: Who's very powerful.

FISHMAN: And who is very powerful. Hey, look how powerful he is right now.

TEACHER 1: Absolutely.

This system was organized around the isomorph of overprotecting Jason. He was being treated as a damaged child who could do no better than he was doing. When the Homebound program failed with him, everyone backed off and he was taken to a series of clinicians, all of whom focused their efforts on spending time with Jason and trying to get him to speak.

Jason was an adorable little boy, with big brown eyes. He reminded me of those schmaltzy Keene paintings that were popular some years ago showing haunting children with wan bodies and large, beseeching eyes. It was not necessary to dig deep to know that what Jason called forth in everyone (myself included) was the impulse to cuddle and protect him.

To challenge Jason was extremely anxiety provoking for us all. This sweet, mysterious boy who shared little made us concerned that maybe we were pushing too hard. But the signs we got from Jason were that he was as much a hostage to his process as we were. Whenever he would show progress—like the first time he spoke out in school—he proudly told his mother to be sure to tell me. Signs like this gave us comfort that we were going in the right direction and that we shouldn't fail him by retreating.

Thus there was a total absence of complementaries in the system. It seemed that the entire system was functioning as the homeostatic maintainer, through the isomorphic pattern of overprotectiveness. To achieve the goal of getting Jason to participate fully in the school program, both academically and and socially, it would be necessary to transform the dysfunctional process of rewarding Jason for not participating; when he refused to do schoolwork, he was still permitted to play Nintendo and other games.

The plan of treatment was therefore to introduce a counterisomorph: Jason's reluctance to speak and participate would be seen on a behavioral level and would be challenged in the person of the parents. The parents accepted the suggestion that Jason be denied his Nintendo and other games and that his access to them be made contingent on his doing work in school. They were pleased with this outcome of the session, and the mother in particular was relieved to be included in the treatment and not blamed for her son's problems, which their previous therapist had attributed to her supposed dependency.

STEP 3: ADDRESSING THE DYSFUNCTIONAL PATTERNS

As we have seen, isomorphic patterns such as the overprotectiveness that surrounded Jason are most amenable to change when all of the right contexts are involved. In this case, a key context was the school. A few days after the initial therapy session, the family went to the school to administer the achievement test to Jason. This was the first time the parents had sat down with Jason to do such a test. Moreover, it was the first time that Jason had even agreed to take such a test. The testing took place in an anteroom off the principal's office.

PRINCIPAL: I'll leave it to you. I hope Jason wants to return tomorrow, and one of the ways he's going to do that is to do a good job this morning. But it will also help us decide whether he's going to go to the first-grade class or the second-grade class. I think he probably wants to go to the second-grade class, but because he hasn't gotten much work done, it may be that the first-grade class is a real good place for him. He'd do all right in the first-grade class, all *A*s. But today is day one. And he's got to start working. Do you hear that, Jason? I hope you're listening to me.

FATHER: The guy's got a purpose.

PRINCIPAL: Quite honestly, the thought occurred to me, and it's really a tough decision, but I would be more than glad to be Santa's emissary on this one, and as he makes successes today, perhaps tomorrow, then he earns those things that right now are not available to him.

And Christmas is something that we go back to: Santa's verse about good boys and girls. Part of being good is getting your work done at school. If you haven't earned it, you haven't earned it. (*Explaining the test*) You've got to skip some places. It is as simple as that. This isn't real hard. There are 650 boys and girls who are getting their work done today. I need 651. Okay, I'm going to close the door. I'll be in my office for most of the time, if there is anything you need from me. And if you need additional guidance, our special ed teacher will help you.

MOTHER: All right, thanks. (*Principal exits.*) Come on, Jason, let's do it.

FATHER: Let's get it over with.

MOTHER: You can do it. Sit down now, because you can't see this if you're standing up. Now sit down, Jason. Come on. Sit here, and let's get this done. Say these. We want to see how many you get right. What I'll do is I'll circle the ones you get right, okay? We'll start with this one. What is that? Come on, say it. Come on, Jason. What's that word? Hurry up, we don't have all day. Daddy has to get back to work. Come on, what's the word? It's just a letter there, what is it? You know that, come on. Come on, Jason. Come on, Jason.

FATHER: Jason, you have one second, then I'm going to take you over my knee and drill your butt.

MOTHER: How come you're doing this? I don't know for what reason, but you know these words. Now say them. Come on. We'll start with one. Do you want to do it with them in here? Do you want Mr. Cohen to come back in and then you'll do it? Huh? Do you? Or do you want to do it right now with Mommy and Daddy here? Now let's do it! What is it?

JASON: (*Whispers.*)

MOTHER: Yes, but I can't hear you.

FATHER: Speak up, please.

MOTHER: Daddy can't hear you all the way over there if you whisper. Say it. Come on, before everyone comes back. They have to use this room, too, not just us. Now come on. What's that word? Say it. You know it, now say it. All right, say it a little louder. I told you I can't hear you. All right, what's this word?

FATHER: I guess he's going to have to go to kindergarten here.

MOTHER: Do you want to go back to kindergarten? All right, say this word.

FATHER: And speak up, please.

MOTHER: Come on, Jason, we don't have all day. Daddy has to get back to work. Let's go. What is that? You said the first one, but I didn't hear it too good. What's this one? Can you say it a little louder? What's that? Huh? What is it? Say it, Jason, come on, you can. Now just do it. Hurry up. I have to get home. Come on.

FATHER: Now, if she has to keep on, Jason, you're going to lose television and Nintendo.

MOTHER: Now you know how to say these little baby words right there, come on. Do you want to start with the first one? Let's go. What's that? Hurry up, what is it?

FATHER: Speak up, too. I know you can do it.

The session continued in much the same vein until the very end.

MOTHER: Say it louder. You've got one more chance, Jason. Now say it! You *know* these words. Now *say* them.

JASON: (*Says word softly.*)

FATHER: A little bit louder.

MOTHER: Right, a little bit louder, that's all. What's that?

JASON: (*Whispers word.*)

MOTHER: Louder. What's that? Huh? Do you know that word? No? Okay.

With both parents cajoling, gently threatening, and working together, Jason finished the test. It turned out that he was not ready for second grade, as had been planned. He was barely doing first-grade work. The treatment team—the parents, the principal, the teacher, and I—were extremely grateful that the parents had been successful in getting Jason to do the test; we all felt it would have been a tragedy if he had been automatically put in second grade, where he was guaranteed to fail. And such failure would only have rendered Jason more mute, because he would have embarrassed himself in front of his peers.

STEP 4: ESTABLISHING AND MAINTAINING A NEW ORGANIZATION

The new organization created in this case was a collaboration between the school and the parents. Both parents became intimately involved with Jason's school situation, and the teacher and the principal functioned as partners in setting up this new system.

Collaboration with school officials is not always the best policy. Sometimes it is necessary to pit the family against the school; in other cases, the therapist works for reciprocal empowerment. Here, however, a conventional collaborative stance was appropriate. The principal was willing to get together with the parents and make special allowances for them to step in and actively participate in the work of the school, guiding and teaching their child and sharing the teacher's plans.

At a session the week following the testing, some progress was reported.

TEACHER: The thing that's happening right now, and it's bothering and worrying me, is that Jason is showing me that he can do very, very well. The problem is that now he is not letting me know what he doesn't know, and I can't help him. That's my big dilemma. Jason, I can't help you. If kids say, "I don't know this word," I can help them on the board. I watch them write it on the board. What does it sound like? Where does it go? What do we know before? Before you know it, they're telling me the word. But I can't help you do that because you don't tell me.

FISHMAN: I think it's time for the big guns. (*To mother and father*) Can both of you go to class?

MOTHER: Well, that *is* the big guns.

FISHMAN: Because you've got to use some verbal communication.

FATHER: Do you want to hear him cry?

FISHMAN: No, I want to hear him talk.

FATHER: So do I. In school.

FISHMAN: Then there is no problem. If at nine in the morning Jason is not participating, you both show up.

FATHER: (*To Jason, in a loving, gently teasing manner*) Mommy and Daddy have to get you in . . . sissy!

PRINCIPAL: That's saying an awful lot. I mean . . .

FATHER: Do you want your mother and father to come up there and hold your hand? I sit on one side and your mother sits on the other side? Huh? Is that what you want?

MOTHER: What do we do?

PRINCIPAL: I think it's a good idea. I think Jason needs to know that this has got to end. Nobody else can do it now.

FISHMAN: And no ventriloquism. Don't allow him to whisper to you and then speak. If he wants to talk . . . does he talk with a real voice at all?

MOTHER AND FATHER: Yes, definitely.

MOTHER: He'll wipe you out. Well, if all day, you mean . . .

FISHMAN: Okay. So no more of that, okay? We're talking the big guns. (*To*

Jason) From what I see, Jason, you've got a bomber's jacket on, right? Pilot's jacket. That's right.

PRINCIPAL: It seems that Jason needs to hear that he must start participating. Mom and Dad coming in . . . maybe that's what is necessary.

FISHMAN: Time for the big guns. Because it's not fair to Jason. Jason needs to know that this is not a way to spend his childhood.

At a session two weeks later, the teacher reported major changes in Jason's behavior at school.

TEACHER: Well, I'll tell you what. We have lots of surprises today.

FISHMAN: Oh yes?

TEACHER: Lots of surprises. Where do you want us to begin?

FISHMAN: Wherever.

TEACHER: Well, what we started this time was that when Jason came in and he was given the opportunity to complete his assignments and the assignments were not completed, or not even started, we took the time to call his dad. And his dad came in . . .

FISHMAN: Our local Saddam.

TEACHER: Right, our local Saddam. He came in, and we have all sorts of great things (*Holding up folder*).

FISHMAN: Congratulations. (*Shakes mother's hand.*)

MOTHER: Thank you.

FISHMAN: I know how tough it must have been for you.

TEACHER: And I even had the young man give me a little beautiful whisper of a number eight, so I know there's a voice in there.

FISHMAN: He talks!

TEACHER: He talks, and I found out he laughs. And the last time I asked him a question, it was about his favorite color, and he had some papers to do where he was supposed to use his favorite color, and they were all colored blue, so I'm assuming his favorite color is blue. One of the great things, I think, is we were even talking about his writing, and . . .

MOTHER: He said, "Will the doctor be proud of me?"

FATHER: (*Chuckling*) That's what he said.

FISHMAN: Jason, I'll tell you what. I'm *very* proud of you. I know how tough it is to change, and you've really been making a lot of changes. (*Father punches the air in Jason's direction as acknowledgment.*)

MOTHER: Well, his Nintendo is out of his room, because that's the one thing . . . (TO FATHER) What happened? One day you had to go up . . .

FATHER: Right. That's the day I went up and I told him, "The Nintendo's coming out, the toys are coming out." Got rid of the dog.

MOTHER: Yes, the dog is gone, but he wasn't staying anyway. But he did get things taken away that he really liked. And we did tell him that as

soon as he starts behaving—he has to work without his father now—
then he'll get his things back.

FISHMAN: Right. And maybe even a special surprise.

MOTHER: Uh huh.

Freud assumed that once a problem was analyzed, the integration of
the analysis would take care of itself; synthesis at the intrapersonal level
was not a central concern of his therapy. In IST, however, therapy is very
much concerned with maintaining change; the forces that are supposed to
maintain the change are not taken for granted. With difficult families, the
support of extrafamilial institutions such as the school is often crucial for
the maintenance of new patterns. If the therapist fails to mobilize all the
social agencies and individuals needed to orchestrate the new patterns, the
change may collapse.

In this case, the collaboration of the school was critical to the success of
the therapy. The task of therapy had to be not only to motivate the family
but also to motivate the people interacting with the family. The school personnel were not only cooperative but were receptive to the father's participation, treating him well when he was in the school and making him feel
like an ally rather than a stranger. In some cases, the outside institution
may be needed to give a parent an extra push or enticement to maintain
the change.

Thus the role of the family therapist is changed from working with just
the family to working at the interfaces—or, even better, mobilizing the
family to work at the interfaces. The therapist must be flexible enough to
be able to do both, sometimes connecting very closely and respectfully
with the extrafamilial institutions and sometimes getting the family to do
its own connecting. And here the therapist walks a fine line. The goal is, of
course, to empower the family and not undermine its authority. With
some unpracticed and unskilled families, however, the therapist must
become an advocate and a friend of the outside agency, sometimes
empowering the family by helping the outsiders to pull on them. With the
difficult systems of today's families, I believe we will see more and more
that the therapist has to stay as a hovering presence, not only helping the
participants to change but also helping to ensure that they have enough
social supports to bolster the change.

STEP 5: ENDING THERAPY

Therapy with the family continued from about Christmas until school
recessed in June. During that time Jason made steady progress in the regular first-grade classroom. By the end of the school year he was participating fully in the schoolwork, although he was still not speaking up loudly

in class but was instead whispering to the teacher. He talked with the other children at recess, however, went to lunch and to the bathroom, and was animated both in and out of the classroom. At this point, the parents were satisfied with their son's behavior and felt there was no need to continue therapy.

Beginning in the fall, several follow-up sessions were held to track Jason's progress. In one of these sessions, Jason's mother mentioned that her older daughter wanted to go to the school to help get Jason to speak. At the time I liked the idea; this seemed to me an ideal way for the family to empower itself and further demonstrate to the school staff its insistence on maintaining control and being involved to the extent necessary to see that their child did well. So Jason's sister did go to the school and apparently was a disaster. The boy clammed up and did worse for the short period of time she was involved. In retrospect, it is clear that this step should have been taken under the aegis of therapy and that the older child should not have been further parentified.

By the end of the following year, Jason was functioning as a completely normal boy. He participated fully in the life of the school, speaking aloud both socially and in his schoolwork. The power of the intervention had been the creation of a powerful therapeutic system that, in a completely coordinated way, changed his potentially paralyzing problem. As I think back on the therapy and the results, however, I believe that it was not only what was done that was successful but also the fact that the family may indeed have been saved from other interventions (medication or in-patient care, for example) that would have profoundly pathologized this youngster. In some ways, this intervention was a preventive one, preventing the iatrogenics of some of the potential treatment.

There is always the question in my mind, with such an extreme manifestation as this, of whether it is fully explained as just a family developmental problem. Clearly, there must be more. Were there biological developmental characteristics that were cursedly connected to the difficulties in the family? Had the family, in its broader context, not been organized in such a way as to accentuate his developmental delays, would the boy not have manifested his symptoms? Very probably, but this is one of the areas that requires scholarly investigation. Clinically, however, this intervention in the broader context, which I have used with other electively mute children, appears extremely successful.

Each subsystem of the broad context has potential for use in treatment, but for each there are specific principles and concerns that should be addressed. It is to these concerns that we now turn in the chapters that follow.

CHAPTER 5

Working with Siblings

And Cain talked with Abel his brother: and it came to pass, when they were in the field, that Cain rose up against Abel his brother, and slew him. And the Lord said unto Cain, "Where is Abel thy brother?" And he said, "I know not: Am I my brother's keeper?"

—Genesis 4:8–9

THE QUESTION of whether Cain is his brother's keeper speaks, I believe, to the issue of responsibility, specifically, the responsibility for one's sibling, which this chapter addresses.

Traditionally, family therapy has paid little attention to the sibling subsystem. Jane Pfouts (1976) and Stephen Bank and Michael Kahn (1982) have deplored the fact that the focus has almost exclusively been on the husband-wife and parent-child subsystems. Even in postdivorce therapy, as William Nichols (1986) has noted, only a few approaches, such as those of Elinor Rosenberg (1982) and Mary Eno (1985), have shown more than passing interest in dealing with the sibling subsystem. Yet sibling relations can be as influential on family members as the parent-child relationship or outside family influences. "In a culture which is increasingly peer-oriented, communitarian, and less hierarchical, the sibling relationship becomes for many the most powerful and enduring intimate connection available" (Kahn, 1988, p. 23).

Ralph Ranieri and Theodore Pratt (1978) have described how working with the sibling group apart from the parents can be a valuable adjunct to family therapy and may be essential to treating the dysfunction of a particular child. They have found that even in hostile sibling relationships, there are positive feelings and that separate sessions offer the siblings a safe environment in which to express their feelings about one another, to try out behaviors that may be used in peer relationships outside the family, and to come to a better understanding of how their behaviors affect one another and the family as a whole.

In Intensive Structural Therapy, working with the sibling subsystem plays a key role in the treatment process. It does not necessarily include separate sessions with the sibling group, however, although such sessions may well be used. As we will see in the case in this chapter, powerful interactions—even reparation of sibling conflicts—can occur in the family session.

General Principles

Children can be used in the therapy session in many ways, as consultants in acquiring and assessing information and as cotherapists. There are several caveats that must be observed, however, to guard the children from being triangulated, protect the sibling subsystem, and foster the bonds within it.

Try to keep children free of quasi-adult roles. The sibling subgroup is a separate system within the family, with its own set of relationships and alliances outside the parental boundary (Lewis, 1988). Sibling bonds can be damaged when a child is pulled into a quasi-adult role. A parent may, for example, form an alliance with one child and use another child as a buffer in the marriage. Both roles serve a rescue function for the parent's own needs; if they are allowed to continue, they will pose a barrier between the siblings. The "chosen" child will be cut off from the more appropriate, mutually supportive sibling subsystem (Nichols, 1986) and may even be continually rejected by the sibling group. Eno (1985) has stated that parent-child coalitions and sibling isolation are two key dimensions of postdivorce family life and affect the ways in which siblings help or hurt one another.

Do not make children responsible for their siblings. Siblings must never be put in the untenable position of taking over responsibility from the parental subsystem, where it belongs. This shift of responsibility is sometimes seen in families with a handicapped child. Milton Seligman (1988) notes that siblings of disabled children often feel excessive responsibility to take care of the handicapped child, a role frequently encouraged by the parents. Contrasting their own healthy or normal lives with that of the impaired sibling, they commonly experience what Bank and Kahn (1982) refer to as "survivor guilt."

In such cases, the impaired sibling is likely to take advantage of the unimpaired child's excessive sense of responsibility and enslave that child in taking care of him or her, becoming helpless in the process. The normal sibling will then develop anger, resentment, and more guilt, and quite possible subsequent psychological disturbance. Elva Poznanski (1969) reported in one study that psychiatrists treated more siblings of handi-capped children than handicapped children themselves.

The same situation can occur in families with a child with behavior problems. The "well" child may be experiencing pain and guilt and may feel responsible for transforming the recalcitrant sibling. Such responsibil-ity can impede and even cripple development in the sibling charged with it. It would be at the very least ironic and at worst criminal for a therapist to saddle a child such as this with further responsibility in the name of psychotherapy.

There is one exception to the principle that children must not be made responsible for each other. In large family systems, much of the socializa-tion and caregiving of the younger children is done by the older children. In a sense, the parents raise the older children, who in turn raise the younger ones (McGuire & Tolan, 1988). As a practical matter, such an arrangement is implicit and accepted, but in dysfunctional families it may become difficult for the younger children to gain access to the parents. As the overwhelmed parents are attending to the "squeaky wheels" in the system, rules of access are established, often enforced by the tyranny of teasing. The younger children may be afraid to challenge the rules for fear of ridicule and may be suffering.

Reestablish the parents as a strong executive unit. The goal of keeping chil-dren free of quasi-adult roles and inappropriate responsibility is, of course, to reempower the parents and liberate the children. Rather than placing the siblings in an executive position, the therapist must help the parents regain executive control. Considering the broader context may reveal what is weakening the parents' sense of strength. Are there relation-ships in the parents' context that are undermining them? If, for example, there is a bitter or embattled relationship with one or both of their own parents, those parents should be brought into the therapy, if possible. If other forces, such as work pressures, are rendering them incompetent, steps must be taken to relieve those pressures. Within the system, one or both parents may be rendered ineffectual by alliances. The therapist supports the parents in a time-limited way in the therapy sessions, all the while scanning the context for areas that can be permanent sources of support.

Part of the work with the sibling subsystem is to help the children help their parents with the task of regaining contol. By the time a family reaches the point of entering therapy, all the family members are super-sensitive. Their nerves are frayed, and they may have given up. The thera-pist can make the children feel confirmed in their needs and can enable them to communicate their needs to their parents in a reasoned way.

Clinical experience as well as theory suggests that the therapist should not model a parental role when working with the sibling subsystem (Nichols, 1986). Seeing children without their parents is, as Karen Gail Lewis (1988) warns, "fertile ground for triangulation" (p. 102). It is all too easy for the therapist to become attached to the children and join them against the parents. But such a bond puts the children in a one-up position and creates conflict between parents and children and parents and therapist. Nichols recommends an avuncular approach, with the therapist acting as a kind of uncle or aunt, to avoid confusion and loyalty conflict. Thus, seeing the siblings as a subsystem can be an important means of assessing information and revealing misinformation, but therapists must be aware of the role they themselves play in treatment.

Look at rivalries within the sibling subsystem. Even though in families there is an inevitability that siblings manifest rivalry and quarreling, children are not born hating one another; something happens within the family system to convert normal sibling rivalry into a destructive process (Lewis, 1988). It is a cause of concern and should be monitored. Two common reasons for it are parental intrusion into the children's relationship and preferential treatment by the parents. The problem can also be traced to alliances between parents and children. Obviously, the contextual therapist treats sibling rivalry in the same way as any other problem in the family system and assesses it in terms of both the family's internal dynamics and the relations between the family and its broader context. Whatever its cause, sibling rivalry should be evaluated carefully in its relation to the entire family system (Lewis, 1988).

Ensure that the needs of all the siblings are being met. One generic and quintessential reason for including the siblings in therapy and carefully assessing their subsystem is to look out for the welfare of all the children. Even though one child may be of most concern, it would be asystemic and ethically wrong to focus exclusively on any one family member. It is common lore in family therapy that while the child who is acting up is getting the lion's share of the attention, the perfect sibling may be more vulnerable. That child must walk a very narrow line, and, as a result, his or her self may be submerged and may remain inchoate and undeveloped.

CASE EXAMPLE: BETH

Beth was 16 years old and out of control. Her parents were divorced. The mother had remarried and had two small children by the second marriage. After the divorce, Beth had at first lived with her mother, as her older sister, Lauren, still did, but the stresses on the family were great. Both mother and stepfather worked long hours at a discount store, on different shifts, and they saw little of each other. The developmental stresses of an adolescent, an older sister starting to leave the system, and two small children, added to the severe financial pressures and difficult work schedules, had made for a highly stressed system.

When the mother found Beth impossible to handle, Beth had gone to live with her biological father. The father's work schedule was lighter, but he worked nights. In his absence, Beth would open her father's house to her drug-using friends. She was also extremely promiscuous and had recently had a urinary tract infection. On one occasion, she told her father she was going to spend the weekend with her mother but went to New York instead and was mugged at the bus terminal. On another occasion, she was picked up in a stolen car, and as a result, a court appearance was pending. She was at risk of permanent expulsion from school because of her frequent absences. She had become very depressed and cried a great deal.

Throughout this period, the family had shown tremendous conflict avoidance about Beth's behavior. There was almost a conspiracy among all the adults not to force the issue with Beth, partly, I believe, because they didn't have the resources to deal with it; they were stretched to the limit. Lauren, the 18-year-old sister, had been instrumental in bringing matters to a head. Her friends had been telling her about Beth's activities, and she had finally gone to the school guidance counselor for help. The session described here followed by one day a session in which the parents were confronted with the facts, when the father, forced to face the truth, had declared, "I can't believe my daughter would lie to me."

Present at this second session were the mother, the stepfather, the biological father, Lauren, Beth, and Beth's friends Kate (who was 21) and Andrea (who was Beth's age). Kate played a significant role in the session —to be discussed in detail in the next chapter on working with peers.

The father began this session by focusing on his ignorance of what had been happening and his hurt at being lied to. He appeared to have taken a protective stance toward Beth, shielding her from the accusations of other family members and finding explanations for her behavior. At one point, he seemed more troubled about the lies themselves than about the alarming misconduct they had concealed. Lauren, however, quickly raised the level of tension in the room with an impassioned, tearful appeal to her sister.

FATHER: I didn't know about New York. I knew about the car and one weekend when she was on the street, because I got mad at her and said, "This has got to stop. Are you going back with your mother? Are you going to find somebody else to live with? Because I'm not going to put up with the attitude any more. If you want to live with me, you're going to have to give me, you know, something back." So she says she's going to stay with her mother for the weekend, but she didn't, and that's when this thing started up. She never told me she went to New York. (*To Beth*) Over the weekend, that Saturday night, when you told me you were going to leave, I asked you to be honest with me. You're not honest with me, and I'm by myself.

KATE: Everybody thinks that he's the bad guy, but he doesn't know what's going on. He doesn't know anything, because everything goes on behind his back.

FATHER: I'm trying to be nice, I'm trying give and take, but I can't take lying. That's one thing I can't take. You can be honest with me, be open with me, we can get things out in the open. I have no grudges, no regrets, no vendettas, but I can't go for lying.

BETH: I didn't say nothing because nothing I say is going to help.

FATHER: If you'll tell me, we can work out our problems.

BETH: Why, so you can make me look like a slut?

LAUREN: We can help you! For Christ's sake, will you open your eyes and look what's going on?!

BETH: Shut the fuck up.

FATHER: Oh, hey!

BETH: I'm sorry, all right? But you're all coming down on me!

STEPFATHER: We're trying to help you, Beth.

BETH: What does Lauren have to do with this? After all, she knew about the stolen car. I didn't know it was stolen!

MOTHER: Lauren is concerned about you. She went down to the guidance counselor's office, she and Kate and Andrea. They were worried. You think they don't care. They do care. It took a lot of guts to go down there.

LAUREN: (*Looking around and gesturing to Beth's two friends*) You know how scared these guys are coming here, Beth?

KATE: (*Crying*) I don't want you to hate me for what I'm doing, I'm trying to help you.

LAUREN: You just don't get it, do you? I wish you would open your eyes and just see that we love you and we care about you and we want you at home and we want a family, but you don't want that. You want to live with your damn friends on the street and do whatever the hell you please, and you don't even care that we're hurting! You don't care, you don't care about Mommy crying at night and Daddy crying and the baby crying. You don't care! You don't care!

BETH: I'm also crying, Lauren. I do so care.

LAUREN: You're really showing us how much you care right now! . . . Beth, we know everything anyway. Why can't you just admit it instead of trying to cover it up? We know about the drugs, we know about the guys . . . I heard you sneak guys in the bedroom, Beth, right? . . . Did you flush coke down the toilet, Beth?

Lauren and the others continued to tax Beth with her behavior, contrasting their caring concern with that of her drug-using friends, who hadn't been heard from since the matter had been blown open. The session became extremely tense. None of the members were dry-eyed. Everyone's gaze went back and forth between Lauren and Beth. Beth for her part had a fixed, almost hard expression on her face as she alternately glanced down and glared at her sister. Lauren finally gave up in despair.

LAUREN: (*Crying*) It's hopeless. This whole meeting, yesterday, everything is hopeless. She doesn't have any love left in her. She doesn't have any caring left in her. We can give and give and give and we can try and try and we're running into a dead-end street. There's a dead end, there's no hope, we shouldn't even be here, because it's not going to help anyway, she just doesn't see. There's no hope for it, it's ridiculous. I mean, why am I sitting here talking to a brick wall? Nothing I say means anything to her!

It was a very powerful scene, a poignant moment that had several people in the room in tears. During the previous 5 or 6 years, and especially with the arrival of the twin children of the second marriage, Lauren had assumed more of a parental role with Beth. Forced into the position of trying to parent a wild teenager, she had taken to abusing Beth verbally. As a result, she had lost her credibility with the younger girl. In order to regain that credibility, it was necessary for her to apologize and make amends, so that Beth would not see her as an antagonist. The next segment of the session includes the beginning of the work of repairing the sibling relationship.

FATHER: You don't like the way she looks. You don't like the way she—

LAUREN: I admitted that. I treated Beth very badly the last couple of years. I put her down a lot, the last couple of years. I regret that, Beth, you know I regret that. You know I said I apologized for that. I'm older now and I realize how immature that was and I should have accepted you for you, but I made that mistake and I apologize for that. Are you gonna make me dwell on that forever, that I put you down that much? I mean, I know I made those mistakes, and I'm sorry!

FATHER: When did you apologize to her for that? Was it after she came to live with me, or before she came to live with me?

LAUREN: After she went to live with you.

FATHER: So when she came to live with me, she was feeling, you know, unloved by you, because you were always—for the last two or three years—you were constantly saying things like, "Your hair's different."

LAUREN: I made a mistake! Don't turn it around on me!

FATHER: I'm not trying to turn it around. I'm just trying to find out—

LAUREN: (*Yelling*) All right, put everything on me, okay?

FATHER: When she came to live with me, she was looking for love.

LAUREN: And you gave it to her by giving her money and giving her the time and the place for her friends to hang out.

FATHER: She found it in certain friends that came around, that's what I'm saying. She was looking for something at the time. I gave her the opportunity to have different friends around, and it just happened they weren't the right friends. She picked the wrong friends, because she was searching, she was hunting. And she made a mistake, just like you made a mistake.

FISHMAN: We don't know whether Beth thinks she made a mistake.

LAUREN: Do you think you made a mistake, Beth?

BETH: I know I made a mistake.

LAUREN: What mistakes have you made?

BETH: My friends.

LAUREN: Is that all the mistakes you've ever made? You told me that your friends don't lead you in the wrong direction, that your friends can't make you. You said to us yesterday that you do what you want, what you please. If you are so independent, then how can your friends have made you make the mistakes? Tell me that much. I thought you led your own life and nobody told you what to do. And now you're telling us your friends made you make those mistakes? You're confusing me a little bit. You know, I may not have been the best sister in the world, but I care, I care enough to be here, I care enough to cry at night because I worry about you. I care about you and I love you, Beth! It makes my heart break when I see you, because I wonder what kind of life you're going to have, if you're going to be happy and live a normal life or are just going to end up on the street. That's how much I care. You don't see that. You just see me how I used to be towards you, you don't see how I want to be towards you.

BETH: You've just proved my point.

LAUREN: What point did I prove, Beth?

BETH: You see what you want to be. You don't see what I want to be.

KATE: What do you want to be, Beth?

BETH: I just want to improve.

LAUREN: But you can't get anywhere by sitting here denying things. Why don't you just tell us the truth? . . . I love you so much, Beth. Why [are you doing this], Beth? We don't hate you. We only want what's best for you. Why do you have to hate us? Why do you hate us so much? It doesn't have to be this way! It doesn't!

FISHMAN: (*To father*) This must be pretty tough on you.

FATHER: It is. I've always loved her. I've always tried to be there when she needed help.

At this point, I felt that the only way for the father to bend was to be supported. If he felt that he was just going to be attacked, he would only become more rigid in his position of protecting the girl from the other members of the family, and it was that very protection that was maintaining the dysfunctional homeostasis. Having supported him by offering sympathy, however, I then challenged him on his priorities.

FATHER: The thing that hurts me is the lies. I could take it if she told me she had sex with ten boys or twenty boys, okay, but to have her say "I didn't have sex at all" and then find out that she had sex at least once or twice, that hurts me more, because it shows that she doesn't trust me as much as I put trust in her.

FISHMAN: (*Incredulously*) Let me ask you, you're not concerned if she has sex with ten or twenty boys?

FATHER: I'm concerned. What I'm trying to say is, if she makes a mistake and has sex and someone confronts me and says, "Your daughter's been having sex with ten guys," and I go to her and say, "Have you had sex with ten different guys?" and she says no.

BETH: It's none of your business who I have sex with.

FATHER: I know, but it's—

LAUREN: Sure it is!

FATHER: It is my business. You're underage.

LAUREN: There's AIDS out there, and all kinds of germs. Doesn't that even enter your mind?

FISHMAN: So you're concerned about AIDS.

LAUREN: Damn right I am.

FISHMAN: When you're using drugs, it's not like twenty years ago. No one's ever been cured of AIDS. Everybody dies.

At this point, I left the room. I felt that my presence was hampering the process that needed to unfold. The girl needed to be challenged even further, and the father needed to change his position. But instead the father continued to call for "talking through things," the mother bewailed not being able to trust Beth, and Lauren repeated her apology and love for Beth. As I observed from behind the mirror, it was clear that more intensity and action were needed.

The crisis induction involved forcing the parents to make adequate arrangements to keep Beth under control. My goal was that by the end of the session, one or the other of the parents (or ideally both) would take over responsibility for putting together a more effective hierarchy. Beth's mother and stepfather did not want her in their home, nor did Beth want to live with them.

The young people left the room, and the father, mother, stepfather, and I began to discuss the possibilities. The mother began by turning to me and asking in beseeching tones, "Is there no kind of facility that can help?" She was looking toward an arrangement that would take the pressure off the system. If this were to happen, however, much of the work done thus far would be undone. Instead, what was needed was to increase the pressure on the system, so that a new structure would emerge, a structure that included a parental hierarchy to contain this wild teenager.

FISHMAN: Oh, she doesn't need a special school. She just needs controls. She needs the three of you to say, "Okay, you can negotiate certain things." But that's later. You can't trust a word she says to you now.

MOTHER: This is the problem I had in the past, when she was living in the house and she was in counseling. Her biggest gripe with us was that we don't trust her, but as soon as we give her this much (*gesturing*) she takes this much; she is not where she is supposed to be. She went to a friend's house—my husband dropped her off—and I said, "Please have the mother call me to let me know if it's okay that you are there." Instead, they took a cab to a party that was not supervised, with over fifty kids, and she had one of her friends call. I felt stupid—I knew this was a kid on the phone—and I had to send my husband to go find her and drive her home. How can I trust her? I take her to the movies right down the street. They don't go in the movies when I drop her off, they go around behind the building and do drugs. This is what I went through. Our life is a wreck, and I feel, like, it's not fair. Okay, I love her, she's my daughter, I want her there, but I have to consider my two babies, too.

FISHMAN: So where else can she go? Do you have any relatives who live in terrible places?

By "terrible places" I had in mind someplace like a very small town in a distant state, a place that this adolescent would find boring and where she would not want to live. Such a prospect would give the parents increased power, because they would have an alternative. They could say to the girl "No, you can't live here" if her behavior was unacceptable.

Whether in a "terrible place" or no, however, the answer for Beth was not a facility such as her mother had in mind. Institutions are dangerous places, especially for an adolescent with Beth's vulnerability to being led astray by bad companions. They are only a temporary solution, and an expensive one at that. And finally, they take the power away from the parents, relieving them of the responsibility for dealing with the problem. I therefore insisted that they themselves look for a place for Beth.

FATHER: Why stick our problems on somebody else?
FISHMAN: The idea is to make her want to live with you, and then you have to say, "You can't do X, Y, and Z, and if you do, then you can't live here." So find a place.
FATHER: My sister has a place in south Jersey. And she is more of a disciplinarian.
FISHMAN: Oh? She could really discipline her? Would she take her?
FATHER: I'd have to talk to her. I don't know if she'll be home now or not.
FISHMAN: Want to call her? You want to be able to say it's a real option when the kids come back in the room. It'll only be temporary.

Using the telephone in the therapy room can move things along rapidly. The idea is *carpe diem:* Seize the day, do it right now. By the end of this session there could be a whole new system in place. The father slowly and with obvious discomfort moved to the phone and began calling while I engaged in casual talk with the mother and stepfather, assuring them, "Believe it or not, she'll grow out of this. The idea is keeping her safe in the meantime."

The father first tried to reach his sister. When his niece said that she was not home and wouldn't be back until late, he sat down, clearly relieved. Dogged clinician that I am, I suggested, "What about her grandmother?" The father gave me a look of defeat and said, "Okay, I'll try her."

Eventually he reached his mother and made arrangements to have her come to his house every week night and stay overnight to supervise Beth. When the young people came back into the room, the father presented the decision to Beth.

FATHER: Beth, you're going to be staying at my house, but Grandma is coming over, and she's going to be watching over you while I'm not there. And on Fridays, when I work days, she's going to come over, pick you up, and take you to her house until I get home. We're going to do this until you straighten out. (*As Beth begins to object*) There's no other alternative . . . You don't want to go back to your mother's house. I'm trying to work something out where you can be where you want to be, and we don't have too many alternatives—either your mother's house or my house or your grandmother's. That's it, there is no other choice.

The description of the therapy with this family is continued in the next chapter, where the role that Beth's friends played in the treatment is brought in. One friend, in particular, proved to be an effective cotherapist. It was the participation of the sibling in this case, however, that began the change process. My pleas and the pleas of the biological mother and stepfather had fallen on deaf ears. The intense therapeutic crisis occurred with the participation of the sister.

In addition to helping precipitate change, the inclusion of siblings in therapy can play one other critical role. In this age of divorce and blended families, as Margaret Schibuk (1989) has pointed out, siblings are essential "units of continuity" long after the nuclear family may have be reconstructed unrecognizably. The siblings can be the anchor to the past and help support the family members as their present system is being transformed.

The addition of siblings, as we have seen, can be dangerous in the sense that the sibling may feel somehow responsible and, indeed, may be the brother's (or sister's) keeper. Nonetheless, it would be absurd to ignore the input from siblings because of the risks involved. As therapists, we must simply be aware of the risks and act to preclude the negative consequences. Indeed, that caveat applies to all our interventions to a greater or lesser degree. IST is a precise therapy that involves close monitoring by the therapist. To dismiss possible interventions because of their potential pitfalls ignores the very premise of contextual therapy—that is, that if we can assess the context carefully and follow the feedback closely, we can safely use more and more aspects of other contexts. This close following of feedback is all the more possible when the therapist seeks to create change right in the therapy room.

Like siblings, peers have, until recently, largely been ignored in therapy. Yet they, too, are important social influences. As people tend to live in horizontal families more and more, away from their families of origin, friends become de facto families. It is to that group that we turn in the next chapter.

CHAPTER 6

Working with Peers

O NE OF THE MOST important extrafamilial resources in Intensive Structural Therapy is the peer group. The inclusion in therapy of close friends—both adolescents and adults—can be invaluable. As we saw in the introduction, today's families tend to be horizontal rather than vertical; that is, the multigenerational system of grandparents, parents, and children is often replaced by a system in which friends take the place of biological family. Yet friends are often overlooked in family therapy, especially the friends of the adults. Although it would be considered a cardinal sin not to mention an adult's parents and family of origin, it is the rare therapist who explores the current friend system. Other than family network therapists, I can find only Russell Haber (1987, 1990) and Margaret Jones (1987) to have addressed the use of friends in the family therapy literature. This chapter considers how friends of both youngsters and adults can be powerful forces in the therapeutic process.

General Principles:
Peers of Children and Adolescents

Peer relationships are tremendously powerful in the social, psychological, and moral development of children and adolescents. In one set of self-report studies (Youniss & Smollar, 1985), for example, adolescents reported feeling that they were better understood by their friends than by their parents and took their personal problems to friends more often than to their parents. They also said that they learned more from their friends than from their parents.

Many studies (reviewed in Hartup, 1983) have demonstrated the importance of peer interaction in affecting behavior and psychological development, in both positive and negative ways. The development of social skills, sex-role identity, moral judgments, and the ability to resolve conflict have all been seen to correlate with successful peer relations in childhood and adolescence. Studies of gang interaction (Vigil, 1988; Hochhaus & Sousa, 1987–1988) and adolescent drug use (Johnson, 1980) point to elements of peer interaction that provide a sense of identity, protection, and companionship.

On the other hand, longitudinal studies have found that poor peer relations in middle childhood are predictive of later emotional and social dysfunction (Cowen, Pederson, Babigian, Izzo, & Trost, 1973). Similarly, poor peer relationships have been shown to predict drug abuse (Oetting & Beauvais, 1986) and antisocial behavior (Roff, Sells, & Golen, 1972).

Family and friends are the two primary systems in anyone's life, and their joint influence can be synergistic. Among one group of adolescents whose mothers wanted them to go to college, only 49 percent had college plans if their best friends did not intend to continue their education after high school, but 83 percent planned to go to college if their best friends had similar plans (Kandel & Lesser, 1972).

It is surprising, therefore, that so little use is made of adolescent peers in family therapy. Both Haber (1987, 1990) and Jones (1987) consider that the neglect of child-child relations is of great concern in view of the powerful influence of friends on psychological development, which can only increase as social changes in today's world—divorce, dual-career families, and geographic distance from extended families, for instance—make friendships all the more important.

Use peers as cotherapists. The key to working with a youngster's peers is not to underestimate the potential alliance between the peers and the family. Therapists have long been hampered by the idea that peers cannot be counted on to support the therapeutic good. As we will see in the cases to be described, however, this is not necessarily so. Even a peer who has been an active participant in the problem behavior can often see that things have gone too far and may be willing to help bring about change.

Youngsters can re-create patterns outside the family that are isomorphic with patterns within the family. When the family is dysfunctional, some of the same dysfunctional patterns are created in the peer group. At the same time, however, a child may try to select some peers to be syntonic with earlier family patterns, patterns that were more appropriate and functional. Such friends share the values of the family and are likely to subscribe to the need for correction. They know what has been going on and can confront the family with the need for change, challenge them to bring about the necessary changes, and support them in their efforts to control the patient's behavior. Especially when a youngster is at a point of transition, of abandoning good friends and joining with more corrupt peers, the good peers can often be recruited to help rescue their friend and can be invaluable to the therapeutic process.

Thus the therapist, by searching for shared values between the generations, can transcend the generational gap. What are generally considered to be two separate processes—peer-to-peer relations and family relations—are brought together rather than treated as divided contexts.

Use peers to bear witness. Often an adolescent's friends not only know better than the family what is happening with the youngster but also are better able than the therapist to bring the message home. Parents are forced to recognize that a child is delinquent when it is the child's friends who say so. The therapist's words and display of authority are never as strong as when they are combined with the same message (or a worse message) coming from the child's friends. Parents know that peers run the risk of being socially ostracized as "finks," so those who bear witness have great credibility, and therapists should make use of them whenever possible.

Do not try to change peers therapeutically. Although the personal information the patient's friends provide about themselves is frequently useful, it is important to remember that they are consultants in the therapy, not patients themselves (Haber, 1987, 1990). Their job is to help the family develop a better perspective of the problem. It is the therapist's job to make clear to everyone the limitations of a friend's involvement. The friend and the friend's parents must be reassured that the youngster is coming in only to help, not to receive any mental health services. Unless this is emphasized, the child may be confused about why he or she is being invited in, and the parents may find it difficult to allow the child to participate. The friend's parents' style of parenting is not the issue, furthermore, and should never be addressed.

Bring in the parents of peers if necessary. When the peer has been involved in the patient's misbehavior, it is often extremely helpful to have that child's parents in the therapy session as well. With both sets of parents present, neither child can use the power of the third ("But Todd's parents said it was okay!"). This larger organization creates a broad net around the children and helps to limit the pull of the peer on the patient. Not only is the behavior of the problematic child changed, but the child's context is changed as the other parents modify their own child's behavior.

Bring in both "good" peers and "bad" peers if possible. As we have seen, the therapist brings in the "good" friends to support the family and to accentuate the positive facets of the patient's life; equally important is to bring in the "bad" friends, if possible. One can then monitor the negative influences and—ideally—intervene to counteract them. At the very least, the clinician can get a sense of what the patient is up against. In the case of children and adolescents, it is more effective to bring in bad peers with their parents. Some of these parents, of course, will take the position that it is *their* perfect little darling who is being led astray, but generally these are not the parents who come in; those who are willing to cooperate usually are able to be more objective about their child.

Be ready to reassure and support. It is essential for the therapist to recognize that participation in a session is potentially disastrous for friendships. In the face of the risk and the generosity the friend shows in participating, the therapist must be available to support the friend without being condescending or patronizing, and without taking the friend's side if conflict emerges.

CASE EXAMPLE: BETH AND KATE

The case of Beth, described in the previous chapter, is a classic example. In addition to the unsavory friends who were using Beth's father's house for doing drugs, Beth had a 21-year-old friend named Kate. Kate had been a kind of big sister to Beth, but in recent months Beth had become increasingly estranged from her as she had become involved with her new crowd of friends.

During a session on the day previous to the session described in chapter 5, the father had refused to believe that his daughter was doing wrong. Kate had then been mentioned as a friend who had expressed concern about Beth, and I had said, "Great, bring her in tomorrow." During that next day's session, Kate bore witness to what had been going on.

KATE: I don't want to get you in trouble in any way. What happened happened because I was trying to get you help.
FISHMAN: What exactly did happen?
KATE: I knew she was having problems—I wish you would talk to her father, because I don't want to turn her against him, but I . . . I know that when she came back that weekend, that she was out of her father's house. Since then I've learned that she went out and hung around with the same friends. She said she is trying to be better now, and she's

assured me that she hasn't been with any of these friends. . . . They (*Beth's friends*) are just using her for the house, because she has a place for everybody to go.

FISHMAN: Where's that?

KATE: Her father's house, and he doesn't even know what's going on.

Kate also took part in the direct appeal to Beth.

KATE: I know you're scared to tell everybody everything, because you don't want them to think bad of you, but it's better if everything comes out, because that's what you need. You need to get everything out. . . . I know you care what everybody thinks about you, because I know that you're not like that, and you care what other people think about you.

Finally, when Beth expressed reservations about the arrangements to have her grandmother supervising her at her father's house, Kate supported the plan.

BETH: So what am I going to do?

FATHER: We're not saying that; we're just trying to get you straightened out.

BETH: I have been straightened out.

STEPFATHER: You just said you had a problem.

KATE: However long you're going to be at your grandmother's, it's okay, because all the friends you did wrong with, they're not going to be there, so who are you going to go out with?

FATHER: Your grandmother's coming over at nine at night, so that when I go to work there is somebody there to watch over you. She's my other set of eyes. I have no other set of eyes except for her. And when she comes over, she will stay overnight, and in the morning when you go to school, she'll go home and do whatever she has to do at home and then at night she'll come back and stay with you. On days when I'm off, it's different. She doesn't have to come over when I'm there. We'll deal with situations as they come up. If you want to go to the movies with someone, fine. I'll take you to the movies, I'll drop you off. But you're gonna be supervised.

KATE: This would be the same thing as we were saying last night, as if we had gotten a nanny or someone to watch you. It's the same thing, but it's your family that's going to be there.

At a follow-up session one month later, the father reported that Kate was going to be staying with Beth in the evenings, watching her during his absences at work. Beth had proposed that Kate move in. The father felt that Kate had been through her own adolescence and was settling down;

she was studying to be a nurse. The mother had some reservations about the plan, questioning what would happen when Kate wanted to go out and whether it was good for Beth to be with Kate exclusively. She wisely insisted that her ex-husband set ground rules for both girls when Kate moved in.

So while Beth had some terrible friends, she also had at least one good friend who represented values more akin to those of her family. One might well ask, "How is it that this kid, who looks so rotten and so immature, selected such a wonderful friend?" The credit goes to the family. Beth's family, with all its limitations, had produced a human being who could appreciate the family's values of concern and protection from danger, and she, in turn, had selected a friend who shared those values.

Such friends have tremendous credibility in therapy, because they are risking a great deal to help the therapist help their friend. They are breaking the adolescent code of uniting against adults and authority, and therefore they stand to lose the very friend they are trying to save. This factor was even more striking in the case that follows.

CASE EXAMPLE: CHUCK

Seventeen-year-old Chuck had spent a little over a month in a psychiatric hospital and was about to enter a long-term program for alcohol abuse. His parents were long-distance truck drivers who worked together and were frequently away. Chuck's maternal grandmother lived in a trailer next to the parents' house. There had been control over Chuck when his maternal grandfather was alive, but the grandfather had died and now Chuck was sneaking out almost every night and using his pickup truck to take his friends to town, staying out most of the night.

The consultation described here included the grandmother, as well as Chuck, his parents, and Chuck's staff therapist. During the course of the consultation, it came out that the grandmother had known more about Chuck's activities than she had revealed to the parents. The mother, for her part, had kept a great deal of Chuck's misbehavior from his father. And the father's response to his son's activities was a proud grin as Chuck's escapades were revealed during the session. Thus there was a pattern of complicity in conflict avoidance throughout this family.

There was one other person in the room who knew what was going on, and that was Chuck's friend Seth. Seth proved to be a courageous ally in challenging the system to change. He disproved the age-old tenet that you cannot trust peers because they are only going to support their friends. He risked breaking the adolescent covenant of youngsters against adult authority and blew the whistle, challenging the parents to regain control over their son.

FISHMAN: (*To Seth*) You're a good friend?
SETH: Yeah.
FISHMAN: You're best friends?
SETH AND CHUCK: (*Looking at each other, smiling, and nodding*) Yeah.
FISHMAN: How long have you been friends?
MOTHER: You've been friends since grade school. (*The boys agree.*)
FISHMAN: Okay, Chuck, how long have you been here?
CHUCK: One month, two days.
FISHMAN: Why are you here?
CHUCK: Because I had behavioral problems, and I'm depressed.
FISHMAN: Who depresses you?

This was a variation of a classic line of Minuchin's (1974): "Who upsets you?" Chuck was a little taken aback by the question. Not surprisingly, his depression had to do with context. Here I was challenging the linearity of the family's thinking. In terms of "who," the response immediately contextualized the problem—it became the whole family's problem not just their son's.

CHUCK: I don't know.
FISHMAN: Guess.
CHUCK: Things I do depress me.
FISHMAN: How about the people in your life? Who gets you down the most?
CHUCK: (*Pause*) Probably myself, because after I do things I feel bad and get down.
FISHMAN: Outside of yourself, who gets you down the most? (*Chuck is silent.*) I'm going to ask your friend. (*To Seth*) Who do you think gets him down the most?
SETH: I really don't know. I guess I do, because I do more running around than he did.
FISHMAN: So he's jealous.
SETH: Yeah, something like that. Sometimes he'd sneak out and get caught. When I'd sneak out, I wouldn't get caught.

As the session continued, the picture of a family system rigidly avoiding underlying conflicts began to emerge.

CHUCK: Sometimes my parents—whatever I do, they get mad and get me down. But they have a right to do that.
FISHMAN: Always? They always have a right?

CHUCK: Always.

FISHMAN: Always? That's unusual. You never get a bad rap? They're always right?

CHUCK: Yep.

FISHMAN: (*To parents*) You must be quite unusual parents.

MOTHER: We didn't think we were; we thought we were doing everything wrong. But all Chuck could ever tell us was that he can't follow the rules. He doesn't object to our rules. He says they're not too strict, not unreasonable, but he just can't follow them, he doesn't know why. If there's something he wants to do, if it doesn't fit within our boundaries, he goes and does it anyway.

If the members of this extreme conflict-avoiding system could not acknowledge their difficulties to themselves, they were not going to be able to acknowledge them to an outsider. I clearly needed an ally, preferably someone who was an intrinsic part of the system—either the grandmother or the friend.

FISHMAN: (*To grandmother*) What do you think? What is your perspective?

GRANDMOTHER: I really don't know. I just don't know why he's over here, I really don't. Me and Chuck get along real good, real good. But then when it comes to following the rules, he just doesn't pay that much attention to them. I've never been mean to Chuck. I've corrected him a few times, but I've never been mean to him. Chuck loves me, and I worship him, and we get along. Only one time that I can think of, and that was just before he came over here. He had a friend with him that I didn't approve of and his folks didn't approve of, and he thought I was wrong in asking him not to come back any more. And that's the only time I can think of that we ever had any problem at all. I knew he was doing things he shouldn't do, but I didn't correct him on it, I never did tell him not to do it. When he would say, "I'm gonna do this" or "I'm gonna do that," I'd say, "Well, I don't think that's right," and that's all I ever say to him.

FISHMAN: (*To father*) What about you? What would you say?

FATHER: Me? I don't know, I swear, I was really astonished by a lot of things that I didn't know about, because I was left in the dark about a lot of things for a long time. And I was disappointed and hurt by him. He's showed me he's making some kind of progress here now. I know that he was pretty depressed, and it seemed like he was angry.

FISHMAN: Why don't you ask him?

FATHER: What he was angry about?

FISHMAN: Yes.

FATHER: I've asked him, but I just can't get an answer.

FISHMAN: Try it here, try now.

FATHER: (*To Chuck*) Can you tell me what you're angry about?

CHUCK: (*After long pause, mumbling*) I'm angry and disappointed by stuff at school . . . and behavior. Just all around. I know I disappointed you.

FATHER: Are you just angry at yourself, or is it me?

CHUCK: Just me.

I saw his response as more conflict avoidance, which did not help me to get the problem into the realm of relationships.

FATHER: You can say what you feel; you're not going to hurt me.

CHUCK: I'm angry at myself.

FATHER: You're not upset with your mother or me? Seth? Your grandma? (*Pause*) For a long time we thought we had the perfect family. Well, we did. Somehow it's just one of the things that happen. (*To Fishman*) I have no answers why, I haven't found out why he's doing it or why he's done it. (*To Chuck*) Do you know the answer to it?

The myth of the "perfect family" is a paralyzing shibboleth for a family. If the members are perfect, they cannot express conflict.

CHUCK: I think because at that time I didn't care what was happening. I was having fun, I was with my friends.

FATHER: Why didn't you care? Did alcohol have anything to do with it?

CHUCK: Yeah.

FATHER: That's what came as a real big surprise to us, believe it or not, his parents and his grandmother. All this time he's been drinking, and we had no idea whatsoever. (*Shaking his head and chuckling*) He's been pretty slick.

GRANDMOTHER: Chuck, did you ever come home drunk? Did you ever come in my house and hug me and kiss me—was you drinking then?

CHUCK: Not in the house, no. There were times where I would just drink in my room. I would lie there on the bed and go to sleep.

GRANDMOTHER: I remember them times. But I just can't figure out how he done what he done and me not know it. (*Father is grinning at Chuck*) I despise it and I can smell it for miles, and I just could not believe that he did this as often as he did.

FISHMAN: (*To Chuck*) Let me ask you a question. Do you feel that in your family you have to be perfect? Your father just said this had been a perfect family. Do your parents expect you to be perfect?

CHUCK: I would say no, not really. They have high expectations of me.

FISHMAN: And you feel you've let them down.

CHUCK: Yes.

The session was starting to move, to build intensity as they talked about the boy. I was beginning to form another hypothesis. My first hypothesis had been that this boy lived in a very rigid system that did not accommodate to his new developmental stage. In a system like that, the adolescent may react with destructive behaviors, creating a crisis that reorganizes the system—ideally one with greater, more appropriate flexibility. My new hypothesis was that Chuck was bristling against being in a system where he had to be perfect. Was it a completely totalitarian system that was smothering him? Was the family driving him out to his peers, and maintaining the problem implicitly through their rigidity and their blindness to his needs? At this point, I had not seen any splits and coalitions within the family system, which included the grandmother. So I now turned to the boy's friend.

FISHMAN: Seth, what do you think? You know what Chuck's coming to, in this family. Is this a tough family to be growing up in?

SETH: Oh, not really. I think he's getting more peer pressure, I really do. He'll go uptown and everybody knows they're in for a good time. They all want to go out to the club, they'll stay out till six o'clock, and they'll wind up sneaking back in.

FISHMAN: How has that had to do with Chuck?

SETH: I don't know how it is, it just seemed like, when anyone wanted to go out of town or sneak out, they'd come find him.

FATHER: Why don't they come get you?

SETH: 'Cause I won't go.

CHUCK: You've snuck out!

SETH: I've snuck out, but I've never gone out of town.

The boys continued to talk about their nightlife, revealing activities that were obviously news to Chuck's parents.

MOTHER: (To Seth) Is this a thing that you've done often, or just one time?

SETH: Just once in a while.

FISHMAN: (Laughing) Well, what's his friend going to say?

MOTHER: I think they're being honest with each other, and they've been talking. . .

FISHMAN: Sure, they're honest with each other!

SETH: (Jokingly) I'm lying and he's not.

FATHER: They have some pretty knockdown dragouts for themselves.

The father's half-jesting comment might be taken to suggest that the boys have a knockdown dragout fight right then. That would certainly have shut Seth up and put an end to the revelations about what had been going on. The boys, however, continued to describe their nightlife and how they got away with it.

MOTHER: Chuck has this curfew, twelve on Friday and Saturday nights, and that's one of the things we have a lot of problems with. A few times he missed his curfew. Very seldom did he miss his curfew, but when he did, he made a big mess-up. So we'd ground him. That's why I can't understand how he can get out of town very often.

FATHER: He told us two weeks ago he snuck out after we went to bed.

SETH: As soon as everybody goes to bed—

CHUCK: I'd come into my room and wait ten or fifteen minutes. Grandma would look out of the window to see if I was there, if the car was there. Then I would turn on my little clock radio and set it to go off fifteen minutes after I leave. Then I'd sneak out.

SETH: We'd just push the truck down the hill and start it and go.

CHUCK: When I came back, I'd climb up the carport and then go in the house. I'd take off my shoes and go in my stocking feet. That's why the dogs never barked.

GRANDMOTHER: There's times I stayed awake until five in the morning out there, and you wasn't in, and that is what hurt me more than anything.

By now my second hypothesis had also been discarded. This was not an overly rigid system that demanded perfection but a system that provided little corrective response to the boy's misbehavior, accommodating his escalating forays into delinquency. I now set out to discern the structural problems that rendered the system so inefficient and the boy so dangerously free.

The grandmother had known what was going on and had never told the parents. The system was organized about this conflict avoidance, and the only person who was willing to introduce conflict was Seth, the friend, who then became a key part of the process of generating a crisis and creating a new hierarchy that would bridle this dangerously out-of-control boy.

As the boys described their escapades, the father continued to grin proudly and supportively. It was time to expose the coalition between the father and son.

FISHMAN: (*To mother*) These two are against you. In the war of the sexes, these two are against you. Your husband smiles. He thinks boys will be boys.

MOTHER: He thinks it's funny. I think it's terrible. I think of the danger that this kid could have gotten into, and the things that could have happened.

FISHMAN: Talk to Chuck Senior [i.e., the father].

CHUCK: The day I told him about sneaking out, he smiled and said it reminded him of what he used to do, and she blew up. It's (*snapping his fingers*) that easy to set her off.

MOTHER: I care about you, Chuck! I love you, I want to protect you from things, and that's what rules are for—to protect you. And that's our problem. You cannot abide by the rules, so here you are. I feel that you do need protection. I don't feel that you are old enough or mature enough to be responsible for your life after one at night.

FISHMAN: (*To mother*) Have you thought of moving out?

MOTHER: (*Crying*) I've thought of running away, many times.

FISHMAN: That's about all you can do. You're a long-distance truck driver. You go a distance, so he goes a distance. Would you move in with your mother?

MOTHER: Oh, I don't want to leave now. (*Crying*) It's my whole world.

My question grew out of a hunch that if the boy was out of the house so much, somehow one of the parents must want to get out. Was the son's running away isomorphic with some fantasy on the mother's part? She was trapped in a family where her husband and her mother were allied against her in dealing with her son. As she sat there with lips tightly clenched, I experienced what she must be feeling in this family—a sense of claustrophobia and a desire to get away. My feelings exemplified the subjective reaction of the therapist that characterizes the fourth dimension of the 4-D model of assessment discussed in chapter 2.

FISHMAN: Is your husband very hostile?

MOTHER: My husband's not hostile at all. And I think it's unbelievable that he just sat here and smiled while he told me what he did. So it's all right with me, I mean—

FISHMAN: It's all right with you?

MOTHER: It's all right because—

FISHMAN: (*To grandmother*) She's a very patient daughter! Is she a Zen Buddhist or something?

GRANDMOTHER: She's kind of like a mother. She can take a lot.

FISHMAN: She's an ostrich.

GRANDMOTHER: She hurts inside.

FISHMAN: Hurts? This is not just "hurts."

GRANDMOTHER: When it comes out, it makes her sick. I know, I've been through it. Not with her—my daughter's a good girl.

FISHMAN: Too good. The girl is too good.

GRANDMOTHER: So when she hurts, I hurt. And I know when she's hurting, I know when she's got something on her mind, and she won't tell me, because she's afraid of hurting me. Well, I'm hurting anyway, so . . . I just can't seem to understand why Chuck has done what he has done. He's had everything, they give him everything.

FISHMAN: I'll tell you why he's doing what he's doing. Chuck has friends in powerful places. He has friends in powerful places in the family.

GRANDMOTHER: But that's not true. Chuck Sr. doesn't—

FATHER: Well, I'm about to get angry at this shit. (*Gets up, walks past me, and leaves the room.*)

At my perturbation, we saw the homeostatic-maintainer father activate to return the system to status quo. Had his support of the boy been dealt with, the system might have changed. His response was consistent with the prevailing isomorph of conflict avoidance. All this time, I was conscious in the room of another parent figure to whom we had to answer: Seth. Were all these adults going to fail his friend again? Seth knew the dangers that Chuck had been exposed to when he was out all night driving around the countryside in his high-powered truck. The fact that Chuck was about to enter a drug-and-alcohol rehabilitation center suggests that there must have been some driving while intoxicated. Seth's watchful presence empowered me as I challenged the system: I didn't want to be one more adult failing his friend.

As we have seen, a key step in IST is to challenge the system so that new patterns can emerge. This was a new pattern. The father's walking out and expressing that much anger was a beginning, but it was still distancing from the problem rather than facing the problem. Again there was an isomorph here: The father vanished, just as the son had vanished instead of challenging the rules of the system and saying, "Hey, I need more freedom."

There was another isomorph in the split between the parents. The mother had kept things from the father, who was now feeling blamed for a situation he knew nothing about. The corrective isomorph was for her to bring him back into the room, just as she had to admit him fully into the knowledge of what was going on. If a staff member called him back, we would again be disempowering the family.

MOTHER: That is not true. Chuck Sr. does not let Chuck get away with anything, but it comes through me first. I have to tell Chuck Sr. Chuck Sr.'s gone [away on trips]. Some things, I think, well, it's not that bad, I won't tell him. I feel real guilty, but I've kept things from him and he's had to catch it secondhand. I'm wrong, I should have told him everything, and I haven't. And Chuck Sr. tries to be a friend to Chuck. And I think that's worse.

FISHMAN: Because Chuck Sr. really doesn't know what's been going on?

MOTHER: Uh huh. And, too, I was there, and I think that at that time I would tell Chuck Sr. about the things that Chuck was doing, and then I'd think Chuck was saying, "Well, Mom didn't get it right. She's been sick, she didn't hear it all."

CHUCK: Gimme a break.

MOTHER: That's the way that I feel.

CHUCK: You don't know what's going on.

MOTHER: I don't like it. And Chuck Sr. felt he was put in the middle. Is he going to believe me or Chuck? And it's upsetting to him.

FISHMAN: So you've been protecting Chuck. So then it's not fair to Chuck Sr.

MOTHER: That's right, and I know that now.

FISHMAN: Why don't you bring him back and tell him?

The mother was gone for about 15 minutes and finally returned with the father, who had calmed down and appeared somber and subdued. His anger was gone, and he seemed placated and even contrite.

MOTHER: (*To father*) There are some things that have to come out, that you have to know.

FATHER: (*Apologizing for leaving*) I'm sorry, but I just couldn't handle any more.

FISHMAN: We don't mean to be disrespectful in any way. It was just a question of how to help control this confused boy. Your wife said something when you left, much to your defense—not that you need that.

FATHER: Why would she do that? She doesn't need to do that.

FISHMAN: (*To mother*) Maybe you could say it.

MOTHER: I've been wrong all these years for protecting Chuck, like I said, and not told you everything. Because I felt, like—I started telling you everything and you would blow up, you would be so crazy out there on the road and I would worry about you out there and you'd come home and the minute you walked in the door I'd tell you the problem and you and Chuck would get together and talk about it, and I thought you were all against me. I felt a lot of times the punishment was not hard enough for what he had done, and I felt that Chuck had talked you out of the punishment.

FATHER: Oh, he's manipulated me, there's no two ways about it. He's good at it, and I'm just a big sucker for him.

FISHMAN: So what are the consequences when he sneaks out?

FATHER: Either his pickup has been taken away or he's been grounded or his telephone privileges are taken away—something like that. It can be anywhere from a few days to a week.

CHUCK: The most I ever had was a month, and I deserved that.

FATHER: And the last time it happened, you had just gotten off. And what did I tell you when I was getting in my truck getting ready to leave, and I turned your mother's car over to you?

CHUCK: You said something about maybe if I give up booze and get a fresh start, I'd get my truck back.

FATHER: Right. And to this day, if I drive your mother's car through the mall parking lot, especially at night, they're checking it out, all them kids. And I just wonder, what has this car been through?

SETH: Everybody just knows it. If you drive that car uptown, I'm going to tell you, you'd be chased by every one of the group, because—

FATHER: You're missing the whole point, Seth. The kids didn't pay that much attention to that car, but I mean it's just that—

CHUCK: Everybody's seen me in that car. They've seen me in the pickup, they've seen me in that car, and now if they see that car—

SETH: They think Chuck's driving. The car disappears, and when that car shows up again, it means that Chuck's back. It's very simple. When that car disappeared, I was still around, but nobody even noticed. I just had to start picking people up. My car was in the shop, so I was driving the pickup.

FATHER: Why ours? Both of you, you both answer the question. Why does authority bother you all so much?

FISHMAN: I don't think it's authority that bothers them. That's why they're hurting. It's the lack of authority. Every adolescent pushes against authority, but the lack of authority, which is exactly what you are saying, could kill.

I had an image in my mind of this boy being killed in his pickup on some rural highway while his parents slept.

MOTHER: Well, what more can you do to them than what we've done to him?

FISHMAN: You've got to answer that.

MOTHER: Really, I've even thought of tying him to the bed. I've thought about a lot of things.

FISHMAN: We're going to step out for a minute, but you talk to your husband about this.

When we returned to the room, the father reported on their discussion.

FATHER: I told him that he is just going to have to make up his mind—and his mother, and I too, and he's got thirty days to think this over—that when he comes home, when he's told to do something or one of the rules is laid down, that's the way it's going to be and there's going to be

no backing off on his part, or ours either. And he made the comment that we weren't there—
FISHMAN: Who made the comment?
FATHER: Seth made the comment that we weren't there to watch Chuck. Well, that's not the way it's going to be anymore. I'll be there, I'll be around.
SETH: Are you going to be home maybe once a month?
FATHER: No.
SETH: We were sneaking back in his room even when you all was home.
FATHER: That's not gonna be anymore. Chuck's room is no longer out there. Chuck is in the house.

Chuck had been sleeping in a room somehow separated from the house, and Seth was pointing out that it was easy for him to sneak out and in, even when the parents were at home. The father declared that Chuck's room was being changed; he would now be in the house with them.

CHUCK: I'll tell you one thing that's not going to change.
FATHER: What's that?
CHUCK: Me going in my room. You were just dead set against me staying in my room. Why? As long as I behave, why can't I stay in my room?
FISHMAN: Chuck, you've got a good point. You have to have a voice. Your parents have to be in control of the situation so you are not out of control and in danger, but on the other hand, you have to have a voice. That can be another session, but of course you're right. It's a question of negotiations.

Why would Chuck's friend do what he did? What was his motivation? Traditional psychoanalysis tells us that the basic motivations of human actions are sex, self-interest, aggression, and perhaps curiosity. I suggest that Seth was motivated by what I describe in the Epilogue as another basic human drive: altruism. This boy, realizing the dangers his good friend's recklessness had put him in, put himself in the position of testifying against his friend, even in a hospital with cameras on him, in a rural community where psychotherapy is not as widely accepted as in some areas.

General Principles: Peers of Adults

With the exception of bringing in the parents of peers, the same principles that govern the work with adolescent peers apply to adults. Adult peers can be used as cotherapists and witnesses as well. Whether they are part of the problem or part of the solution, they can make a significant contribution to the therapeutic process, so both "good" and "bad" peers should be included. But they are not there to be changed themselves, although the relationship between the adult in therapy and a friend can be— and often should be—addressed and changed. In addition, there are several other points to keep in mind.

Assume that the contexts of friends are as complex and conflicted as those of the patient. The adult in therapy may be the patient, but the friend may have problems that are closely related to the influence he or she is having on the patient. An understanding of the forces that are at work in the friend's life can help the therapist to join with the friend, to determine what can and what cannot be asked of that person, and to assess the likelihood that the friend will be able to change in ways that will help transform the system.

The therapist should look for patterns in the friend's relationships that are isomorphic with patterns in the adult family member's relationships. Similar patterns may be seen in their marriages, for example. Some years ago I was working with two couples. The therapy was separate, but it happened that the two wives were close friends. Couple 1 had an extremely hostile style of fighting: The woman would stand back on her heels and assail her mate, who would counterattack in an exquisitely passive-aggressive manner. Couple 2 had a very different, more respectful way of handling conflicts. But on days when the two women had lunch together, if I saw couple 2 the same afternoon, they would display the same fighting style as that of couple 1. I surmised that the conversation at lunch had concerned the two husbands and that the wife of couple 2 had, at least for that day, been strongly influenced by her friend in adopting her stridently confrontational approach.

Remember that men and women tend to have different styles of friendship. Carl Whitaker (personal communication, 1980) says that men tend to be in love with things, while women tend to be in love with relationships. The truth of the first part of this formulation was well illustrated in a conversation I had with a psychiatrist friend some time ago. He mentioned that he had gone on a camping trip with his brother and a friend and that, all alone in the north woods, they had had the conversation of a lifetime. "That's great," I said. "What did you talk about?" "We talked about our dream cars."

Whether or not these men were unconsciously referring metaphorically to deep structures of the human psyche, the discussions that women have with their peers have more implications for our work. These relationships are likely to be more complex than those between male peers, and the clinician should be aware that a woman's friends are likely to be exerting an influence on her family relationships—and on the therapy. For that reason, it is more frequent for a woman's peers to be included in the therapeutic process than for a man's.

Be aware that friendships today are complex relationships. Many friendships today represent situations that may limit the degree of freedom of the participants to change the nature or the quality of their relationship. Most notably, many friendships develop in the workplace. Where people's livelihoods are involved, the context is less flexible and less forgiving. Nevertheless, the friendships may be enduring and supportive. Chapter 7, on the work context, will take up this situation in greater detail.

CASE EXAMPLE: JOYCE AND KATHY

Joyce, at age 38, had been severely bulimic since she was 12 years old. Her life had taken what outwardly would appear to be a normal course: She had married, had four children, and held a job as a substitute teacher. Yet she continued to be severely symptomatic and had been hospitalized numerous times every year, with little abatement of her symptoms.

What follows is a segment of a consultation I did for one of the psychologists in the hospital in which she had been confined for 3 months. There was a significant split in the hospital unit: The adjunct therapists and the family therapists wanted a contextual approach, whereas the medical director was insisting on doing individual psychotherapy with her. The split was mirrored when I called the medical director and invited him to participate in the session. As we spoke, it became clear that we had different ideas of what a consultation is. I saw the meeting as an opportunity to help a system that was, to use a sailing term, in irons—that is, paralyzed. His major concern was that the consultation not be a venue for "patient stealing." When he said he could not attend the session, I promised to call him afterward and to send him a written report for the record.

The consultation, which was the only time I saw the family, lasted 7 hours over 2 days. During the course of it, I worked with a number of different subsystems as well as with the entire system, which included Joyce's husband, three of their four children, Joyce's mother, both of her husband's parents, her boss, and her best friend, Kathy.

During the course of the consultation, it became clear to me that many of Joyce's relationships were organized around her eating disorder. The important people in her life were all caring for her, putting her in the one-down position of being the patient, beholden to everyone else. She therefore was not free to speak up and try to alter her relationships to meet her needs better and make them more appropriate.

In my experience, bulimia is a result of conflict avoidance. To the extent that conflict is not expressed, it is manifested in eating disorders. It was therefore important to enable Joyce to challenge the important people in her life. Her friend Kathy had set herself the mission of saving Joyce from her eating disorder. My goal in the intervention described here was to help create a boundary and to empower Joyce so that she would no longer be in the fixed position of the patient and could establish the relationship on a more equal basis. Present at the session, in addition to Joyce and Kathy, were Joyce's husband, Walter, and a co-worker.

As the session began, I was struck by Joyce's birdlike fragility, which was evident not only from her appearance but also from her tentativeness. Like a bird at the seashore, she hesitantly approached and almost instantly retreated at the slightest motion. Her husband's crewcut boldness was in stark contrast.

FISHMAN: You think that Kathy needs you to talk about it, don't you? That you're doing it for Kathy.

KATHY: I think that she feels that I need to talk about it, and that's why she . . .

FISHMAN: But aren't you in some ways giving to her by doing that?

JOYCE: I don't know. You got me on this one.

FISHMAN: So, can you tell her that you don't want her to talk about it?

JOYCE: Well, that's not always the case.

FISHMAN: Well, then, you'd have the opportunity to bring it up, but that's different from her bringing it up.

JOYCE: It's kind of my life now, and I think that when she calls that's how she feels.

WALTER: Would it be easier if Kathy said, "How are you today? Is there anything new to talk about?" or "Do you want to talk about it?" It would give you the opportunity to say, "No, there isn't, and let's go on to something else" or "Yes, there is, and . . . "

Joyce's husband was functioning as a cotherapist at this point. He understood that the rigidity of the system had forced Joyce into an extremely untenable position.

JOYCE: Well, normally what she does is, she calls and says, "How are you?" and I'll say, "Shitty," and that begins the conversation.

WALTER: Okay, but you could say, "Shitty" and "I really don't want to talk about it anymore today."

JOYCE: Okay, I can do that.

FISHMAN: When you say "today," it gives her the opportunity to have something to look forward to, that maybe she can hear about it tomorrow.

I was being a bit wry here. I was struck by the emptiness of her life and its material manifestation, her self-starvation.

FISHMAN: (To Kathy) I was also going to ask you a question. Are you clear, exactly, on what Joyce would like?

KATHY: Well, how about if I rephrase it . . . I'm unclear.

FISHMAN: Ask Joyce. See, everybody speaks for Joyce. Joyce is very lovable, and everybody wants to help Joyce, and to the extent everybody does, Joyce doesn't grow.

KATHY: (To Joyce) No, I'm not one hundred percent clear. I have to say that. No.

JOYCE: What are you unclear about?

KATHY: What you expect. What you want me to do about, like, talking about your eating disorder. Do you want me to not bring it up?

JOYCE: I think you can say to me, "Do you feel like talking about it today?" And if I say yes, then I'm being truthful with you, and if I say, "No, don't even talk about it, because I've had enough of it today," then we'll go on to other things. I thought it was pretty clear.

FISHMAN: It sounds pretty clear to me.

KATHY: I got it.

FISHMAN: (To Joyce) But is that fair to you?

JOYCE: What do you mean?

FISHMAN: Well, saying "Do you want to talk about it today," or even bringing it up, somehow suggests that you're a patient. I don't know that you need to be a patient. Is that fair to you? What you said I think is fine. I think it's clear, but how about going even beyond that and saying, "Let's be friends, not on the basis of my being a patient"?

Joyce looked puzzled. It was a unique suggestion that she might have a relationship based on anything other than patienthood. As it now stood, people were tethered to her through her symptoms. How could she trust a relationship based on true equity, where people were not locked into taking care of her and could even leave her if they chose?

JOYCE: Do you think I could trust that?

FISHMAN: I think that the really loving way—and I know this is done out of really caring—that a really loving way is to challenge Joyce so she has to say, "Get the hell out of here." Just like she should say to her husband when he starts to intervene, "Not your job, mon." Like they say in Jamaica, "Not my job, mon," "Not your job, mon." Can you do that?

JOYCE: But I do do that.

FISHMAN: Why don't you try it now? (*Joyce gives a big sigh.*) But the idea is, Joyce is going to say . . . (*To Joyce*) go ahead and try it now.

KATHY: You mean like a role play, like, "Hi, how are things today?"

JOYCE: Fine. That's a joke, because all the patients . . .

KATHY: How's your eating?

JOYCE: I'd rather not talk about it right now, okay?

KATHY: Normally what I do, I would not let that go.

FISHMAN: Okay. Okay, don't let that go.

JOYCE: Shoot.

KATHY: But the agreement is, though, to respect that.

FISHMAN: But to really help Joyce you shouldn't respect her. You should do exactly what you've done in the past. So go ahead.

JOYCE: I'm really confused about this.

If Joyce and Kathy were confused, it was hardly surprising. My goal was not to set rules at this point but to stir things up with some therapeutic sleight of hand, to create a conflict that would build intensity and bring about some affect.

KATHY: I asked how your eating was going, and you said, "Not so good, I don't want to talk about it." Why don't you want to talk about it?

JOYCE: Because it is not going so good. I'm just disgusted with it, and I'd rather not talk about it. I'd like things a little more up.

KATHY: But that's ignoring the problem. How does that help?

JOYCE: Bug off! (*Laughter.*)

This was the beginning of laying on an interactional template. Clearly it had the quality of playacting. Nonetheless, if Joyce could begin to challenge and, in many ways, redefine her relationship with her friend, she could indeed be her friend in a much more functional way.

The therapist needs to be extremely sensitive to the homeostatic mechanisms of friends. Both adolescent and adult friends can be instrumental in maintaining a dysfunctional homeostasis, and if at all possible they should be included in the therapy. But friends can also be salutary in creating new, more positive systems. As we have seen in the cases of Beth and Chuck, some peers have the same positive values as the family. They subscribe to the family's belief in the need for correction and can be used to provide a link between the patient and the family, bearing witness to what is going on, confronting the family with the need for change, challenging them to bring about the necessary changes, and supporting them in their efforts toward better control of the patient's behavior.

CHAPTER 7

The Work Context

I don't like living in reality much, but it's the only place you can get a good steak.

—Woody Allen

WORK IS A REALITY that family therapists must make the most of. Indeed, work and the family tend to be the most influential forces maintaining a person's identity. In addition to providing economic sustenance, work can provide personal identity through one's contribution to society. Finally, it offers a social context, a culture of co-workers who confirm us as people.

Sometimes a job is just a job, and a person's identity remains quite separate (Montalvo & Guiterrez, 1983). People in some circumstances cannot see the job as an extension of the self; when jobs are tenuously held and may be lost tomorrow, or when a worker has to go from one job to another, people cannot afford to look at the work domain as a major descriptor of their identities.

Whether it is a major source of identity or not, therapists have treated the world of work as essentially walled off from the therapy domain. Therapy, they seem to believe, requires sterile procedures that isolate the people from the arenas in which they make their living.

Of course, this a bit of an overstatement. All therapies review the work context when trying to ascertain the mental health of the client and the effectiveness of therapy. But only in treating the most disabled psychiatric patients is vocational rehabilitation considered a central area for intervention.

This blindspot for the work context can result in serious oversights. The pressures and patterns of an individual's work world can be instrumental in maintaining a dysfunctional status quo or in causing chronic destabilization of a system. Conversely, successful intervention in the work context can greatly enhance the therapist's work.

Because the work environment is affecting the family unit with ever more intensity, increasingly, work and family are the two central institutions in people's lives (Mortimer, Lorence, & Kumka, 1986). In the past, such unwritten rules as "Never bring family concerns to the office" or "Put in long hours regardless of family responsibilities" dictated the separation of work and family (Magid, 1986). These old edicts, however, are becoming intolerable and impossible for workers to observe in a society where work occupies a more and more central role. According to Lennart Levi (1990), as many as 75 percent of those who consult psychiatrists experience problems that can be traced to a lack of job satisfaction or an inability to "unwind" after work.

The traditional picture of the husband as the sole wage earner now depicts only 11 percent of all U.S. families. Women accounted for approximately 60 percent of the total growth of the U.S. work force between 1970 and 1985 (Committee for Economic Development, 1987). About 40 percent of the work force is composed of dual-earner couples (Friedman, 1987) and, by all accounts, the estimates are conservative. These changes in the work force are accompanied by changes in values that create a new emphasis on the work life and its influence on the family.

In spite of these changes, "work" and "family life" have been studied as separate worlds. Chaya Piotrkowski (1978) comments that the family is seen as the realm of intimacy, personal expression, and significant relationships, as opposed to the work world, which is characterized as impersonal, competitive, and instrumental. She criticizes mental health practitioners for viewing the world of work as a dimension of life that has little relevance. A major concern for other critics is that the current literature does not express the different *meanings* of work for women and men, either at home or at the employing organizations (Zedeck & Mosier, 1990).

Some sociologists and psychologists agree. Their research shows that attitudes at work become ingrained and carry over into home life (Staines, 1980). It is asserted that each environment induces similar structural patterns in other environments (Parker, 1967) and that both work and family life influence each other. For example, job stress can displace positive family interactions as family members expend their energy to help the worker manage stress. Alternatively, boring or mundane work can enervate the worker so he or she will lack energy for the home and family. Sheldon Zedeck and Kathleen Mosier (1990) propose further research that views the person in the family environment *and* in the workplace, with the two environments joined in a dynamic reciprocal relationship. What happens in the workplace can be a consequence or antecedent to what happens in the family.

Yet many clinical psychologists, like family therapists, have virtually ignored the issues of occupational stress (Ilgen, 1990). Neal Miller (1983) pointed out that the workplace can be an important context for decreasing stress, but most clinicians do not focus on how work is related to a presenting problem. Instead, they focus their interventions on one specific problem, such as substance abuse or smoking (Ilgen, 1990). As employee assistance programs (EAPs) become more commonplace, more opportunities arise to examine how the workplace directly affects employee mental health (Keita & Jones, 1990).

The workplace has tremendous influence on individual mental health. In general, it can be concluded that if a mismatch exists between the worker and the job, or if the worker feels unable to control his or her work conditions, copes ineffectively, or lacks social support, potentially pathogenic reactions may occur.

As early as 1966, Robert Rapoport and Rhona Rapoport used the term *isomorphism* to indicate similarities in behavior and modes of interaction between work and home settings. Chaya Piotrkowski (1978) collected data from 30 members of 13 families and was the first to systematically study the interfaces or connections between work and the family. Three interface patterns were revealed: positive carryover, negative carryover, and energy deficit. In each area, Piotrkowski provided valuable evidence that job satisfaction initiated positive interactions within the family, while job stress was a major source of conflict within the family system as a whole. Similarly, being "physically or mentally drained" at work in a strenuous or boring job led to unavailability by workers to deal with the emotional and physical demands of the family.

Aside from Piotrkowski's 1978 study, there has been no research in the family literature that has attempted to bridge the gap between work life and family life. Perhaps the material lies between the lines in related fields, such as industrial psychology, industrial medicine, or personnel psychology rather than in family therapy. "Despite the obvious importance of the job in people's lives—as judged by the amount of time spent working—mental health professionals have been remarkably oblivious to its possible effects" (Piotrkowski, 1978, p. 4).

General Principles

Evaluate clinical situations with an eye to being available to address the work context in therapy. The workplace can be as dysfunctional as a family system, and our tools of intervention may be required. This is especially true in family businesses, which can combine a double whammy: a structurally impaired business *and* family. This consideration of the workplace is a newly developed concern, calling for new therapeutic skills. Some of these skills are well developed by EAP clinicians.

Explore whether the work context is supporting dysfunctional family patterns. The assessment techniques described in chapter 2 should reveal whether the job context is isomorphic with the family system. Sometimes the similarities are obvious. In one family, the mother commuted 3 hours a day. The isomorph was distance: emotional distance in the marriage and geographic distance in the work context. Of course, the two were recursively connected; the mother and father were not together enough physically to get together emotionally.

The more common situation is the embattled couple bringing the hostility to work. For example, a colleague told me recently about the terrible time she was having with the principal at the school where she works as a counselor. It was so bad, she said, that she goes directly to the superintendent of schools when she needs something for a child.

When, during an informal consultation, I described a program I thought might benefit her and her co-workers, she challenged everything I said. She summarily dismissed the enhanced home school partnership I described, saying, "It couldn't possibly work," while two of her co-workers and her boss said that, on the contrary, their school would be a very good place for such an approach.

A few weeks later, I learned that her own home situation was full of conflict. She had a history of dismissing her husband as she was dismissing me. The other isomorphic pattern was her lack of confidence; she was negative to my proposal as she was negative to her husband. Here we see the same isomorphic pattern in three different contexts: school (work), consultation, and home.

It is important for clinicians to ascertain if this isomorphic mirroring is present and, if possible, to probe all the contexts. Of course, it isn't always possible in situations where an inquiry could jeopardize the job.

Consider whether another job will elicit more functional facets of the patient's self. When a family member is not working, or is working in an unsatisfactory situation, a positive change in the job status introduces a change in the family system because the individual presents a different persona to the family, thus challenging and changing the family system. The person sees himself or herself as more competent by being a productive member of a work team. Indeed, work is more than a place for financial reward; it is also an essential context for confirmation of self.

It behooves the contextual therapist to determine whether encouraging the work context to become an avenue for confirmation is a good idea. Some jobs are just deadening, so the therapist has to support the client to search elsewhere for confirmation. There are those who believe that the act of working adds an essential emotional dimension to a person's experience. I once heard the renowned cyberneticist Humberto Maturana ask his audience, "Why do people go to work?" After entertaining a number of responses, he surprised the audience by advancing his own premise, paraphrased thus: People go to work because what they get from their co-workers is a kind of love (personal communication, 1983).

Establish appropriate boundaries between work and personal life. As we saw in the Introduction, work tends to be an increasingly jealous suitor of people's time. As our country gets poorer, the job market more competitive, and companies less paternalistic, work occupies more of our time and thoughts. The boundary line is shifting, with work steadily encroaching on personal lives.

In more subtle ways as well, the boundary line can be a problem. In some cases, there is too permeable a boundary between work and family. Co-workers or bosses become involved in personal concerns, for example, or a very close relationship between workers creates dysfunction in the workplace as well as at home. At the other extreme, the boundary is so rigid that the needs of one are attended exclusively, to the detriment of the other context. The stress on the family is increased when a spouse is left out of major decisions, such as relocation or job changes, or is not allowed to share work concerns even when doing so would be reasonable and would make for better understanding of the worker's moods or physical exhaustion. There are work contexts, of course, in which discretion and even secrecy are necessary, but in those circumstances the rules are generally accepted and respected.

In each of the cases that follows, the first type of dysfunctional boundary—one that is too permeable—was present. It is not surprising that these are the cases presented here, even though they may be less common than cases of rigidity, for these are situations in which members of the work context can be readily involved in family therapy, which is obviously a part of the personal realm.

CASE EXAMPLE: PAULA AND HER BOSS

Paula, age 37, had been bulimic for 30 years. She had a surprising appearance: On the one hand, she looked like a well-dressed, fashionable suburban working woman; but on a closer look, one could see that she had the eyes and the gauntness of a chronically ill person. What was distracting was that she was like that old gestalt picture of the woman who can be seen as either an old woman or a young girl. And once you have seen one image you cannot see the other without turning your eyes away and looking back again. The other part of the surprise was her husband, who was dark and boyish. Their tow-headed kids completed the picture—except for one daughter, who was very quiet and had a troubled look in her dark eyes. Paula's symptoms had waxed and waned over the years, subsiding when she had had her 3 children.

During the last 5 years, her bulimia had been very severe again. She was hospitalized three times, each time for a 2-month period. On bad days, she would force herself to vomit up to 30 times, as well as use laxatives. Paula lived with her husband and two children. He worked in a large corporation, she in a doctor's office.

I saw the family as a one-time consultation. In deciding who to invite, I inquired about Paula's various contexts and asked if we might include Paula's boss. From the discussion of Paula's job situation, it was clear that her job would not be jeopardized by an invitation, and I had a hunch that the invitation would be accepted.

The work context was thus included because it was an important part of Paula's life. I thought that Paula's boss might be a helpful participant in the therapy. I had not, however, expected to find the extent of the dysfunction that was revealed in the relationship between Paula and her boss.

At the therapy session were Paula, her husband, her boss, and her best friend. About half an hour into the session, we addressed a major issue: that everybody seemed to be compelled to talk to Paula about her symptoms. Her bulimia tended to be the essential part of conversation between herself and her best friend, and between herself and her boss.

Paula's supervisor, a woman in her early 30s, was the office manager. She was extremely conscientious, friendly, and fastidious to the last detail. One such detail was being sure that Paula was doing well and that she had someone to talk to about her eating disorder at least once a day. That behavior reflected extreme pathological enmeshment on the part of the boss. A healthy employer-employee relationship has more appropriate boundaries.

BOSS: I'll ask her how she's doing and how she's feeling. But I never ask her how her . . . Well, I'll ask her what she eats, to make sure she's eating right. But I never really talk about the bulimia.
PAULA: Right.
FISHMAN: Do most of the employees—also the supervisors—in your clinic ask their employees if they're eating right?

HUSBAND: If they knew they had anorexia and bulimia, they might.

FISHMAN: But otherwise not. It's not standard.

BOSS: We talk a lot about food because I'm obsessed with it, and dieting. So, I mean, it's not unusual for us to say, "What'd you have for dinner?" or "How's your eating going?"

OTHERS: Right.

BOSS: Even with, um, the other woman that is in our office. Yes, I want to know—Paula, I should ask you—if there are any signs that I should look for if you're having problems during the day. I also need to be able to trust you and you trust me that when you're having a problem . . . well, we had this conversation a few days ago.

FISHMAN: Let me tell you what, shall I? I think you need to do everything you can to treat her like everybody else. And any moment you are treating her differently, that's bad for Paula. (*Pause*) There's someone else in your department?

BOSS: Uh huh. There are a few people.

FISHMAN: Okay, so you talk to them exactly the same way. Don't find yourself in a position where you treat her specially.

PAULA: I don't think she's . . . No, I think she's been pretty good about that.

BOSS: I agree with you, and I feel comfortable with that. I guess that my concern is that since I'm normally spending eight hours a day with her, should I be looking for things?

FISHMAN: What would you look for?

I was amazed by the level of overinvolvement.

BOSS: I don't know. I mean I asked her. The first time she told me it was like . . . Should I watch every time you go to the bathroom? I didn't know. It just really struck me that I didn't know.

FISHMAN: You see, I wouldn't pay any attention to the bulimia. It is not your job.

This was the first time that Paula's boss had heard that she should observe a boundary between work and Paula's bulimia. She looked at me with questioning surprise. The contextual therapist works surgically and unequivocally. This severing of the world of work from the world of family was, of course, an extreme antidote to severe behavior. In more functional situations, such drastic surgery would not be needed.

BOSS: That's easy to say. It's hard to do, for me, because personally, you know, I think we're friends.

FISHMAN: But the bulimia is just a . . . habit. That's how she chooses to live.

The relationship between Paula and her boss masqueraded as support, but it breached the border into intrusiveness for Paula. This pattern undermined her sense of confidence and helped lead to the maintenance of the symptoms. I believe that patients with eating disorders have severe difficulties expressing conflict; they manifest symptoms instead of addressing conflict. In the system here, Paula was living a life in which she felt beholden to everyone for the help they gave her and thus could not confront the issues and people making her angry. The identical isomorph was seen between Paula and her friend, Paula and her boss, and Paula and her husband.

In a later session, Paula's husband was inspired to do some problem solving and some pulling on his wife, disengaging her. I challenged him not to help her out of this situation. He even sounded like a cotherapist, oriented philosophically much like the therapeutic team. This was a change, since he had been acting before as the homeostatic maintainer, buffering his wife from the travails of life that would, if she mastered them herself, enhance her confidence to address conflict. (To the extent that she was not addressing external relationships and conflicts, she was failing to transform her internal isomorphic pattern of conflict avoidance.)

Paula's case demonstrates that dysfunctional isomorphs in the work situation can be mirrored by those at home, and vice versa. Enmeshed at home and at work, Paula had become similarly paralyzed in both environments. Her rigidity had impelled both her husband and her boss to deal with her in a similar manner, and they maintained her in that position.

Boundaries had been blurred, and Paula had become more of a patient than an employee. The astute therapist watches for ways to transform the basis of such a relationship. Eventually, then, the question "Is she essentially a friend or an employee?" will be moot, liberating all parties to be themselves.

CASE EXAMPLE: GEORGE AND HIS DAD/BOSS

We met George in chapter 2. He was 40 years old and worked with his father in the family business, lamp manufacturing. The family had moved from California 5 years earlier. George lived alone but in close proximity—emotionally and physically—to his parents. His parents made the initial call. They were acutely concerned about their son because of his heavy use of cocaine and because he had been unable to establish a lasting relationship.

The parents had been in therapy as a couple for 20 years. George had always refused to be involved in any family treatment but had had many years of individual therapy (paid for by his parents. This was a family that was very therapy savvy—as well as therapy weary.

Present at the first interview were the parents, a couple in their early

70s, both very thin and fashionably dressed vegetarians who were exercise fanatics; and their son George, who was a tall ectomorphic blond. Dressed in a turtleneck and dark pants, he looked for all the world like a ski bum or a 1950s beatnik. Tension filled the room, and I sensed that these extremely therapy-savvy individuals were accustomed to directing things.

FISHMAN: What are your goals?
GEORGE: My goals are to straighten things out with my father.
FISHMAN: Not with your mother?
GEORGE: One comes with the other.
FISHMAN: Not necessarily. They're separate issues.
GEORGE: Not in this case. Believe me when I tell you. . . . If there's one, then it comes with the other. It's like winter, then comes the snow. That's a bad analogy.
FATHER: That's why I'm here. Supposedly, I'm the cause of his problems; that's what his mother says and that's what George says. And this is born out of a poor communication or reading the book improperly or properly, I don't know. How do we communicate? How do we cement our relationship so we can talk to each other, not yell at each other?
FISHMAN: Has he been late for work?

My sense was that—to repeat a phrase I used earlier—these people were not in danger of going off the deep end; they were in danger of going off the shallow end, and the same applied to the therapy. At this point in the session, I was trying to be as direct and forthright as possible, and also congruent with their values, which were those of the father: ultrapragmatic business values. I was also attempting to eschew psychologizing. It was the lingua franca of homeostasis and inaction for this family. The father dealt with my question about the son being late to work.

FATHER: Yes, many times. He's been an avoider, complete avoider. And that's why I get really up on him.
GEORGE: With good reason.
FATHER: George is an avoider. He makes appointments, promises, he constantly avoids. He buries himself in his apartment . . .

I pursued the subject the father had introduced.

FISHMAN: Do you have any friends?
GEORGE: My father says there are no friends in business.
FISHMAN: Well, how about outside of the business, like on Saturday night?
GEORGE: My mother and father, they're my only friends. But this has nothing to do with Daddy and I. We're bringing in too many ingredients. This is just between me and Daddy.
FISHMAN: I'm afraid I don't think I can help you.

This was crucial for the therapy. I shocked them. They expected me to be just as enmeshed as they were. This man thought he could direct the therapy—and buy me. After all, his family had been seeing therapists for 20 years. To distinguish myself from their other therapists, I used one of the few tools therapists have: ourselves, and our willingness to continue their game. If I let that happen, I served no one's best interests.

The therapist should be extremely careful at the beginning of therapy: The initial gambit should be on the therapist's terms. If I had accepted the young man's opening strategy and accepted the enmeshment of the system, my effectiveness would have been neutralized. They needed an opposite isomorph—distance—to correct this system.

FATHER: All right. Gimme a critique. I don't agree with him [George].

FISHMAN: You don't need a therapist; I think you need a business consultant. First of all, I'm not going to have anybody tell me, after all my years of experience of doing therapy, how to do therapy. If you can get someone that will allow you to direct the therapy, grab your hat, because that person is not going to help you. *(To father)* Number two, if he's an employee, he's an employee: If he's late for work, or doesn't come to work, you fire him! If he does come to work and produces, fine. Business and family are two different things.

GEORGE: Well, if you work together, though, you can't separate them . . .

FISHMAN: Who's the boss? *(To father)* You're the president, you're the founder. Did he sign the income tax form?

FATHER: No.

FISHMAN: What's the problem? What's complicated? If you treat him like an eleven-year-old, he'll act like an eleven-year-old. You don't need therapy; you need a business consultant.

GEORGE: *(Looking puzzled)* I don't understand what he's saying.

FATHER: I got it, I got it. By the way, that's very good therapy, what you just told me.

FISHMAN: It's common sense. It's reality. Business and family are different things. Business—there are no friends in business, right? There are employees, though, right? If he's an employee, he acts like an employee. But you allow him to act like a little boy.

I was deliberately polarizing, like a ray of light breaking down the parts: polarizing the enmeshed, lumped system and setting boundaries. This would be my general intent throughout the therapy.

FATHER: How do you attack the problem? Well, you simplified it very much: You're a boss; you need to be the boss.

FISHMAN: George has a choice. He can either work for you or not. Listen, he acts like a child, he's treated like a child. He doesn't even have to make friends.

GEORGE: What's he saying? (*Again 11 years old.*)

FISHMAN: Listen, everybody has to make friends, unless they're treated special. You're difficult to deal with. You know what that means? You feel you're special. There's only one reason you're feeling special: Somebody is treating you special.

I was conducting family therapy one-on-one. I was asserting boundaries and dealing with the developmental issues in terms of George's age while fitting my comments into the pragmatic perspective of the business man.

FATHER: So, very simply, you transcended two or three years of therapy. You came down to the bottom line, which is: If you're a boss, be a boss; don't treat him like a child. Well, whether you treat us as a group or not, I got something out of this. So what George says is partially true; I am really the cause of the problem.

FISHMAN: That's the only thing I agree with. Are you pretty successful?

FATHER AND GEORGE: Yes.

FISHMAN: Then, do what you do best. Be a good businessman.

MOTHER: It's hard to separate when it's your own flesh and blood.

FISHMAN: I'm not denying that. If it weren't, you wouldn't be here.

MOTHER: If I told you today that when George first came to work for his father, he knew nothing of the business, that he received a monstrous salary. He said, "That's my son. If I can't do it, who can?"

FISHMAN: It's the same pattern.

FATHER: I know when we set down these ground rules what I should do. But it's hard; I don't know if I can do it.

FISHMAN: I'll tell you what Aristotle said: "If you want to change a habit, you just change it." Nothing gradual. Employees are employees. I mean, he may be somebody who can really make it in life.

MOTHER: Do I have to go away from here and have the feeling that something can't be done for him?

FISHMAN: On the contrary. Something profound is being done for him.

MOTHER: So if my husband changes, that will be the whole answer? All his problems will disappear, the drugs . . .

FISHMAN: It will be the first step toward change.

MOTHER: I just want to tell you. When George was little, and he used to use bad language toward me, he used to curse me, insult me. And my only recourse was to go tell my husband. And I would say, "Aren't you going to do something? He's cursing me, insulting me." My husband would never correct George. He used to say to me, "I don't want to correct him in front of you."

In other words, father and son are the couple.

FISHMAN: I hear what you're saying. I think it's important but I think we've done enough for today. I think it's a question of you doing what you do best. Being a businessman. And your son, I think, if you can really follow this, your son will be fine.

My intervention was simply to create a boundary between work and family. I used the father's own language, as George had quoted him earlier in the session: "There are no friends in business." In other words, there was a boundary between the two different worlds. The mother, while concerned about George's drugs, seemed, by the end of the session, to be greatly relieved that the father was finally responding to a therapeutic intervention that would help to separate him somewhat from his adhesion to his son.

A week later, I saw the family again. At my insistence, the session included George's younger brother, who was also unmarried.

FATHER: Sunday, at home, he wanted to talk business. I said, "Business is business; we'll talk about it at the office, and I don't want to hear about it, period." So I told him that he's an employee and that if he fouls up, I put him on notice; if he fouls up again, he's fired. It's like any employee; I can't tolerate it, good-bye, good luck. So then he calls up the next day and says, "You won't believe, I've got a temperature of a hundred one; I won't be able to come to the office." I say to him, "I don't care what you do; be in the office at nine tomorrow morning." The next morning we had a big altercation, but the bottom line was I told him, "I'm putting you on notice." So that's the thing, and (*To Fishman*) you were the motivation for this because you told me you gotta separate business from family.

FISHMAN (*To brother*) Do you think what your mother and father did for George is good?

BROTHER: It's a start. I told them long ago George needed to be handled firmly. I thought that years ago he was still an adolescent. Then George wanted to live with them, and I told them, "Fine; let him live with you, but treat him like the child he's acting like. Give him the discipline that he needs and the love and companionship, also."

A crisis had been induced by creating a polarity between father and son regarding work and family. As a result of these two sessions, the system began to change. Family members made the boundary between work and family clearer to George. The father told George that if he continued to come into work late, he would suspend him without pay.

After the second session with the family, the son said that he did not want to see me again. The parents called and I agreed to see them if they wanted my consultation. "But," I added, "you probably do not need more therapy. You know what to do."

I heard nothing from the family for a month. George's behavior had changed. He was much more responsible. Then he didn't come to work for two days, and the parents came to see me. The father said he knew he should fire his son, but he couldn't bring himself to do it. The father's behavior presented a classic display of the homeostatic maintainer in operation.

I said it would be best if he did act decisively, but there was no rush. There would be other opportunities. The father decided to give the son a second chance. Then another crisis occurred. This time, homeostasis did not prevail. The father acted "decisively" and told the son that if he did not get treatment, he could no longer work with him. The father's response was at least some change. Although he was still excusing his son, he was demanding George to accommodate.

The mother called me saying that George had agreed to enter a drug treatment facility. She asked if I had any suggestions regarding the institution. I replied that the site for the treatment was not the issue. The important thing was to have a coordinated treatment approach, one that worked effectively with the entire family system, including after discharge. This would be vital if the parents were to achieve a resolution of their "Hundred Years War."

The mother's reaction was very revealing: "Oh, so you don't agree with hospitalization. You were the one that got things moving—by getting my husband to change—and now that I have gotten George to go into a facility, you are not supportive!" She was now acting as his doctor. When I insisted on the need for a coordinated system she repeated, "So you don't agree with hospitalization!" and hung up. Her reaction was clear evidence of homeostasis at work again—"my son has been wronged."

This case demonstrates the power of *work* as a lever for change. The full weight of the "work culture" was evident to me when the son repeated his father's dictum: "There are no friends in business." Work had the force of a religion for these men. Their relationship, which was so intertwined that it violated a cardinal tenet of work—that business and personal affairs do not mix—was the dynamic lever to budge the system. But as the system budged, other homeostatic forces were reactivated.

CASE EXAMPLE: BILLY AND HIS FRIEND/BOSS

Billy, age 36, was referred to me after being discharged from an alcohol rehabilitation facility. Prior to his hospitalization, he had tried to control his drinking, but he had had three serious lapses when he drank heavily for weeks. The most recent episode had occurred after his girlfriend, Marcia, had broken up with him at a time when he was also undergoing intense pressure at work. After 6 months of heavy drinking, he had gone to his best friend, Keith, who was also his boss, and said, "I need to go into a drug rehab facility. I'm killing myself."

Billy was the fourth of five children from a Roman Catholic family. He had no contact with his father, but he was quite close to his mother. Billy was unmarried and lived alone. He had had a number of relationships, but none more significant than the one with Marcia, a 25-year-old clerk at the store where Billy worked.

In the first session I met with Billy and Keith. As I assessed the context, it became clear that a major source of Billy's stress was his job and his relationships in the workplace. The two men had been friends since early childhood, and for the last five years Billy had managed Keith's small department store. Keith expressed his concern for his friend and employee and made clear that he wanted to do anything he could to help him. He willingly took an active part in planning Billy's rehabilitation. He would take Billy away for weekends, and he was always lecturing him on how he should change his life, become religious, take more vacations, and start to exercise.

This kind of closeness between a boss and an employee is not as uncommon as it once was. It implies a new twist on an older view of pathology. From a traditional psychoanalytic viewpoint, Billy's behavior could be viewed as an extension of a dependent personality, prone to make quick transference relationships. In brief, Billy could be seen as turning his boss into his father.

But to me it was not that simple. Keith was not just a blank screen on which projections occurred; he loved to be Papa. His own context was decidedly attenuated. He was divorced and had no children. He depended greatly on Billy for emotional support. For him, as for Billy, the business was his family. He liked to relate closely to his employees' needs, and he did not respect boundaries. During an early session, I suggested that the two sounded much like a married couple arguing, and Billy, laughing nervously, agreed.

The business relationship between Billy and Keith was characterized by an isomorphic pattern of conflict avoidance. Keith constantly questioned

Billy's managerial decisions, but in a roundabout way, going to Billy's employees to check up on what he was doing. Keith spent much of his time traveling, in what appeared to be an effort to avoid confronting Billy with their differences. Billy also avoided conflict. If he challenged Keith's interference in his business decisions, Keith would respond, "How can you say things like that, when we're such good friends and I care so much about you?" Billy therefore risked both job and friendship if he confronted him. Yet if he did not, his effectiveness as a manager was severely compromised. He was thus caught in a highly stressful no-win situation, which led inexorably to his heavy drinking. (Anger, it has been said, is soluble in alcohol.)

The second most important person in Billy's life was Marcia. Their relationship was also convoluted and fraught with ambiguity. Was he Marcia's boss, her lover, or her friend? In this store, the three roles, sometimes contradictory, formed a tangled web.

Billy's problem was thus a broad systemic issue. My goal as therapist was to disentangle the complex web of relationships, facilitating disengagement in inappropriate relationships and restoring more appropriate roles. His entire emotional life was focused on the business, where the enmeshed roles and ambiguous boundaries had led to profound emotional distress. Billy had to be helped to keep the job from being an extension of the self.

At the beginning of treatment, Billy said that even though he was depressed, he was the master of his soul ("because I make a good living"). I saw this as a convenient self-deception. He was not the master of anything. His livelihood depended on the company, which was torn by conflicting relationships. To restore his functioning, he needed to gain a sense of genuine control over his life.

The therapy proceeded smoothly at first. The sessions included not only Keith and Billy but also the office manager, Arlene. Arlene was married but appeared to be more emotionally involved with Billy than with her husband; she described Billy as her best friend. She was also very close to Marcia.

As therapy continued and increased emphasis was placed on boundaries, Arlene and Billy gradually became estranged. His new sensitivity to boundaries made Arlene feel rejected. She would then call Marcia and complain to her that Billy was harassing her, and Marcia would call Billy with conflicting messages regarding her availability. (At the same time, Keith became so impressed by the changes in Billy that he asked me to see *him* for therapy. I saw him a few times, alone and with Billy, his only available context. He then went on one of his long trips to explore wildlife.)

About a month into treatment, there was a single, extremely dramatic session with Marcia and Billy. About 2¹/₂ hours long, it played like a Shakespearean tragedy. The two were obviously very emotionally involved with each other and bewildered that their relationship kept falling apart despite repeated efforts to get back together. But the degree of misunderstanding and the intrusion of others proved to be insurmountable barriers for the couple. The session ended with an agreement to take a walk together, as friends, but they never did. Somehow, when they told their best friends, Keith and Arlene, of their plans, the idea of the walk was scuttled.

In the course of our work, in weekly sessions over a 3-month period, Billy became better able to separate business and his personal life. After what seemed like a period of mourning for his business family, he began dating women who were not involved with the business. In essence, a new isomorph was established in Billy's life—that of maintaining boundaries. With this new concept, he was able to improve his work performance, greatly improve his social life, and stop abusing alcohol.

Be prepared to deal with the effects of menial jobs and joblessness. In the limited number of cases we have examined here, work was generally accepted as a central and positive institution, and the jobs had presumably been chosen from among multiple options. Obviously, this is not always the case. Some jobs—when they can be had—are more to be endured than embraced. And some people hold jobs by a thread or are jobless, suffering the pressure of trying to hold soul, dignity, and family together without an adequate income.

Braulio Montalvo and Manuel Gutierrez (1983) have studied the Hispanic community for many years, with valuable ideas for the therapist working with jobless individuals when the world of work is unresponsive. They describe a series of maneuvers by which the therapist moves the investment away from the all-encompassing task of compulsively looking for a job to the minute details of everyday life. They encourage practicing time distortion (making a lot of time look like a little time) and shifting the view so that the patient's self-esteem does not hinge completely on what the job market or work conditions may dictate. Montalvo and Gutierrez (1983) support the deinvested attitude of the working man that "a job is just a job". This idea totally counters what our culture has maintained for hundreds of years: that a person's self-worth is contingent on his or her place in the work world. In the current economy, with joblessness so prevalent, Montalvo and Gutierrez's thinking is refreshing, supportive, and healthy.

I would add other techniques for bolstering the spirit. For example, the unemployed person can expand the concept of work to include such items as the many things to do around the house, or logging the household budget, or making four or five telephone calls to follow up job application status, thus treating work as a transitional activity and reaffirming the other home activities as the core of the person's identity. Performing volunteer work can also reaffirm self-esteem.

Since unemployment means losing the social context of the workplace, the client and the family should be encouraged to build a larger social network, including a nonvocational community and perhaps other unemployed people. The goal is to establish a framework for elevating self-esteem and mood while the job search goes on, mindful that the patient may not be able to resurrect the work context soon.

Meanwhile, therapist and patient alike must not focus exclusively on the external world. The therapist needs to recognize the tremendous pressures on the internal dynamic of the family itself that can result from joblessness. Montalvo and Gutierrez (1983) describe one case in which the wife would not let her jobless husband go out, because she thought he'd become (again) an "alcoholic bum." She confined him to the apartment, where the poor fellow felt cooped up and depressed. Finally, the wife realized that he was about to become violent, so she let him go out for an occasional beer. No disaster ensued. Instead, the man's mood lifted, although there had been no change in the external context. His *relationship* to the external context changed, not the context itself. During the year it took for the man to find a job, he had become a less violent person.

Conclusion

Work and the workplace often supply vital missing elements in applied therapy. The therapist needs to determine what dysfunctional isomorphs may be operating between the work situation and the family and then to help the patient challenge and transform these dysfunctional isomorphs. In other situations, transforming the system by changing isomorphs will not work until the client and the family are newly introduced to a work situation.

For example, I have designed an eating-disorders program that provides sessions with a vocational counselor. To produce lasting amelioration of severe eating disorders such as bulimia, anorexia, or compulsive overeating, the work environment can help provide a context that confirms the individual as a person. The workplace can also give patients with eating disorders the confidence to challenge in a functional way the central personal isomorph of eating disorders: conflict avoidance.

Furthermore, the work situation can offer different and less isolating isomorphs than those operating in the family, particularly if a *psychosomatic* family is making change even more difficult.

Assisting the patient in breaking old molds may require the help of a member of the workplace who may be reinforcing the negative isomorph. This can be accomplished best by constituting a therapeutic unit that includes the family plus key representatives from the world of work.

CHAPTER 8

The Legal Context

INSTITUTIONS outside the family sometimes dominate the lives of dysfunctional families, so the case histories of families in IST may include the school principal, the corrections officer, the residential treatment staff, or the hospital administrator. Olof Ulwan, a pediatrician and family therapist in Sweden, compares today's dysfunctional families to royal families: The more disturbed they are, he says, the more people and institutions they have serving them (personal communication, 1992). Whether the setting is a royal court or an inner city, the coordination of many "server entities" can become Byzantine.

The therapist must examine the family's institutional contexts to identify the patterns: Are they isomorphic with the family's dysfunctional patterns, thereby maintaining the system's dysfunctions, or are they providing corrective influences on the family's deficiencies? The multifaceted forces can be so complex and conflicted that even adding a systems therapist can be dangerous for troubled families with multiple institutional relationships. The therapist can, unintentionally, triangulate the family system and increase the stress on the unit. A basic caution for the therapist working with families and their institutions is to be keenly sensitive to the pressures that impinge on the family from many sources.

Historically, families and institutions have been viewed as having contrasting—even antithetical—atmospheres. Boundaries between families and larger systems in the institutional sector are marked by an unusual combination of diffusion and rigidity. Family members and members of the larger system often harbor myths about one another and about their relationships. These myths may preclude flexibility in meeting a family's specific needs for change (Imber-Black, 1990).

Part of the clinician's job is to do motivational groundwork to unite the institutions that surround the family. While we as therapists take it for granted that getting a consensus is essential, we need to educate others about how invaluable consensus is as a therapeutic platform. A key step in working with institutions is to get from all participants a commitment to work together.

As a preliminary step toward getting this commitment, participants should be encouraged to critique their own performance in the case to date. This honest self-appraisal is not necessarily designed to lead people to helpful insights but rather to help them recognize that they have reached a dead end. Careful probing can help an institution realize that its efforts are not achieving the desired goal. By asking for frank selfassessment "Is this working?" and "How is it going to help?" we can collect evidence of institutional effectiveness and ineffectiveness, which diagnoses and treats the problems of the institution as well as of the family. We can then move forward and suggest trying a new behavior, after openly reviewing the possible negative consequences to both the patient and the institution of staying on the same track.

In working with any institution, the issue of power becomes a key question for exploration. First, it is important to identify the power in the institution or, more specifically, at the interface of the institution and the family. Who is the real decision maker? Is it the administrator or official in the institution? Is it the higher bureaucracy? Or is it a member of the family system who is deeply influential in maintaining the status quo with the institution?

Second, what is the extent of the clinician's freedom to intervene? For all concerned—therapist, family, and institution—power is often tempered by political considerations. I once was consulted in the case of a family with a 17-year-old son who had been starting fires. The authorities were involved through a county agency that controlled the funding for treatment facilities. At a multidisciplinary meeting where the boy's treatment was to be planned, I intended to propose Intensive Structural Therapy, working with the family and providing some essential recontextualization for the boy through his interest in drawing (we had some contacts at the county art center). The family was interested in my suggestions; they felt that they could keep everyone safe, and they saw this as an opportunity to do some much-needed work as a family. They were also influenced by the agency representatives present, however, and it became clear not only that there were strong feelings for long-term institutionalization but also that hospitalizing the boy was a fait accompli. The agencies had more influence with the court; moreover, the family had no more insurance, and if the boy was hospitalized, the county would pay for everything.

Finally, it is crucial to determine the ideas, orientations, goals, loyalties, and concerns of the institutional personnel that may affect their attitudes and actions. The therapist must understand, empathize, and at times be wary of the basic orientations and major concerns of other professionals. Will they tend to mobilize change or paralyze change? If they will endanger or undermine the clinician's work, then direct discussion and resolution will be called for. If there are conflicts or hidden agendas within an institution or conflicting loyalties between professionals, it will be important to identify these counterproductive pressures and resolve them. The goal is consensus.

Family therapists all too frequently see the damaging results of inept and inappropriate encounters at the interfaces of institutions and families or individuals. A classic example of negative consequences is when the authorities burst into a home, without due process, ostensibly to check the children for bruises, threatening to take the children away from the parents and making an alliance with the children against the parents. The balance of forces can also go awry when the institutional forces reflect patterns that are isomorphic with those of the family—excusing the chronic misbehavior of an adolescent, for example, and treating the youngster as a mental health casualty instead of making him face the consequences of his actions.

This chapter takes up the issues in dealing at the interface of the family with the legal system as an outside institution. Other chapters will consider the school system, hospitals, and social service agencies.

The focus in this chapter on the courts, as with other contexts, is on the family as though it were interfacing with one agency only. In reality, the interplay between the family, the school, the social service department, and court often involves multiple conflicting agendas. The challenge for the clinician is to work with the institutions so that they facilitate one another's tasks.

General Principles

Try to win over a "hanging judge" to the mental health perspective. Since the creation of psychiatry as a discipline, tension has existed between the legal and the psychiatric systems over the issue of whether problematic behavior is "mad or bad." The legal system tends to focus on the rights and responsibilities of the individual, whereas most mental health professionals see a person's problems as psychologically determined or contextually influenced, depending on their orientation. Similarly, there is a major contrast in the views of the legal system and the mental health system concerning the degree to which people can change. The law works with snapshots of people, whereas clinicians work with people in the process of change, so we see more change.

Indeed, in spite of our efforts, there are sometimes situations when the court refuses to acknowledge the validity of the views of the mental health expert. I once testified on behalf of a couple who had lost custody of their two children on the basis of child abuse allegations that had never been proved. I saw a truly loving relationship between the father and mother and their children, and I showed the judge a videotape of the father interacting with the children in a clearly caring manner. The judge seemed impressed, but nevertheless he ruled to sever the parents' parental rights forever. (Fortunately, their lawyers appealed the case and won.)

There are no quick and facile solutions to ease the tension between the conflicting world views. In the preceding case, there were experts that conflicted each other at every turn. My sense was that the only possible hope I had was to go to the level of interaction and have a videotape for evidence. After all, it was videotape that convinced numerous cynics that family interaction profoundly influences behavior. I reasoned that perhaps the skeptical judge could be convinced of the quality and importance of the relationships by seeing a tape. In retrospect, I think it was not enough—there were too many conflicting agendas for the judge, like his relationship and dependence on the social service department, which helped him with his most difficult dispositions.

Generically, the most effective tools I have found are these: make a complete evaluation—see as much of the system as possible; closely analyze interactions—documenting statements by citing interactions; use enactments of conflicted relationships with embattled parents who are fighting for custody; try not to get symmetrical on the witness stand; and do not put yourself in a compromising position where you feel like a hired gun.

Broaden the focus to include the family context. The goal of the therapist should be to influence the court to the extent that, at the very least, it is aware of the effect of its actions on the family. In cases involving children, for example, the court often follows a course that does little or nothing to strengthen the parental hierarchy. Clinicians equipped with a lens that takes in the entire context have a powerful perspective to bring to bear on the case. While focusing on the best interests of the child is essential, it is equally important to help the court expand the "best interest" concept to include the family. This broader perspective also admits the longer-term reality that families tend to stay in some proximity to one another for the rest of their lives, for better or for worse, despite what courts and therapists might prescribe. As my friend David Treadway says, "Blood is thicker than therapy" (personal communication, 1988).

Counter excessive leniency on the part of the court. In the history of the U.S. court system, courts have always tended to take a nonpunitive approach to children. Today, a court may be so accepting of a minor's limitations that it is rendered ineffectual, and so elastic that it may meet neither the specific needs of the family member nor the needs of the family system. We are also witnessing a period of increased leniency in the adult court. For example, the Philadelphia prisons are so overcrowded that only the most serious criminals are ultimately confined.

The therapist must determine whether the judicial system is leaning too far in the direction of the mental health perspective, so that the patient does not have to face up to the consequences of his or her behavior. In such cases, the court is unwittingly serving as homeostatic maintainer, replicating the dysfunctional pattern within the family. Just as we sometimes need the court to be flexible, we sometimes need it to be firm, adversarial, and unyielding.

In working with the court and the judicial system, the first step for the clinician is to diagnose the problem encapsulated by the specific judicial subsystem and the family. The following case examples highlight the importance of the therapist's various positions with, among, and between the court and family members. In the case of Tony, the judge was advocating change, but he realized as the session proceeded that he had been an agent of the status quo. By his continual acceptance of Tony's excuses, he had helped maintain the system as it was. Most frustrating of all, the therapist (and his supervisor) were so vague and inept that the system obliged the judge to give this very clever addict yet more slack.

In the second case example, that of Debbie, a young girl's probation officer and her pastor were enlisted to counterbalance her overindulgent parents. The officer of the court, with some guidance, became the enforcing agent of an authoritarian hierarchy to help Debbie take some responsibility. This was accomplished by initiating a crisis—dramatically threatening Debbie with court proceedings. Ultimately, Debbie's parents were enabled to reassert their authority over their wayward daughter and make it stick. By working together as a cohesive unit, the court officer, the pastor, the therapist, and the parents "captured" Debbie in an escape-proof safety net and taught her a much-needed object lesson about accountability.

CASE EXAMPLE: TONY

Tony, 35 years old, had been abusing drugs and alcohol since his teens. He had been in treatment facilities many times and had served time in jail for drug-related offenses such as stealing. In his last run-in with the law, he had been given probation on condition that he receive a psychiatric evaluation and undergo treatment.

In our first session, Tony asked to be sent to a detoxification center. When he came out of detox, he said, "Listen, I can't make it unless I have a job." The therapist and I (as supervisor) agreed. A trainee who was observing through the one-way mirror was a school jobs counselor, and he helped Tony find a job the next week.

By our third session, Tony was working. Meanwhile, we had enlisted a new team member, the judge. The judge had been increasingly irritated because Tony had failed to comply with court orders, yet he apparently was continuing to give Tony every opportunity for a second chance. We were pleasantly surprised by the judge's willingness to work with us. Ironically, his eagerness to accommodate us seemed to mirror his willingness to acquiesce to Tony's demands and to overlook Tony's incidents of irresponsibility. The judge was functioning as a quintessential homeostatic maintainer.

At the session were Tony Wilson; his wife, Joy; their two children, the therapist; and Judge Thompson, who was on the speakerphone. As supervisor, I was present behind the one-way glass for most of the sessions. In the first part of the session, we gently maneuvered the judge to evaluate his own participation in the homeostatic maintenance.

THERAPIST: Judge Thompson, tell me, if you would, what the situation is and how serious it is right now.

JUDGE: Right now. Well, I'm a little bit concerned because I don't have any proof of compliance. I have set Mr. Wilson under court order to obtain an evaluation for substance abuse and also to give the court a report of some sort on what the evaluation showed and what is the course of rehabilitation that is necessary for him. I haven't been able to get them from him yet. [*The judge recited a series of incidents of not getting information or verification.*] I didn't mean to indicate that I didn't believe him, but we do, in the courts, work in terms of proofs. The better the proofs are, the better the credibility is; and, you know, I still don't know exactly where I stand in terms of knowing enough about Tony Wilson and his problem . . . I am still waiting to get information and I expect him to comply.

THERAPIST: When he is missing meetings and things like that, what is that saying to you?

JUDGE: Well, that makes his situation a little shaky as far as I'm concerned, to the extent that I wrote a letter to him today . . . (*Reading from letter*) "This is to advise you, Mr. Wilson, that you remain under court order. You must actively participate in substance abuse rehabilitation and produce evidence of same. Additionally, you must produce for the court a report of your evaluation and recommended treatment. The evaluation and recommendation report must be done by a certified substance abuse counselor. The court is aware that you have not met two scheduled appointments with the therapist at the Institute for the Family, and the court is therefore rescheduling you and Mrs. Wilson for a hearing on the question of your compliance with the court order."

THERAPIST: So this is a very serious situation.

JUDGE: I think it is. And I intend to enforce my court orders, but right now I have been somewhat lenient with Mr. Wilson . . .

Tony Wilson lived in an isomorphic world in which nobody held him responsible. The people in his world somehow bought his excuses and made their own excuses to keep him from changing his behavior. Even the judge confessed he had been too lenient.

THERAPIST: Along those lines, what are we looking at in terms of . . .

JUDGE: Well, we're looking at the court finding that he is not in compliance with the court order and he can be held in contempt of court. I'd like to avoid that, but there are sanctions that go as far as putting him in jail until he decides to comply. Now you asked me what could happen and I'm telling . . . I don't like to make threats because I don't believe that that's the way to deal with it, but that certainly is one of the classic judicial sanctions.

THERAPIST: Okay, okay.

TONY: Well, excuse me, Judge Thompson.

JUDGE: Yes, sir.

TONY: This is Tony. This is the first time you asked me to bring something from the meetings and stuff.

JUDGE: No, I sent that in writing to you, Tony . . .

TONY: Yeah, and this is the first time . . . (*Judge tries to interrupt*) Excuse me, can I finish? 'Cause the first time you said, you asked me to bring my sponsor's name, right?

Tony exhibited great dexterity in organizing contexts. Here, he had cut off the judge, who could put him away for a long time, because he felt the man was interrupting his speech.

JUDGE: Yeah.

TONY: And I asked you: Do you want me to bring it in? Now, you just told me Friday to bring in a list. I went and got that list, with meetin's and stuff I went to. I got my own job. All of this stuff that you wanted . . . and now listen, being that we're on this, I can't come Friday. I could come tomorrow 'cause I'm scheduled to work on a job that I went and got myself. So if I'm not complying or doing what you say, you're gonna have to send me to jail. I'm doing the best I can do! I mean, do you understand what I'm saying?

Tony was an expert dissembler; years in the streets had taught him to be fast on his feet and fast with his mouth. Yet in some definitive ways, Tony appeared to be on a positive path. He had a job and wanted to regain the respect of his family. Having a job is definitely a first step to recovery. The loss of the role as breadwinner is one of the most devastating and devaluing events in the life of a man like this. A program of detox or counseling alone is therefore insufficient; he needs to be reintegrated so that he is earning a living and is not totally dependent on the family.

As I observed Tony from behind the mirror, I believed that while he was not to be trusted, some of his recovery was genuine. At this point in therapy, we were trying to coordinate the members of the system to support his progress.

THERAPIST: Okay, so . . . what I hear you saying is that if Tony continues with the AA meetings and continues to get reports from our end and along those lines, that he's moving in the right direction.
JUDGE: Well, yeah, that's all I want out of Tony, you know. I want Tony to help himself. And that he stays right. And I think that is a positive step.

Using the judicial system as an arm of the therapy has provoked controversy for many years. Some judges wonder whether the system should be responsive to the mental health needs of its subjects and whether the court has any business doing anything other than supporting the system; others dwell on how to proceed when you cannot count on spontaneous compliance from the participants. They wonder how coercive and punitive the judicial system should be in those instances.

While some delinquents, addicts, and other offenders will accede to therapy voluntarily, many must be ordered to do so. Then the therapist must turn the required process into a positive engagement in which the results begin to persuade the subject to "buy into" the therapy process.

In all cases, we want the offender not simply to satisfy the court requirement by showing up but also to actively engage the family in the recovery process, helping the subject in such matters as preventing relapse or maintaining a job. One of the therapist's tasks is to diagnose whether the family is there only to keep the offender out of jail or if they are there to work positively on a variety of issues. The therapist is also in the uncomfortable position of deciding whether the subject was sincere or not. In Tony's case, it was hard to sense whether he was moving toward accepting and using therapy to help himself. Even his children and wife didn't trust him to be truthful. He had promised many times before that he was going to change and then relapsed.

For therapy to be truly effective under this system, the therapist needs to espouse a family therapy perspective, including, when necessary, granting the benefit of the doubt. We could not prove that Tony's abuse and potential manipulation of the system would not continue. But we could, by espousing a systems therapy position and following the microtransactions in the room, monitor whether real change occurred in some of the dysfunctional patterns, such as conflict avoidance.

It is important here to draw a clear distinction between therapists as an arm of social control versus therapists as the confidential helpers of their clients. Under the court system, we are not working strictly for the family; we are working for the judicial system also. Sadly, the therapist usually becomes an arm of the judicial system. This adds a dimension of the "con game" for many offenders, who develop cunning habits as they may fake their way through the court-ordered process looking sincere, knowing that their probationary status depends on their therapists' giving good reports to the judge.

In Tony's case, the pervasive pattern was being bailed out. Tony had not been held accountable for dates, places, meetings, and continuances. He had become an expert in avoiding conflict as well. Our goal was to get the judge to echo the family therapy prescription—that is, to hold this man accountable. During the sessions, we supported the wife, who, for the first time, was holding the husband accountable by saying to him: "Straighten out, or it's goodbye."

But before the therapy could obtain clarity, the judge's ambivalence needed to be corrected. At times it was hard to tell whether it was the judge or the patient who was withholding information and whether the judge was criticizing the patient or the therapist for nonresponsiveness. The judge seemed uncertain where to apply the squeeze. In such a scenario, the therapist is sometimes cast as the go-between for the family and the helping agencies and must help straighten out mix-ups in roles while attempting therapy.

In Tony's case, things became so confused that no one knew whose responsibility it was to write the report on his compliance. The judge didn't know, and almost accused the therapist of dereliction of duty; Tony didn't know; and even the therapist exhibited self-doubt, not knowing whether it was his responsibility or the judge's.

As strange as it sounds, this kind of situation is not unusual. The problem stems primarily from lack of organization at the critical interfaces. It is almost as if the system is set up to foster illegality or deviance. The therapist can barely get to the internal family issues, so great is the thicket of dynamics between court, home, and therapy.

Inevitably in these cases, the moment arrives when the therapist must judge whether the client's behavior is changing. Does he want to work on internal family issues, not because the judge insisted, but because he genuinely wants to regain his family and his self-respect? In Tony's case, the dysfunctional homeostasis—supported by the indulgent judge and the unclear therapist (and supervisor)—seemed to be changing, but I suspected that much of the change was a facade and not reality. Still, incremental progress and clarification were evident.

TONY: I got me a job, and everything I'm doing, I feel good about myself. Maybe it's not great—I should have been doing this years ago. I'm *totally* aware of that. But right now I'm doing it. So I don't choose to be threatened . . . I don't mind doing *any* of the . . . court-ordered procedures. I don't mind 'cause I want my family—because I want to do it, not because I'm afraid somebody gonna lock me up. I mean, half my life I've been institutionalized, so that's not nothing. I mean, I want to do this myself. And I appreciate what you're doing, but I'm trying to say to you: You could work with me, too, a little bit, you and the therapist. That's where it slipped my mind about bringing in writing, because I figured that's where they was involved in it. You know. So maybe that was my mistake. I didn't show a responsibility there 'cause I should've brought you the paper 'cause you told me. But I thought being that he got involved through the hospital—he got me in there, that was enough for that. I haven't went to therapy just like I was supposed to all the time 'cause I just got the job.

JUDGE: I'm not here to threaten you, but I want you to know . . .

TONY: Yes, sir.

JUDGE: . . . that I am a judge and I do have certain authority, and I do expect my court orders to be obeyed. That's not a threat; that's something that everybody is told, not just Tony Wilson.

Tony had learned, it appeared, to use the disarray—the lack of definition of roles between the two institutions, the confusion between the judicial and the mental health systems—to squirm out of responsibility; and he did it by defending his rights. The delinquent had capitalized on the disorganization while he legitimately asserted his misunderstanding and his rights. He tried very hard, and succeeded for a time, to use the confusion between the two systems to escape. The ambiguity of the institutional interface is ready-made for delinquents to manipulate both systems.

At a session a week later, the therapist directed attention to the isomorphic pattern of conflict avoidance between Tony and his wife, Joy.

THERAPIST: *(To Joy)* The fact is that unless things change in terms of—Tony knows that you're serious, dead serious, about meetings and stuff like that—that unless you challenge him, unless you confront him, what's gonna change?

JOY: Well, I mean . . .

TONY: Do you understand what he's saying to you?

JOY: He's saying that I need to challenge you.

TONY: That's something that we never did. That's all. Give it a shot. He might be right. You know, you never did, actually. I mean, why don't you just do it like he's saying, you know?

JOY: I say what I want to say.

TONY: I'm telling you . . . just go on yourself. You know I do it, believe me. So when you feel like it, just get your stuff off. I think it's all for the better.

THERAPIST: See, he's got you 'cause he knows you're not going to challenge him.

TONY: Shit, that'll do it.

THERAPIST: He knows, he knows. You're furious with him. But yet you're not going to challenge him. You're going to let him go just where he wants to go. Yeah . . . a smile . . . he's such a good-looking guy and he's got a tongue of quicksilver. He's good; he's got you. But you're furious at him, yet you can't . . . you need to challenge him.

TONY: Yup, you do.

THERAPIST: So, he thinks it's a joke. He doesn't think you're serious.

TONY: No, no, don't rub it in like that. See, you know what he's doing, he's instigating. You know? He is, he really is.

JOY: I just . . . you know, I worried a couple times about what he was doing and where he was going and if he had been drinking . . . and, you know . . . I don't have time for it no more. You know, my mind now is just focused on . . .

During the remainder of the session, the wife challenged her husband to a limited extent. As the supervisor, I was aware that she had reservations: Historically, Tony had, on occasion, been a time bomb (we didn't fully know to what extent). It was this characteristic of Tony's that kept people, especially his family, from challenging him. It was time now to foster more support for Joy from the extended family and from the community—to enable her to challenge her husband more effectively.

In this family, Tony was a dissembler and a con man. He talked about his sense of responsibility, yet he had missed three appointments. He had learned to *say* the right thing but couldn't do it.

The therapist faced a dilemma. Could he be a strong advocate *and* a therapist? If he acted too much as advocate for the man, he undermined the therapy. After all, the aim of therapy was to allow him to experience the consequences of his actions, not to bail him out. The therapist needed to stand up for Tony in some areas, while being firm in others.

In retrospect, I believe that the therapist should have pushed and confronted Tony harder: "If you're so committed to doing what the judge requires and so committed to your family, then why in hell did you miss three appointments with me? When you miss appointments, you're playing with your freedom. You rely too much on your ability to convince people with your lip. You must do what you promise. Your actions speak louder than your words."

Unfortunately, in this case the therapist's behavior was an isomorphic modeling of the family's pattern. The therapeutic team, like the family, had bent over backward to cushion Tony. In order to protect him, we needed to challenge him every time he did anything to impair his freedom. We also needed to be watchful for a similar isomorphic pattern at his workplace. How would Tony induce the people in his work setting to treat him specially, until the boss finally got mad enough to fire him?

So far, in Tony's work context, he had held on to his job and had not shirked responsibility. So in terms of three discrete systems contexts—family, court/therapy, and work—only Tony's experience in the workplace seemed stable. The inescapable task for the therapist is to make available the interface opportunities to view the isomorph in multiple contexts. The therapist's true understanding of the nature of the systemic dysfunction becomes possible only when the therapist has quick access to all the systems in which the man is failing.

The wise therapist intervenes, opening the curtains between systems that are usually closed to each other. In this case, Tony should then feel more exposed and less able to get away with fast-talking shenanigans and other intrusive avoidance ploys. The idea is to provide no hiding place and force him to deal with the isomorph.

The advantage of this type of intervention is that it would clarify for all participants where Tony was able to deliver and where he was not. For example, Tony's wife became more aware that he had not changed as much as he claimed. With further intervention, she might have become more watchful and more helpful to him in meeting his responsibilities.

The therapist aimed to build a system that exposed the isomorph and the homeostatic maintainers in different contexts. The possibilities and applications are interesting, since delinquency is often nothing more than the capacity of the delinquent to avoid responsibility and to render impotent a variety of people in different contexts, keeping them uninformed of what is happening in the other contexts. The skilled delinquent keeps the boundaries between each context so that he can fool the people in all of them. Note that the family, in theory, should do the work, not the therapist. But since all families have their own histories, internal dynamics, quirks, and baggage, the systems therapist is left to assess the condition of the family at the interface and to prepare the family to meet with the outsiders and to use them well.

CASE EXAMPLE: DEBBIE

Debbie, an acting-out 13-year-old and the second of three children, had run away so many times that in desperation, her parents had resorted to the court system to see if they could get some help in establishing an executive hierarchy. A probation worker was assigned to Debbie, and at first the parents were pleased that he had very good rapport with their daughter. It developed, however, that the probation officer saw himself more as a therapist than as an arm of the law. He failed to support the parents' desire to create a safety net around the girl and to get her to comply with society's expectations for her behavior, as well as their's. The result was a pattern that was isomorphic with the parents' own relationship with the girl: overinvolvement, indulgence, and a lack of consequences for misbehavior. At this point, I was invited to enter the case as therapist.

With adolescents such as this, it is essential to touch their narcissism, their belief that they are special. They must experience developmental estrangement (Fishman, 1988), the realization that they are responsible for their own actions and that their parents are not always going to bail them out of difficult situations. When several attempts to strengthen the parents' control had failed, therefore, an intervention was arranged to provide feedback that would change her behavior as well as her sense of herself in the world.

At the consultation were Linda, the mother; Andy, the father; the probation worker; and because the family was very religious and had a good relationship with their pastor, I also included him. Debbie, predictably, had refused to come to the session.

FISHMAN: You represent the court?

PROBATION WORKER: Yeah, I'm a crisis counselor, with the crisis unit, family court.

FISHMAN: And you represent the church? (*Pastor nods.*)

FISHMAN: (*To parents*) And you represent the most disenfranchised sector, the most helpless . . . ?

FATHER: We feel that way. I guess Debbie decided she wasn't going to come today . . . that's just typical of what's been going on. She will not take any direction . . . anything she's asked to do, she basically does the opposite.

MOTHER: Andy says she acts like she's living in a bed and breakfast. She comes in to eat and to sleep, that's all. Most of the time she just does what she wants to do.

PROBATION WORKER: She's on a withdrawal. She's withdrawing from the rest of the family, isolating herself, doesn't want to do anything. And I've tried to talk with her, reach her somehow. I felt she was going to respond in a way, was going to . . . I tried to talk to her like a counselor. I tried to talk to her like a daughter. We even touched a little on the spiritual aspect—not much, because of my relation to the court . . .

FISHMAN: (*To probation worker*) You may have guessed that we have a different vantage point. You see, Mr. and Mrs. Foster need some help. They are completely overwhelmed. They are very caring people. In some ways, too caring. They work too hard for these kids, who in some ways take advantage of them.

MOTHER: I don't think anybody can do too much for their kids.

FISHMAN: If the kids are convinced that you're going to do too much no matter what, then they've got you. Adolescents, I love them, they're wonderful, and they grow out of it, but they're mercenaries. And if they think they've got you—and Debbie thinks she's got you—you're lost. She thinks there are no significant consequences to her behavior, and she's always thumbing her nose because you bend over backwards. Now here's where the court can help.

PASTOR: Is there a difference in loving them and doing too much for them? I mean, you can love them an awful lot and care for them a lot, and express that love to them. But what you're saying is, "You can do too much for them, even though you're expressing that love."

FISHMAN: Is it possible, if the family were to ask, to have two policemen come over to her house and take her to see you?

MOTHER: When she wouldn't get in the car today, I said, "What do I have to do, call a police officer to pick you up and force you to go?" and she just took off.

FISHMAN: Perfect. We're talking in the same direction. (*To pastor*) We're going to help empower the parents. And Mom and Dad need support. They need to have some leverage with this girl. The church is very important, because you can support the parents . . .

PASTOR: And hopefully we are.

MOTHER: They are.

FISHMAN: Yes, in your hour of need . . . and a thirteen-year-old girl who is in an hour of need. She'll grow out of this and she'll be a lovely daughter—great, certainly. The question is how to get her from here to there.

MOTHER: It's just so hard, because I don't want to hurt her.

PASTOR: Debbie's getting to the point now where her actions really produce harm to herself, and sometimes we have to let that hurt happen.

I marveled at what a wonderful cotherapist the pastor was proving to be. He had all the credibility and authenticity, in terms of the family's culture and values, to help transform this system.

FISHMAN: It's not hurting her anyway. It's helping her. It's making her life more orderly.

My statements stemmed from the desire to help normalize what the parents were experiencing in developmental terms. I was operating on the assumption that adolescents need a coherent context of adults to support and oversee them. We were about to enlarge this system of supportive adults to help supervise this girl—and to help support these parents. The probation worker was mobilized to start court proceedings.

PASTOR: What is going to court going to mean?

PROBATION WORKER: We have to file a family crisis petition, which has a format: we have to state the reason why, what we have attempted to do, and give the court some recommendations.

PASTOR: She has to actually go in to court?

PROBATION WORKER: Yes, I'll send her a summons. If she doesn't show up, then the court will issue a bench warrant.

PASTOR: And this is for family court?

PROBATION WORKER: Yeah.

PASTOR: And she'll sit down for a pre-court review with a . . .

PROBATION WORKER: No, she'll go straight to court before the judge, and I'll present the case to the court—why we are there, why the petition was filed, and what we want from the court, what our recommendations are: for her to obtain counseling, for her to do her house chores, for her not to leave the house without her parents' knowing where she is going, to keep her curfews. All that is put into an order. And the court will tell her, if she doesn't follow through, she has to be back in court and the court's going to put her in the youth house.

PASTOR: Similar to what they'd do to someone under probation. The same type of thing.

PROBATION WORKER: Yeah, more or less the same.

MOTHER: So, the first time she comes—if she runs like she did today, you would send a . . .

PROBATION WORKER: Well, the first step, I would send her a summons . . .

FISHMAN: It's important that two policemen stop by the house with a squad car and come into the house and present this.

FATHER: The police have been there a couple of times.

FISHMAN: This is different. And ideally, have her get into the back of the squad car and take her. We need some theater.

The mother looked at me with some surprise, as if to say "Do you really mean theater?" I did mean theater. I was thinking of a case described by Carlos Castaneda (1968) in which a father who was having severe problems controlling his son hired someone to intervene to scare the boy. At this point, I was looking for the police to help this family in exactly the same way, by dramatically reinforcing the parents' power.

MOTHER: If she doesn't go the first time, are you saying? Or do you want this regardless?

FISHMAN: What do you want?

MOTHER: I don't know if he (*Pointing to probation worker*) can do that.

PROBATION WORKER: What we have to do is send her a summons.

FISHMAN: Who'll deliver the summons?

PROBATION WORKER: I mail it to her.

My heart sank. What we needed was a therapeutic crisis, which could be created by a theatrical staging of the delivery of the summons. I therefore conveniently misunderstood what the probation worker had said.

FISHMAN: Would it be possible to have a couple of policemen come along?

PASTOR: Would it be possible if I can get the two policemen and we present the summons through the policemen?

PROBATION WORKER: Yeah.

PASTOR: You wouldn't get policemen she knew . . .

PROBATION WORKER: I think it can be worked out with the youth section of the police. They go to my office every day.

FISHMAN: If the pastor can work it out, there has to be ceremony: a knock at the door, she's given the summons, and that begins it.

I wanted the pastor to help coordinate the delivery of the summons, so that he could also be supportive of the family when it happened.

PROBATION WORKER: If she doesn't show up, then the court can issue a warrant, and she's picked up—from school . . .

FISHMAN: (To parents) So you should have some support. (To mother) There's really no reason you should run away from home. [The weekend before, the mother had been so despondent and overwhelmed that she had left and gone to a friend's house.]

MOTHER: I know.

PROBATION WORKER: Well, I'll talk to my supervisor. I have to go through him.

MOTHER: If you get the initial summons and the police come . . .

PROBATION WORKER: I'll file the crisis petition for next week, because I have to give her notice, by law. The summons I can do tomorrow.

FISHMAN: And Pastor, you can arrange . . .

PASTOR: I'll call tonight.

FISHMAN: And the parents will let you know exactly where she's going to be.

MOTHER: We don't know where she's going to be—that's the problem. We'll eat dinner and she'll come in maybe an hour or two later and make a mess and kick off and leave again.

PASTOR: Can they issue a summons at school?

FISHMAN: I think it would embarrass her too much. It's too tough on the kids. It's just not fair to embarrass her in front of her friends.

MOTHER: How about seven thirty in the morning, just before she leaves for school, or . . .

FATHER: Right after school . . .

FISHMAN: It'd be nice to stage it. (To pastor) Are you ever there in the morning, at breakfast time?

PASTOR: I'm in and out all the time.

FISHMAN: (To parents) Maybe you can have him drop in for breakfast one morning, and at seven thirty the police will knock at the door. Everybody sit down for breakfast—that's a rare entity in America these days, but . . .

MOTHER: (To father) You'll be gone by then.

FATHER: Maybe supper together.

PASTOR: What I can do is call a sergeant on the police force who could help us out.

PROBATION WORKER: Because there are some officers from the juvenile section who are plainclothes . . .

FISHMAN: We don't want that. We want the meanest-looking policemen . . .

PASTOR: I think we can get Sergeant Sherman to help us—maybe get two fellows to help us out on this—and just pull up with a car in the morning. Anything to break the pattern on this.

FISHMAN: Give the parents the sense that they are in charge. (*To parents*) Because your daughter needs this.

Two days later, another session was held, at which the parents reported on the confrontation, which had taken place the evening before.

FISHMAN: Tell me a little about when the subpoena was delivered.

MOTHER: I went to the church and said to the pastor, "Is everything hooked up for tomorrow morning?" and he said, "Well, can you come in the study a minute," and he had this police officer in there, who said, "It's going to be rather difficult to do it in the morning, because of the shift change. Can we do it tonight?" I said, "I don't know if she's even home." He said, "Will she go home after youth group?" I said, "She's not here," and he said, "She's here." I said, "She's here? She hasn't come into church in two weeks." And he said, "Yeah, she came ten minutes late, but she's here," which surprised me because at supper time she was saying, "Now, how many people in the church know about me?" She was trying to feel us out . . .

Clearly, a new system had been created. The mother, pastor, and police were working closely together.

MOTHER: A little later, the pastor and policeman asked if she would be home by now, and I said, "I have no idea; I don't know if she's there." So then I got talking to somebody else, and I went out and asked these friends if they'd give me a lift home, and we pulled up in front of the house and the police were already there. And I, like, panicked, because Andy didn't know they were coming tonight. But it probably worked out just as well, because he was totally surprised . . .

FISHMAN: What did they do?

FATHER: They knocked, rang the doorbell, and I'm going to answer the door, and Debbie's upstairs and she says, "I didn't do it, I didn't do anything." I let them in and they asked for Debbie, so I called her down, and she took it. She's looking at me, "What's this?" Then she took it upstairs, she read it, and I went up because they wanted her to know what it involved, and she gave it to me. I told her it meant she had to go to court on Tuesday. At that time, there were some tears. I told her, "The policemen still want to talk to you downstairs." She said she wasn't going down. I went back down and asked them if they wanted to go up to her room, and they said no. She came down in a couple of minutes, and they explained to her that if her behavior did not change, she would have to go to court, and if she didn't go to court, they would have to pick her up and mentioned about the youth house—that it's not a nice place to be. Then they left . . .

FISHMAN: How did she react after that?

FATHER: She was angry . . .

MOTHER: She went up to her room. Then she came down and said, "I'm not ever going to speak to you as long as I live," and she went out the door. We're saying, "Where's she going to go?" and we were praying for her, "Lord, protect her, wherever she is." About twenty minutes later, she came back.

FATHER: About fifteen.

MOTHER: She went back up to her room first, then she came down and said, "All this talk about me starting my lessons again, all these books you bought me, they're not going to do any good." And she took them to the trash compactor, and she said, "As long as it's going to be my last night here, I may as well make use of my time," and we thought, "Oh, no, what's she going to do?" She goes up to her room, and I go upstairs to her room, and she didn't say anything—oh (*To father*), she walked into you and said, "Watch where you're walking, you big pig. . . ."

FATHER: You went up, and she went to the basement and put her sneakers in the dryer, and then she went to her room. And I let the dog out and set the dishwasher up and ran it, and turned the lights out and went up. About a quarter after ten, her lights were out, and she was in bed. I peeked into her room. She was asleep!

MOTHER: So it was, like, explosive initially, and I don't know if she lay there and worried about what was going to happen, but today she was fine.

The creation of a new system was not by any means the conclusion of the therapy. Considerably more work was necessary, and the addition of the pastor and the court contributed significantly to supporting the parents during subsequent therapy. The recontextualization of this family was important not only in creating the transformation through the crisis— the staging of the confrontation by the police—but in maintaining the transformation, as the girl continued to be monitored by both of these outside institutions in support of the parents.

In closing, I would like to address a problem that every therapist struggles with: how to work with families ordered by the court into treatment who do not want to be there.

The therapist accepts the bona fide arrangement that "you have been forced here," but he or she also states, implicitly or explicitly, "I don't want to work with you forever on that basis. So let's see if we can find some issues where we have some genuine agreement that we can work on together."

The task is refining and reframing the auspices of the work. The hard reality is that we are being sent, in part, to watch the family. There is an unspoken, "If you don't behave I'll report you to the judge." We implicitly say, "Look, if we can do something, great, but if we cannot work together, then I am obligated to say that to the court."

There are cases where reframing is not possible, where the therapist works with people who feel forced. There are times when the therapist tries not to identify with the courts: "I am independent, and we're here to help explore and figure out what's going on."

But then there are cases of chronic addiction or time-tested intractable abusers, where you welcome the fact that they feel forced and are using the specter of the court. This is a very welcome force when you are dealing with chronic, delinquent behavior with people who are known to snap out. And with certain very difficult cases, like a chronic sexual abuser or a man who beats his wife routinely, the therapist does not want the court to go away. The auspices of the court can facilitate the therapy by forcing compliance and enhancing the therapist's power via reporting responsibility to the court.

In other cases, we may try to develop a new basis of work—searching for some reciprocally agreed upon basis to proceed. For example, "You know your wife is going to leave you and that your kids hate you. If you keep pushing heroin your health is going to go or the Mafia will kill you." Suggestions like this, involving the broader context, can generate enough intensity to get some cooperation. Closely following feedback, you try to find some other reason for mobilizing the possibility of change.

The generic issue really comes down to the classic task of family therapy, to contextualize the problem. In many of these cases, the goal of the therapy is to affect the deep structures of the self—those mechanisms that maintain morality. We want to organize a system that no longer supports the immorality.

Here the tenets of IST can be invaluable. We organize a broad, coherent system that is united with its message. This coherent larger system can be invaluable in recruiting the family to work honestly on its problems, even if the first contact was made by the court.

This was demonstrated in the case of Luis, mentioned in the introduction. The presence of the probation office, his public defender, and his teachers rapidly transformed this family from a position of wanting to send their son away and going on with their lives. The input given from the professionals made it clear to the family that there was a great deal that they could do for their son; and to the extent that they were acting differently with their son, they were open to further family change. In this case, it was like the old story of a camel pushing his nose in a tent. Once his nose is inside, it will not be long before the entire camel is in the tent. It was the same with this family: By the end of the first session they were dealing with one of the pivotal problems in the family, the relationship between the boy and his stepfather; they had forgotten that the court had mandated them to come.

CHAPTER 9

The School Context

A MONG OUR NATION'S many institutions, the school is one of the most prevalent and inescapable. Every family with children must deal with schools. When there is dysfunction in the family, problems are frequently manifested in the school behavior and performance of the children. Yet many families feel estranged and intimidated by the school system and are easily overwhelmed by it. Parents may be anxious or even phobic about school if they had problems in school themselves. (Olof Ulwan, in a study in Sweden, found that the best communication between parents and teachers took place in the parking lot, after the formal meeting [personal communication, 1992]).

When the patient in family therapy is a child or adolescent, the school becomes an important subsystem for inclusion in the therapy. Both family therapists and school personnel are becoming increasingly aware of the interrelationships of the family and school systems and the desirability of bringing them together to handle children's problems. Several models of intervention have been described by family therapists (Aponte, 1976; Tucker & Dyson, 1976; Lusterman, 1985; McGuire, Manghi, & Tolan, 1990). Similarly, school personnel have recognized the importance of involving the family in solving children's school problems and have drawn on family systems theory for conceptualizing dysfunction in the school ecology (e.g., Johnston & Zemitzsch, 1988). In general, however, school psychologists and counselors see family participation only in terms of ameliorating the presenting problem, without recognizing that one cannot engage the family without in some measure changing it. Whether they realize it or not, school personnel who bring the family into their interventions with children are doing family therapy.

School counselors are in difficult positions, as are child study teams. Their charge is to evaluate the child, and although they can usually have outside experts evaluate the external context of these youngsters, it is not always a simple task. First, it involves a change in paradigm for many individually trained professionals to look beyond the child. They are firmly convinced that the site of the difficulties lies in the sulci of the child's brain. Over the years, I have read countless school reports that are the equivalent of "the sound of one hand clapping"—the child without a context. An additional problem is that of confidentiality. I am always reluctant to put much too detail in a school report about the family, since it becomes a part of the youngster's permanent school record. The issue here is to inform the school of family problems without the specifics, and then to describe strategies that involve all the systems.

Therapeutic interventions that involve the school can apply the same general principles outlined in previous chapters for dealing with other institutions. Again, the overall goal of the therapy is to rebalance the forces at work. Thomas Power and Karlotta Lutz Bartholomew (1987) describe the ideal relationship of family and school as collaborative; the boundaries are clear but permeable, and parents and teachers respect each other's authority in their respective domains. Information is freely shared, and each side initiates interactions when the need arises. Later in the chapter, we shall discuss this type of parent-teacher alliance. The enhanced home-school partnership is designed to fine-tune the adults' sensitivity to the child, so that instead of isolating the youngster, the parents work very closely with the child. Thus, both parents and school become very responsive to their joint charge.

Too often, however, other patterns of family-school relationships prevail, which Power and Bartholomew (1987) describe in terms of their structural features (such as boundaries) and transactional features (such as symmetrical and complementary functioning). One common trap is a competitive relationship in which the boundaries are diffuse: school personnel and family members intrude upon each other's domains and try to achieve a dominant position. In another pattern, domains of the family and the school are not clearly delineated: parents and teachers merge their efforts in an alliance that results in *isolating* the child. In a complementary form of this pattern, to which single-parent families may be especially prone, the parent tends to leave to the school more and more of the responsibility for managing the child. In each of these dysfunctional patterns, the balance of forces needs to be righted. In contrast, the enhanced home-school partnership, by definition, establishes a collaborative, non-symmetrical relationship, in which the roles are defined clearly from the outset.

The patterns just described are found in families at all social levels. But there is another situation that is being seen more and more frequently in poor urban schools. In a revolutionary new attitude toward school, the child in an extremely dysfunctional family sees the school and school authorities as a refuge. For such children, the street and the school become sources of stability and safety, showing more concern for developing the child's potential than the family is showing.

In one big-city high school, a 15-year-old boy came to the School-Based Youth Services Program, a social service agency located in the school, complaining that his mother had lost her job and was prostituting herself in their apartment; his father was in prison for a knife assault.

The agency was able to get the mother a job, and although the boy said that things had improved, he kept coming to the program office several times a day. After his father told him he should always protect himself with a knife, he began carrying a knife on his person and keeping it by his bed at night (perhaps to protect himself from his mother's visitors).

The boy became more disorganized, and the family was referred for therapy, but only the older sister showed up. Meanwhile, the youngster kept hanging around the youth program office. One Friday, when everyone in the office had left, he stood outside the school for a time and then went to his gang (his pseudofamily). That night he had a fight with another boy and killed him with a knife.

From jail, the boy wrote to the staff at the School-Based Youth Services Program, "I don't know what happened. I never did anything like that. I'm not like that"—which was true. In spite of being in a gang, probably for self-protection, he had never been in trouble. The program staff were heartbroken. If they had been able to stay open all weekend and been there for him, the tragedy would never have happened.

In situations like this one, where the family structure is frail and provides little support to the child, the youngster may have more loyalty to the school than to the family. The family, in turn, may feel that they have been co-opted, that their child is being stolen away from them. This kind of triangulation presents a new challenge to family therapists, who tend to see the child as embedded in the family, when in fact the family's influence on the child may be feeble.

There is thus a broad spectrum of arrangements between school and family. In working at the interface of home and school, the therapist must consider them all.

General Principles

As with all work with institutional contexts, the key to promoting success-ful change is to empower the family. This basic principle underlies many of the principles that follow. There are times when the clinician must help the family redefine itself and bring in other members of its network to help, but the message to be conveyed is that the family is not frail and is very capable of handling the problem if empowered to do so.

Ensure that the therapist, not the school, determines the agenda for the ther-apy. By the time the therapist comes to the interface of the family and the school, the school authorities may already have been pushed to their limit. Their agenda may be to turn the responsibility for the youngster over to some other institution. The clinician trying to normalize the situation must work to establish a different set of goals for the therapy.

Most school authorities are willing to cooperate with the family thera-pist and work with the family to find a solution that will keep the child in school. If they can be gotten to the therapy session, they will generally be willing to agree to a concrete set of arrangements that show promise of ameliorating the problem. If they have completely written the child off, however, then the therapist must work with both sides much as with a divorcing family, for the good of both the family and the school.

Explore the parents' attitudes toward school and school authorities. Many parents are still reeling from their own experiences in school. If their child-hood problems brought them in conflict with the school authorities, they may have been left with negative attitudes that, whether expressed or not, may be conveying messages to the child that are contributing to the prob-lem. The family's set of beliefs about school, and about education in gen-eral, should therefore be explored, with an eye toward identifying misun-derstandings and conflicting values. The therapist should make sure that the family is not habitually criticizing the school in front of the child. Whatever his or her problems with the school authorities, the child identi-fies with the school and has loyalty to it. The *blanket* support of a child against teachers and school administration is the "Bermuda Triangle" of child rearing. It leads to disaster, not only because it lets the child off the hook but it also creates a conflict of loyalties between home and school.

Assume that the child is strong and that the problem is one the family can han-dle. The focus should always be on the strengths of the child. Both the school and the family may perceive the child as being frail and may therefore hold limited expectations for the youngster. If expectations are too limited, no one will push the child to stretch. The youngster will then buy into the notion that little is expected and perform accordingly, without challenging himself or herself. The end result will be confirmation of the limitations.

The best example of stretching is the classic Oaktree study (Rosenthal & Jacobson, 1968), which demonstrated how limited expectations become a self-fulfilling prophecy. The Oaktree School experiment consisted of 650 students and 18 teachers. At the beginning of the school year, the faculty was told that an intelligence test that had been given to all the students had determined that 20 percent of the students would make rapid and superior intellectual progress during the year. The teachers were told which students were expected to excel. Actually, the students named as superior were chosen at random by the researchers rather than on the basis of any test. At the end of the school year, the students were given the test again, and the "gifted" ones did indeed perform in the superior range. While there are many explanations for this outcome, clearly the most obvious is that the teachers treated these students in a different way. They had greater expectations for them, and apparently the students rose to meet the challenge.

Search for conflicting loyalties and hidden agendas. The therapist always needs to be aware of the agendas of the various people in social systems. In many instances, conflicting agendas are profoundly injurious to the family, and in the school setting, it can lead to severe educational retardation. To illustrate, I once dealt with an 11-year-old boy who had serious behavioral difficulties in school. Almost daily, he was sent down to the counselor's office, where he talked to a young graduate student. The boy's stepmother, who had been a teacher, became very suspicious when she heard how the boy was spending his day. She challenged the school, saying that the boy was being rewarded for misbehaving. Rather than working in class, he was spending his time talking with the counselor.

I asked for a session at the school. Through questioning, we learned that the graduate student/counselor was writing her thesis on boys of this age. She was using this opportunity to delve into the youngster's innermost thoughts, and the two became very close. As the stepmother had suspected, this relationship benefited only the counselor's academic career; it actually hindered the boy's education and socialization. Moreover, the arrangement telegraphed an unhealthy (albeit unintended) message to the child: "Act up and you will be rewarded." When the practice was stopped, the boy's behavior improved immediately.

Conflicting agendas frequently represent opposing orientations, which can result in confounding interferences. For example, some states appoint teams of professionals to assess children who are having difficulties at school. Such teams generally take an approach that is diametrically opposed to systems-oriented therapy, assessing the child in isolation and not exploring the possibility that the child may be responding to a dysfunctional context. The result can be a serious misdiagnosis that compounds the problem and hinders the work of a systems-oriented therapist who is working to heal the system.

Encourage an attitude of shared responsibility and involvement between the family and the school. When a child is failing in school—receiving poor grades or misbehaving or both—there is frequently a dysfunctional relationship between the family and the school authorities. Parents may lack skills in dealing with teachers and school administrators, avoiding contact with them and leaving their children to deal with school personnel alone. They often perceive the school as "one undifferentiated mass that represented authority over them" (Tucker & Dyson 1976, p. 139).

In most therapy situations involving children and schools, the single most important objective is to bring the parents to an understanding of their crucial responsibility for their child. Parents must clearly accept and share with the school the responsibility for dealing with the problem instead of leaving it entirely in the hands of the school. The school, for its part, may tend to place the blame for the child's behavioral problems squarely on the family, although, as Johnston and Zemitzsch (1988) note, staff members are likely to claim the credit when the child's behavior improves.

The family and the school must be made to see each other as positive forces, with the potential for mutual enhancement. Tucker and Dyson (1976) describe a three-way change of perceptions that must take place. First, school staff members must begin to perceive the child as part of a family rather than as an isolated entity. The family must come to see the school personnel as resources and contemporaries who will not judge them but who are available as sources of strength and confirmation. And the family, in turn, must be seen as an essential source of strength available to the educational system.

Clarify boundaries and roles. The child is a member of two organizations, the family and the school. The challenge for the therapist is to bridge these two subsystems and create a dynamic interactive system in which the family and the school function in some similar and some appropriately complementary ways. This goal can be achieved only if all the participants agree on the boundaries between them and the roles each is to play.

The boundaries and roles decided upon are, of course, specific to individual cases. In general, however, the pedagogical area is in the school's bailiwick. The school determines the curriculum, although when courses of study branch out in adolescence, the input of the family may be needed. Similarly, the school is responsible for determining its own rules and administering the consequences of infractions of those rules.

For its part, the family is responsible for the consequences of misbehavior in general. When the child does not respond to the school's discipline or when truancy is a problem, it is up to the family to determine the consequences according to its own values. The therapist must work to block interference with the family's decision making if school professionals offer unconstructive criticism or if parents assume that it is the school's responsibility to correct the child's behavior. A balance must be struck that does not undermine the parents' position of authority.

Obviously, the boundaries and roles are set in the context of development. There must be more parental involvement with the school when children are young. As children grow into adolescence, they can assume more responsibility for themselves, but problems can never be left solely to the adolescent to solve.

Establish an alliance between parents and school. The goal of the therapist is to recognize and nourish transactional patterns that are collaborative in nature, with boundaries that are permeable. The parental system and the school system can then be encouraged to develop a working alliance in which each supports the other but exercises ultimate authority in its respective domain.

Sometimes it is enough to establish an atmosphere of collaboration in which there is a clear message to the child that the parents and the school are united in their determination to solve the child's problem. With this combined support, and with no opportunity to play one system against the other, the child may spontaneously improve his or her performance, academically or behaviorally or both. Other cases call for a more intensive intervention, with very specific steps agreed upon by the school administration, teachers, and parents. A procedural model called the enhanced home-school partnership provides a protocol for organizing both sides and enabling them to assume joint responsibility.

The enhanced home-school partnership is a formal alliance between the parents (or other representatives of the family) and the school in which the parents become intimately involved in the child's education. They oversee the child's homework and sign off on it every day and receive regular communications from the school—weekly, daily, or even several times a day—on how the child is doing. If necessary, the parents come into the school to work with or help control a troubled child. Indeed, the threat of the parents' presence can be enough to straighten out a recalcitrant adolescents, since adolescents would rather have their parents be a "gray" presence: Having parents around is humiliating to young people who are struggling to become autonomous to these same people.

For many parents, especially among the working poor, a commitment to be in the school would jeopardize job security. Even in such cases, however, the demand for a physical parental presence can be met with the help of other members of the family. The important thing is that the parents or a parental substitute show up. The therapist should hold firm that this is absolutely essential, pointing out that not doing so could endanger the parents' job security later through the disruptions that an unruly youngster's behavior might create.

The school must also be persuaded to accept the pact. In this task, the higher and more powerful the administrator involved, the greater the chance of success. In a session held at the school, the therapist assembles the family, the child, the teacher, the guidance counselor, and, if possible, a higher-level administrator. Getting the principal to the session may seem like a tall order, but I have been pleasantly surprised to find many high-level administrators willing to participate either in person or by speakerphone.

Immediately after the ground-breaking meeting, daily communication between the school and the family should begin. If the presence of the family in the school is not required, telephone calls will serve, but there should also be frequent conferences to assess progress.

It is often helpful to establish a support group for the parents, and perhaps one for the child. Groups of parents who are involved in similar partnerships can be brought together, with some sessions including the children and some without them. Support groups reinforce the efforts of the parents or children and give them the sense that they are not alone in this somewhat unorthodox way of working to solve school problems.

The case of Jason, described in chapter 4, made very effective use of the enhanced home-school partnership. Jason's parents were permitted to come into the school to work with their son, who was diagnosed with elective mutism, making possible his return to a regular classroom.

The following case, this time involving an adolescent, typifies a number of strengths and difficulties of working in the context of the school. It features a heroic teacher who was willing to go to bat for and with the family to change the practices in the school. This example demonstrates many of our therapeutic principles in action, as the school's therapeutic team and I intervened on behalf of the child and the family in a troubled system.

CASE EXAMPLE: VINCENT AND HIS TEACHER

Vincent, age 17, had been hospitalized in a nonprofit psychiatric institution for 6 weeks as a result of severe behavioral problems. He had been fighting with other students at school and had been completely unruly at home. He lived with his father and his stepmother, a woman much younger than his father. The father, who had been married several times, had been married to his present wife for about 3 years. Vincent's biological mother had left when Vincent was age 3. Every 6 months or so, she would call and say she wanted to see her son, make arrangements to do so, and then fail to appear.

Many pressures impinged on this family. Besides the usual developmental stress of an adolescent son growing up and potentially leaving home, the father's recent remarriage added tension. The behavior of Vincent's biological mother in promising to visit and then not appearing added further pressure. The prevailing structural difficulties included isomorphic splits: the marital splits between the father and his first two wives; the split with his present wife over how to handle Vincent; and a split within the school as well, in which administrators and teachers disagreed about how to handle Vincent.

As the session progressed, a homeostatic maintaining pattern became clear on the part of the school and Vincent's father: both had been bailing Vincent out of his behavioral difficulties—his father by excusing Vincent, probably because he felt guilty about his multiple marriages and the behavior of Vincent's biological mother; and the school by sending Vincent to an outside therapist instead of imposing punishment for his misbehavior. Common sense directed my intervention: a boy like this, who had done fairly well during 11 years of school, probably did not need an elaborate educational evaluation before proceeding.

The hospital had found no evidence of pathology, and Vincent was about to be placed in a partial hospitalization program. I met with Vincent and his family while conducting a demonstration interview at a hospital in the Midwest. I presented a quandary to the family; the boy had been an inpatient, with no changes made in the systems. The hospital was about to discharge Vincent to a partial hospitalization (day hospital) program. Vincent was scheduled to be the first patient in this new program, so I was instantly aware of the conflicting agendas. I felt that Vincent, as a high school senior, should, if possible, graduate from high school with the taste of success. But when I suggested that he be sent back to school immediately, tension mounted in the room.

The consultation included Vincent, his father, his stepmother (Sally), his younger sister, his maternal grandmother, and the therapist from the hospital unit. Also present was one of his teachers from public school, a young woman who had been identified by the parents as the teacher most involved with Vincent. She had taken an interest in Vincent's problems and had readily agreed to attend the session. She had often said that she felt Vincent was capable of doing much more than he was doing, and she was eager to see him return to school.

About 35 minutes into the session, the father had been making every possible excuse for his son's problems.

FISHMAN: Does this make you feel guilty?

FATHER: Vincent's got the IQ and the physical makeup to do it, so he seems wasted. I'm doing the best I can. I've had them since they were three and four years old. We're just trying as hard as we can to change Vincent's attitude so he doesn't drop out or get involved with drugs or anything like that.

FISHMAN: You say he was spoiled?

GRANDMOTHER: Vincent is constantly watched, and everybody's very concerned about not upsetting Vincent's feelings. He causes a lot of conflict in the house. He thinks, "I can't do anything. Why don't they trust me?" but he hasn't earned it. If you catch a kid playing with matches, then you don't give him matches, and you're always watching him. It's just gotten into a vicious circle: He wants a little more trust, and they can't trust him. It just doesn't work. He's been going to a child psychologist for five or six years now.

A new agenda had emerged. Hearing that Vincent had been in therapy for years raised two questions in my mind: First, why was that clinician not here, and second, had that therapy been part of the system that had made the father so guilty and paralyzed regarding his son? If the father had been told that Vincent's difficulties were the result of mistakes that he and his former wife had made, then he would have a difficult time distancing himself enough to discipline the boy appropriately. It would also weigh heavily in the conflict with his present wife, who felt he was a pushover with Vincent. It certainly added to the complexity of the system and the importance of including both the biological family and the professional extended family in the treatment.

FATHER: Longer than that. It doesn't seem to help. I don't think I can say.

FISHMAN: Listen, we're not sensitive here.

FATHER: Well, it hasn't really helped. This has made the child feel better about himself short-term, but a few suggestions here and there, "Do this, this, this, and this . . . "

GRANDMOTHER: He goes to Mrs. Peck [his regular therapist] on Monday, and then he gets kicked out of school for two days. What Vincent wants, Vincent gets, and that's it.

FISHMAN: So Vincent is bull-headed and Daddy is guilty.

GRANDMOTHER: No, Daddy's not guilty. He's done a good job.

FISHMAN: (Turning to father) Are you guilty?

FATHER: A little bit.

FISHMAN: You said you would like to talk about suggestions. Is that right? I know that you go to a lot of therapists.

FATHER: After the divorce—I don't know what it is—I had some real terrible times adjusting, just like they did. His mother said she's going to cry
and cry until she dies and she don't talk to them for six months at a
time. They've had a real volcanic upbringing.

FISHMAN: When you talk about that, does it hurt you?

FATHER: What's that?

FISHMAN: When she made that promise that she was going to cry and cry
and she didn't call, does that hurt you?

FATHER: Well, when you catch Vincent in the closest crying, it does hurt
me; it makes me feel terrible. We are all willing to do what is necessary
to help the situation. I don't think he's a real bad boy; I think he's gone
off the path a little bit, you know, problems he's had at school, around
the house.

FISHMAN: So are you ready to make some changes? I have some expertise
with situations like this. We've had a lot of experience. I do have a suggestion, but it's not going to be easy.

FATHER: We realize that.

At this point I was attempting to support the family to make its own
decisions.

FISHMAN: It's taken this long, and there's been so much work done, and it's
been tough.

FATHER: We're not going to let anything drop. We're continuing forever.
We've given you at least enough, maybe too much. We've been told
and we've had confidence to do this and that and nothing happens. My
wife has done a real good job in terms of "clean your room or you can't
watch TV at night." Him and Sally get along a little better because I've
started to take a little more authority. Usually Sally is on the line.

SALLY: There was no problem with either of us with the boy.

FISHMAN: I'd say that was before the hormones kicked in.

SALLY: Yeah. After about three years, I started having real difficulties
supervising and instructing Vincent. (*Looks out of the corner of her eye at
her husband.*)

FISHMAN: Where's Papa?

SALLY: (*Laughs, tilts her head down slightly and looks at ground*) Watching TV or
something. I'll tell you, though, the last month it has really been pleasant.
His father has taken over and started checking rooms, doors . . .

Apparently in the past, the father had been unavailable and had given
all the boy's supervision over to his wife. This was difficult for her, not
only because he was not supporting her but also because she was closer in
age to Vincent than to her husband. Of course, her statement was a bit

wry; the last month had also been different because Vincent had been in the hospital.

FATHER: He's been doing fine the last month.

FISHMAN: (*To Vincent*) You're what, seventeen? (*To parents*) I think what Vincent needs—we've talked a lot about the case; it's not as if I just met you. I have the benefit of the records and the hospital's experience with your family, and here's something that you have to do. Are you willing to do it immediately? It's not going to be easy, because it's going to be a real change. I think you are a very caring, loving father, and all the adults, including the teachers, are very concerned, but you've been so concerned that you've been hoisted by your own petard. In spite of your best efforts, it's backfired, it's boomeranged. (*To father*) What you need to do, as the biological parent, you have to think about what you can do to return him to a normal life. All this other stuff is not normal. What does it mean to have a normal life? What do normal adolescents do? Talk to the group about it.

This was the creation of a new reality. In spite of having been in therapy for many years, this boy, whom the father had seen crying quietly in the closet, could be normal. The job at hand was not to cure any arcane mental illness but to get this teenager back to a normal situation. I understood the crying in the closet as a manifestation of the boy's unhappiness and isolation. I also saw it as a potentially powerful communication to his father: "Treat me special, after the tough life you have given me." Either way, the focus needed to be on transforming the system and then watching to see if the boy remained so sad.

FATHER: I only know what I did, and you'd probably not approve of it that much.

FISHMAN: How do other kids live their lives?

FATHER: Dirty room, go to public schools . . .

SALLY: They go to public school. They take care of themselves until their mothers get home.

TEACHER: They go to school, and they go to regular classes.

FISHMAN: Can he go to regular school?

TEACHER: Yes.

FISHMAN: I'm concerned that he's losing the socialization he gets from school, and that's dangerous. He's falling behind his peers socially, and it's hard to catch up.

FATHER: Apparently he's not fitted in here real well, but there's not a whole lot of kids his age. We were looking for him to have some problems here, for the cure. But he's done quite well, and he's doing quite well.

FISHMAN: Why don't you talk to Grandma? Does she have some ideas?
GRANDMOTHER: About what?
FISHMAN: How to normalize his life.

Again, to enhance the family's sense that they could handle the problem, I asked the father to get a consultation, right in the room, from the grandmother.

GRANDMOTHER: He's had several stepmothers who gave him instructions for his life. I think he should go back to school and be with kids his own age and shouldn't be so protected. He should learn to cross the street and not just stay on the same block.
FISHMAN: Does your ex-son-in-law agree with you?
FATHER: Well, I think he's overprotected.
FISHMAN: The danger is, if he's treated special, not like any other kid, he doesn't grow up like any other kid. Why don't you talk together, all of you, about how you can normalize his life? If you treat him normally, chances are you'll have a normal kid. Make some decisions on how you can act today, and the teacher can advise you what the single most important thing is in his life. (*Leaves the room, as does the hospital therapist.*)

During the discussion that followed, the teacher supported Vincent's return to school, expressing her faith in him and her belief that he could do much better. I recognized her as a cotherapist who could help to normalize the boy. As a teacher, she had a powerful position in the parents' eyes. Not only was she an educated person but she was also someone who knew their son in a different context and was therefore aware of facets of his character that were out of their purview. Her views carried a considerable weight with the parents—in fact, more weight than the therapists'. We hardly knew the boy, and we certainly hadn't seen him in school. The hospital staff had also seen Vincent in a different context, but that context could not be generalized to the boy's future, as the school context could.

FATHER: Would you like to go back to Boone School?
TEACHER: You have to make your schedule. This is your big chance. What do you think?

Vincent shook his head, indicating he didn't know. His eyes had begun to well up, and he wiped his eyes and mouth. He was clearly having an emotional reaction to this session.

GRANDMOTHER: Shouldn't he be put in mainstream classes, like everybody else?
FATHER: (*To teacher*) That's what you said when we first went over there.

Clearly, the father and the teacher had had a similar discussion in the past. I wondered whether the teacher's words had been drowned out by all the other professionals in the family's world.

TEACHER: The normal situation would be for Vincent to talk with the teacher about what he wants and not for the whole family to tell you what you want, Vincent, but for you to give some input. You have to pick your schedule; you know what's going on in school, you know my class, you know me. Would you rather try regular classes?

Later in the session, after the system had discussed Vincent's options, especially his going back to school, the therapist and I stepped back into the room. I continued to pursue the theme of normality, searching for strengths and for the positives.

TEACHER: One teacher caught Vincent shoving in the hall one day, and when he was doing it again the next day they were looking out to see if he was doing it, but Vincent was so good in the classes . . .
FISHMAN: Are you saying that he is smarter in class?

Obviously by asking if he was "smarter in class," I was implying that the pushing was just not very smart behavior. With this challenge, Vincent sat up straighter in his chair and became more attentive and less restless.

TEACHER: Oh, yeah, he participated and he was given great reviews.
FISHMAN: What's happening is that he's losing the opportunity of really shining in front of his peers and in front of his teacher. (To father) Are you a man of your word? Do you want to have a normal boy?
FATHER: You bet.
FISHMAN: Can he start school tomorrow?

This was the creation of the crisis. I was focusing on the immediacy of the need to return to normality. This session would be considerably more powerful if, at its end, there would be a decision for Vincent to be in school the next morning. The teacher, my cotherapist, helped.

TEACHER: He can start Monday, if we can get the paperwork done today.
FISHMAN: Can you push it? We don't want to lose any momentum here.
TEACHER: Well, I can certainly try. I think we can get this together by Monday.
FISHMAN: But don't do it for us. It's if the parents want it.
FATHER: If that's what we need to do.
FISHMAN: You've got to treat the kid as normal.
FATHER: I agree with Vincent's attitude that he's got a tough life and stuff. I

feel that I'm fairly normal, and my life was no picnic growing up. And my parents stayed together. I would've probably been a lot better off if they'd split up, and that's the truth. Be a lot better off.

FISHMAN: Will Sally support you?

FATHER: (*Turns to his wife, who nods yes.*) No matter what happens, we decided that we're going to stay together. We've had these discussions, and she's had some thought about it. It's not such a good deal, you know, having the problems that we're having. (*To Vincent*) You want to be normal, don't you?

GRANDMOTHER: Do you want to go to school tomorrow? (*Vincent shakes his head no.*) Why not? We're trusting you. They say they never trust you in public school.

TEACHER: You say it's too early?

VINCENT: (*Nods yes.*) I don't want to rush it.

FISHMAN: Is this always the case—you let him make the decisions?

FATHER: I don't think he made the decision to go to the boys' home.

The suggestion that Vincent should go back to school right away had ushered in the current crisis. An isomorphic pattern was emerging in which Vincent expected to be different and to be treated as different. After all his talk about normal and having people trust him, he now *declined* to go back to school. Of course he didn't want to go back; it was too comfortable for him in the hospital, too easy. Just as his father gave him special treatment because of the painful circumstances in his young life, so the hospital was treating him specially. He was being treated as a patient, not as a normal, confident person.

The teacher had provided the direction for the therapy, with her encouragement of Vincent's returning to class as soon as possible. It was now important to help the school—represented by the teacher—recognize that the family system could be the stalwart context that would be needed to transform the boy's educational experience. The family itself would have to change, to break the isomorphic pattern of treating Vincent as special.

FISHMAN: If you want a normal kid, treat him normal. (*To Sally*) Are we hearing that this has hurt your marriage?

SALLY: It has.

FISHMAN: How threatened is your marriage?

SALLY: I think we're over the hill.

FISHMAN: I guess it's taken some pressure off since he's been in the hospital.

SALLY: It's been a lot nicer at home lately because he's been in the hospital.

FISHMAN: So why don't you talk together about what you should have

done, how to treat him, how to get him to be normal by treating him
normally?

SALLY: I don't really know what to do.

FATHER: He can go back to school, and we'll treat him normal.

SALLY: What do you think, Vincent?

VINCENT: (*Shakes his head.*) I don't know.

FATHER: I guess one of the main problems is figuring out what's normal
and what's not normal. I'm from the old school. Personally, to me, the
hat is not normal. [Vincent was wearing his baseball hat turned around
so the visor was at the back.]

VINCENT: Does that bother you?

FATHER: It makes you stand out in the crowd.

FISHMAN: Is this what happens? You guys start to make a decision, and
before you know it, you're talking about something else? You were
making a decision to determine how to return him to a normal life, and
you're talking about the hat.

FATHER: To me—what I'm trying to express is—it's abnormal, but not to
her.

SALLY: What's normal?

One difficulty for the parents was that they frequently got lost in the
forest and spent more time looking at the trees. Their problem stemmed,
in part, from an ignorance of child development and normal adolescent
development, which could be addressed later. The result, however, was
that there seemed to be no hierarchy of concerns. The children were confused as the parents meandered hopelessly from priorities to peripherals.

Vincent returned to school and did well. The teacher made it her business to see that he maintained his good behavior there. She proved to be
an essential part of the therapy, functioning as de facto cotherapist and
moving the system along, which, as I commented previously, was also
split. In a sense, she herself was empowering the family to wrest more
control over Vincent's education. The parents became more involved in
helping the boy in school, and—as part of the process, I believe—they
themselves changed. Follow-up 18 months later revealed that Vincent had
graduated and gone off to college, and the parental marriage had been significantly strengthened.

Conclusion

Including the school context can be invaluable for the therapist in transforming the total system. Just as we saw in the eating-disorders example

that the work place can provide a significant and appropriate system for intervention to change the entire system, so too can school serve as a powerful context toward total transformation.

One tenet of this book is that the family of today is changing drastically because its infrastructure, like the infrastructure of society at large, is, in many ways, eroding. One symptom of the profound change in the institution of the school is the decreasing tax dollars available to many schools, especially in poorer districts. Today's therapists need to be aware of the eroding infrastructures and of the increasing pressure that schools and school personnel are under. For example, one big city school I work with has 2,900 students in a building designed for 2,000 as mentioned in the introduction. According to one administrator, there is an almost conscious effort to get students to leave school. Another fact, which may or may not be related: in a recent semester at that school 2,000 students got at least one *F*.

Our work with schools is more important than ever, and perhaps more sensitive now, when budgets and, frequently, tempers are already stretched to the limits. As the economy is rapidly changing and there are fewer jobs for the undereducated, success in school becomes all the more essential.

CHAPTER 10

The Hospital Context

THE PRACTICE of psychiatric hospitalization is based on the disease model of medical illness; like patients with tuberculosis, people with psychiatric problems are sequestered from their social contexts. Such isolation cannot possibly meet the needs of the psychiatric patient for change in the social context. Yet the American system of mental care continues to uphold two conflicting paradigms: the medical model, which treats the problem within the patient only, and the contextual therapy (or social psychiatry) model, which mandates that services address the broader social context—the maintainers of the mental symptoms. These opposing views lead to much of the interdisciplinary conflict and subsequent dysfunctional service that characterize the field.

Even in the case of schizophrenic symptomatology, which is often associated with biological substrate damage, there is strong evidence that the expression of symptoms is sensitive to the context. Research by Christine Vaughn and Julian Leff (1976) indicated that high levels of expressed emotion in families correlated with the exacerbation of schizophrenic symptomatology. More recently, the work of Gerard Hogarty, Carol Anderson, Douglas Reiss, and their colleagues (1986) and Ian Falloon, Jeffrey Boyd, and Christine McGill (1984) demonstrated that psychoeducation and family therapy—changing the way the family treats the patient—can positively affect the expression of symptoms. No rest cure, nor even a social milieu cure among strangers, will significantly change the stress the patient was experiencing upon hospitalization. A basic question emerges:

When the underlying problem is an inappropriate fit between the patient and his or her context, can any mode of therapy based on isolating the patient from the family and the broader system be conducive to restoring patterns of positive social interaction with the outside world?

In an atmosphere of isolation and freedom from all responsibility, everything invites the patient to continue playing the role of a mentally ill person (Elizur & Minuchin 1989). The family is often left without authority or responsibility as nurses, doctors, social workers, and hospital staff assume the parental role in the eyes of the patient (Bradshaw & Burton, 1976). At the same time, the hospital communicates to the family that the responsibility for healing the patient is no longer theirs. They are supposed to wait, ready to resume their functions when the hospital has completed its work. As Joel Elizur and Salvador Minuchin (1989) point out, however, the discharged patient returns to a different social organization, since the family and other social systems may have reorganized without the missing member.

Once a patient has been labeled, the societal reaction solidifies the diagnosis, and all behavior is defined within the confines of that diagnosis (Elizur & Minuchin, 1989). Labels tend to confine the patient to a diagnosis without regard to the social context—or even to his or her behavior within the hospital. In a well-known study titled "On Being Sane in Insane Places" (Rosenhan, 1973), eight researchers gained admission to 12 hospitals by claiming to hear voices. Even though they behaved normally when they were admitted, all but one were labeled schizophrenics, and their histories were distorted by staff to fit that diagnosis.

Elizur and Minuchin (1989) describe the changes in the relations among the patient, the family, and the society that occur when a patient is "initiated" into hospitalization: "Once initiated, patients are enveloped by a total institution that seeks to indoctrinate its inmates with the ideology of mental illness and to rewrite their life scripts" (p. 113). Supports are suddenly removed, and the new inpatient may lose accustomed rights or privileges. As the patient adapts to the rules of the new hospital environment, he or she may lose social skills as well. The family may respond with alienation and withdrawal. Many hospitals do not foster family involvement in treatment, nor are they interested in true systemic transformation. Moreover, the very act of hospitalization can weaken the family's urgency for change. To use a term that Carl Whittaker (personal communication, 1981) is fond of, the family has "detumesced."

Many factors in a medical setting may prevent the family from participating in the treatment. The medical model, as we have seen, disempowers the family and absolves it of responsibility. The hospital staff may differ with the family therapist in identifying the locus of the problem as in the patient rather than in the social context (Polak, 1970) or in expecting to ameliorate only the patient's illness rather than the broader context (Shapiro, 1980).

In truth, families and institutions such as hospitals need each other; they are interdependent. Anyone who works in a hospital knows that an alliance between the family and the hospital is clearly related to a more effective outcome. Yet even though coordination is essential, a true collaboration between the two systems seldom occurs.

Early pivotal work on hospitals and family therapy was done at the Colorado Psychiatric Hospital in the late 1960s. In a project described by Donald Langsley and David Kaplan (1968), 150 patients evaluated in the emergency room as in need of immediate hospitalization were randomly divided into two groups. The 75 patients in the experimental group were given family crisis therapy instead of being hospitalized, while the 75 in the control group were admitted to the hospital. The experimental group received an average of 4.2 office sessions, 1.6 home visits, 4.5 telephone calls, and 1.3 contacts with other social agencies, over an average of 22.7 days. The patients in the control group were hospitalized for an average of 26.1 days. While 14 of the 75 experimental patients were subsequently hospitalized at some point during the next 6 months, the 6-month follow-up showed that over 80 percent of the experimentals had never been hospitalized, whereas 100 percent of the controls were admitted initially, and 21 percent were readmitted during the first 6 months after treatment.

These figures demonstrate that hospitalization is not essential for stabilizing individuals in crisis. Equally important, results showed that the families of the subjects in family therapy fared better than those of the hospital subjects, both in gaining the insights and advantages of family therapy and in avoiding the ill effects of hospitalizing a family member, including the economic pressures and the social disapprobation.

Clearly, there are times when hospitalization is necessary. The key issue is safety. In the emergency room, I organize as many family members as possible and pose the all-important question: "Can you keep this person safe?" If the answer is yes, I ask in detail what they will do. Who will be responsible? Who will support the family members?

The family may say, "Yes, but we need a break. We are exhausted." This can be a compelling argument, but it begs the question. It suggests that the family's own support system is depleted, and the real issue is how to shore up their resources, not whether to hospitalize the family member. At such times, other relatives or friends may be able to lend support by taking the family member for a short time while the immediate family works on bolstering its resources. Occasionally a short-term placement or an alternative living situation, arranged through social service, may be needed.

If the patient cannot be kept safe, hospitalization may be the best solution. There is no place for heroics. But other justifications sometimes offered for hospitalization are short-sighted. In the case of eating disorders, for example, psychiatric hospitalization is not the answer. A patient who has a severe eating disorder and is medically in danger should be in a medical hospital. If the patient is not in danger, some form of outpatient treatment will be more effective, because it will deal with the patient in vivo.

There is one other type of system dysfunction that may call for some form of institutionalization, which may include hospitalization. In cases of delinquent behavior where the family's way of dealing with the problem is to shield the child from the consequences, keeping the youngster in the community may amount to bailing him out and indulging him. If the family's protection only reinforces the child's grandiosity and tacitly grants him permission to take advantage of the world, then the therapist must work to change that pattern. The responsible approach may be to help the family stand aside and let the child come face to face with the demands for drug detoxification, for example, and the judicial and other consequences of his behavior, even to the point of institutionalization.

General Principles

The job of the therapist working at the interfaces of systems is to sense what would be the more productive scenario. In one case, it may be to hospitalize the patient; in another, it may be to send the patient home or to some other noninstitutional setting. If hospitalization is inevitable (and it sometimes is), several principles can be applied to minimize the deleterious effects.

Utilize the hospital as a safe, positive place for short-term therapy. When extremely tumultuous and dangerous situations make hospitalization necessary, the IST therapist can make positive use of the personnel and facilities of the institution to begin the work of transforming the family system. The therapist and the hospital become partners in stabilizing the system, as the hospital provides a refuge for the patient and a respite for the family, and for the therapist, a bit of breathing space in which treatment can be planned and initiated at a predictable pace. The therapist's position is that the hospitalization is no more than a stopgap measure, a brief period for regrouping the therapeutic forces.

Family members should be actively involved from the moment the patient is hospitalized. For example, if there is a need for a suicide watch, I always attempt to get the hospital to allow the family members to provide the security coverage. This step in itself tends to create systemic change. Moreover, it provides safer coverage; I would rather trust a caring family than an impersonal bureaucracy to keep a loved member safe. Of course, the therapist must be vigilant and not turn the sheep over to the wolves, as in a case of sexual abuse. The patient must not be robbed of the chance to extricate himself or herself from a bad situation.

The question arises, naturally, of the hospital's willingness to go along with the IST therapist's approach. Ideally, hospitals will initiate it as standard procedure. Most professionals working outside of the institution, however, will first have to get the assent of the decision makers to consult on their own patients and then work to win over the hospital staff. It may be necessary to involve a hospital psychiatrist as the contact person.

In one case, an anorexic 13-year-old girl was extremely frail medically. Through a pediatric colleague, I arranged to have her hospitalized in a children's hospital so that she could have close medical monitoring. Within this safe context, I had the parents present at every meal, to feed the girl if it were necessary (it rarely was). The family's presence was so essential to the amelioration of her symptoms that when one parent sent an employee in his stead, the child lost weight that day. When both parents were present, she consistently gained. But the nurses were very uncomfortable with the arrangement. They were accustomed to taking an active role in the treatment of such children, using feeding tubes or parenteral nutrition. At one point there was a revolt, and I had to meet with the entire hospital nursing staff to explain the treatment. The lesson was clear: The hospital staff must be involved intensively in treatment plans from the very beginning.

Just as in outpatient therapy, it is useful to establish the "hit list" (described in chapter 4) of members of the patient's system who can be recruited and incorporated into the treatment process. Upon admission, or even prior to admission, the new, enlarged system can be encouraged to be involved while the patient is in the hospital. Indeed, the threat of hospitalization can be a powerful force in mobilizing the significant members of the prospective patient's context.

The first session with IST is really a discharge planning session. The therapist, the patient, and the family system contract with the hospital staff clearly definable discharge parameters. These parameters must be observable and must be agreed upon by all the participants.

Once the situation is stabilized, the steps for transforming the family system, described in chapter 4, can begin. The comprehensive system, including key subsystems, is assessed for isomorphic patterns and homeostatic maintaining forces, and a crisis is induced that will help to catapult the family toward change. The hospital, with its support staff and its potential for separating family members if necessary, provides a safe locale for the playing out of the crisis.

The safety factor is doubly important in the case of suicidal patients. Obviously, suicidal patients must be kept from self-harm. But what has often made them suicidal in the first place is the extreme rigidity in the family system. In a system that has such a high threshold for change that it takes an act of desperation to communicate the need for change, it will be necessary to create a great deal of intensity to break down the homeostatic mechanisms.

Reorganize the patient's home context to ensure viability in the "real" world. The hospital can be an invaluable context for reorganizing the system to which the patient will return. From the moment of hospitalization, the period of internment should be used to create a new system. As we have seen, the significant people in the patient's life should be brought together in the hospital setting to agree on what has to change in order for the patient to be discharged and how they will be involved in that change. These decisions imply an agreement on how each participant will be involved when the patient goes home. By the time of discharge, a new system should at least have been initiated, so that the patient "hits the ground running." Changes that have been practiced in the hospital will then have a better chance of continuing at home.

In addition to addressing the homeostatic maintaining forces and isomorphic patterns in the external context, the clinician can use the authority of the institution to mobilize support for the family, so that the patient returns to a context that is richer in social resources than the one he or she left. In the case of 12-year-old Edward, the hospital provided important assistance in recontextualizing a family greatly in need of social support.

CASE EXAMPLE: EDWARD

Edward was a shy, intelligent, sensitive boy who had had a psychotic break. His great-grandparents had raised him since he was 8, when his mother had left him (he never knew his father). His great-grandmother had died the year before, and he was now solely in the custody of his great-grandfather, Martin.

Over the last few months, the boy had increasingly isolated himself from his family and friends. He believed that people were ridiculing him, and he felt that his great-grandfather could not protect him from the ridicule. He began to rant and rave at home to the extent that Martin could not contain him and had had to call the police. Eventually the boy felt so out of control that he ran to the old man saying, "I need help," and was hospitalized. I saw the family as part of a consultation at the hospital.

Fortunately, everything in this hospital was supportive of IST. In particular, there was a social worker from another unit of the hospital who knew that Edward's psychotic reaction was related to his great-grandmother's death from cancer. She clearly valued the boy and volunteered to attend the session, where she immediately allied with me as cotherapist.

It quickly became clear that a central isomorphic problem for this pair was their isolation. Other members of the family had backed off when Edward began to act out. Many of Martin's former friends had died or moved away, and their present neighbors had failed to come forward to help. The two had had counseling at the school and at a local guidance center, but Martin felt that the counselors were not supportive, that they had dismissed him as a doting grandparent who would only spoil the child. Martin had recently begun seeing a woman friend but considered marriage out of the question because Edward would not like it.

The goal in this case clearly was to create a new social system for this isolated old man and young boy and to minimize the iatrogenic social paralysis that can follow from inpatient psychiatric hospitalization. If we could diminish their isolation, we would reduce the stress that was contributing significantly to the boy's symptoms. Ruth, the hospital social worker, became my ally in intervening to reconnect the boy and his great-grandfather to their own peer resources and not let the hospital system capture them. During the consultation, she helped them to consider the various possible resources in the community and to persuade both Martin and Edward to involve them in the therapy.

The 85-year-old great-grandfather was a frail, hunched man who wore a plaid flannel shirt. He had a stubby white beard and was surprisingly spry. As the session proceeded, he sat leaning forward, since his hearing had deteriorated markedly over the last year. His great-grandson was a slight boy who looked young for his age. During the session, they made frequent eye contact, constantly monitoring each other's feelings. My sense of them is that they were two people who had learned to cling to each other for survival after the great-grandmother's death but that this very clinging led to the exclusion of the outside world and thus to their problems.

FISHMAN: (*To Martin*) Are you willing to do pretty much what you can for this boy?

MARTIN: Yes.

FISHMAN: Okay, it looks like it. One thing that would help him—if there are difficulties with him on the unit, would you be willing to come in and bring people in to help?

MARTIN: Bring who?

FISHMAN: Whoever you think is necessary—whoever you think you can get to help.

MARTIN: How do you mean "help"?

FISHMAN: I mean to help control him.

SOCIAL WORKER: Edward does really well with one-to-one attention, and sometimes he requires that, and it sounds like he's built up some good memories having other people involved. He kind of likes to talk about family and those meanings, and I think that's why Dr. Fishman's asking would you be willing to get some other people involved.

MARTIN: I don't know who—I mean, my sister Belle is too far away. Anyway, I can do it alone, but . . .

FISHMAN: Well, no, you've got a neighbor, you've got a daughter.

MARTIN: Neighbor, yeah, well, daughter . . .

FISHMAN: You've got a pastor.

MARTIN: I tried to get him; he's involved. He hasn't been out here since Edward's been here.

FISHMAN: You've got your lady friend.

MARTIN: They wouldn't be able to get along.

FISHMAN: Don't be so sure; don't be so sure. At least give her a chance. It's kind of tough on you to be caught between the two—that's not fair. You know, just like you've got to let him grow up, Edward's got to let you grow up now.

EDWARD: Well, I think that you should, like, see all your friends you have, like the one that lived real close to us, that talked to us. Well, all your friends are gone now. That's 'cause you outlive most of them. But I think you need to get some new friends. You need to go out and look for new friends.

Following the consultation, the social worker continued to work with the great-grandfather, arranging for him to bring people from the community to sessions at the hospital. She helped him to reconsider some of the people he had dismissed and to pay attention to their advice; perhaps he *had* spoiled Edward. All the participants in the therapy—Edward, Martin, the hospital personnel, and the outside forces—agreed that what needed to happen was for Edward to reenter the mainstream as quickly as possible. To accomplish this goal, it was necessary to provide a social context to support this enmeshed dyad. The hospital allowed Ruth, the social worker, license to assist this family, which was not part of her professional caseload, and she greatly facilitated the process of linking Edward and his great-grandfather to the outside.

Ruth is a superb social worker. She works within the system as well as at its boundaries. If there were others like her in the system, hospitalization would be needed less often. In this case, if IST had been available at the point of crisis, Edward might not have had to be hospitalized at all. An IST therapist would have convened the entire system: any family available (maybe even a wayward biological parent), his teacher, any friends, the pastor, Martin's woman friend. The very act of convocation would have addressed the most pernicious isomorphic patterns in the system—the isolation.

Indeed, the hospitalization, for all its positive aspects, contributed isomorphically to the isolation. A psychiatric hospital is not a naturalistic situation for a family. What was created in the hospital was a frail structure; a more stable structure might have been ensured if the great-grandfather's daughter had said, "Why don't you both come and live with me for a while, and we'll all figure out how we can help *our* boy."

Always attempt to re-empower the family. Hospitalization is a profoundly political act. At presentation in the emergency room, a number of decisions must be made not only on the basis of the patient's well-being but also in terms of the institution's medical and legal responsibility and vulnerability. In that atmosphere, empowering the family system can become a more difficult task for the therapist. A large and intimidating bureaucracy can mute even the most assertive families.

Throughout the hospitalization, the therapist must work to keep the hospital from displacing the family. From both sides of the hospital door, there are always forces at work that must be countered to keep the responsibility for the patient where it belongs—with the family. To the exhausted family, the hospital offers relief from the overwhelming stress that had preceded the hospitalization. Family members are often all too willing to agree to an unspoken treaty: The institution will take them off the hook and take over responsibility for the patient, if they will be nice and compliant and go along with with whatever the institution wants to do. When that happens, the therapist must drive a wedge between the institution and the family and help the family to understand that their member is still their responsibility.

The family can also be disempowered by another kind of alliance, this time between the patient and the institution. Such a development occurred in the case of Michelle, described in chapter 2. This youngster had learned how to manipulate the hospital personnel and, in particular, had established a close alliance with a young male staff member. The parents began to be treated coldly by some of the staff and even eyed suspiciously, as though they were guilty of some untoward acts toward their daughter. And as the girl's influence in the hospital grew, she had less and less regard for the authority of her parents.

It is the job of the therapist to break such treaties and to work to bar the experts from encroaching upon the family. Such work does not always win friends among hospital staff and administration. Even the most sympathetic worker has self-interest and institutional loyalties. The decision to hospitalize a patient can have implications for the institution as well as for the patient. In the case of Edward, for example, it was decided in the consultation that the boy would be released from the hospital and returned home. I walked out of the session to find two staff members in tears; Edward was to have been their first patient in a new treatment program.

It is sometimes necessary to work against the institution in order to keep or restore power in the hands of the parents. The therapist may have to act aggressively and quickly to prevent a person from being removed from the family and institutionalized. Or the therapist may have to do battle to have a patient returned home. In such a case, the therapist must present a clear message to both family and institution: "The family can do better. This patient cannot grow up here or make a career in here."

Conclusion

The era of automatic hospitalization appears to be drawing to a close. Until very recently, inpatient stays were profitable for hospitals, and patients were routinely admitted for a variety of mental ills. In their efforts to keep their inpatient beds filled, psychiatric institutions were even known to extend the duration of hospital stays by intentionally putting extra pressure on patients just prior to discharge, exacerbating the patients' symptoms, and delaying their return home.

In the last few years, however, as insurance companies have reduced their reimbursements for psychiatric care, profit margins from inpatient care have turned into losses, and hospitals are looking for new sources of income and less costly alternatives, which together make up a "continuum of care" (Cooper, 1993). In many cases, inpatient stays are being replaced by a variety of less restrictive treatments, such as partial hospitalization: day or evening treatment, from which the patient returns home at night.

At first glance, such care is an obvious improvement, since patients are not sequestered on the "Magic Mountain" but are forced to deal with their real-life family relationships while receiving intensive treatment. In some situations, however, this could be a disadvantage clinically because the home environment could be extremely toxic and damaging.

The move to partial hospitalization has been motivated not by any breakthroughs in clinical assessment but by financial considerations. This treatment is thus just as acontextual for troubled patients as was the routine 28-day hospital stay. What the field of psychiatry needs is a refined diagnostic system based on relationships. Such a system, utilizing a sensitive instrument, would evaluate the patient's context, not simply the patient's reaction to the context. That evaluation would, in turn, identify for the clinician the treatment site and treatment goals most appropriate in a given case.

For example, on small scale we utilize an instrument that we designed for eating disorder patients to triage them regarding disposition: inpatient, partial hospitalization, or outpatient. This scale assesses not only the symptom—severity and chronicity—but also social factors that function as determinators of risk. These are examples: living situation—isolation represents the greatest risk; ability to recruit social support system into the therapy; and financial status—how much debt is the patient in? Other factors are intersystemic conflicts (do therapists disagree?); conflict at home; and conflict in the family or extended family. On the process level, what are the dysfunctional interactional patterns in the family? For example, is it a psychosomatic family system? With these and other factors, we rate the risk level and make a determination as to disposition. This instrument then determines the treatment goals. For example, the goal could be to work to transform the psychosomatic family patterns or help the patient recruit a larger social support system.

CHAPTER 11

The Social Service Context

O N THE WHOLE, the influence of social service agencies on families' lives is greater than that of hospitals and courts. It is not uncommon for members of families to spend many years, if not their entire adult lives, in close connection with social service agencies. While such organizations have a huge impact on certain families, this is an era when social service agencies are witnessing diminishing budgets and burgeoning caseloads. There are critical voices on all sides. Too many children are taken from their homes, only to become lost in the system. Other children are left in the home when they should have been removed. Family therapy, in spite of its expertise in assessment, seems unable to make significant strides in helping the traditional social worker.

As noted in chapter 1, many central tenets of family therapy, such as working within the broader context, are rooted in social work. Yet family therapists have become increasingly isolated from many of the problems faced by social workers. William Doherty and Sandra Burge (1987) comment that family therapy, while attempting to include much of the social context in which social services operate, has lost touch with the reality of family services in the community. Traditionally, therapy and social services tend to coexist—but not necessarily in a complementary way. The "right hand" (mental health worker) doesn't always know what the "left hand" (social worker) is doing, and so the two elements of treatment are not coordinated.

Tension exists between people with a family therapy perspective and those with a traditional social service orientation, each feeling on some level that the other is missing the essential issues. Traditional family therapists focus on solving the problem within the family, while traditional social services are often more inclined to look to an external solution—pulling a child out of a family, for example. James Whittaker (1985) reflected this split when he proposed that youth care focus not on "child saving and child rescue," a jab at the perceived social service orientation, but on supporting and helping the family. His attack is predicated on the (often erroneous) assumption that social services function acontextually and do not appreciate the systemic nature of families.

More recent criticism of social services comes from the feminist view. Kathryn McCannell (1986) holds that the conceptual barriers in psychiatric theory presented in male-oriented language create a problem for the delivery of high-level services to individuals and families. She posits that the masculine orientation emphasizes separation, autonomy, and individuation instead of relationships and connections. The underlying assumption is that greater emphasis on a more democratic relationship-based system will foster greater empowerment of families, that is, that families and agencies will foster a complementary relationship. The goal becomes mutual empowerment rather than a hierarchical organization ready to "save the poor family."

Other recent thinking also encourages a broader perspective that promotes empowerment of families. A program in Toronto called Interface (Integrated Community Resources for Family Assessment, Consultation, and Education) works with systems in transition. It helps families stay together despite stress, and provides consultations to agencies, including other treatment facilities such as schools and children's aid societies. The program, as described by Marshall Dorosh (1986), provides assessment and consultation.

Similarly, the state of New Jersey has created in troubled communities a program called Interact, in which all agencies working with a family meet and coordinate their services. The program is designed to avert the kind of problem that I encountered recently in the case of a child who was in both individual and family therapy. Paul, age 12, had an impulse disorder and mild brain damage. He had engaged in fondling behavior with his 3-year-old stepbrother and was in individual therapy, ordered by protective services, as well as in family therapy.

The goal of the family therapy was to create a hierarchy in the family and to help Paul internalize boundaries. In his individual sessions with a female therapist, he was encouraged to delve into his sexual fantasies. Clearly, the professionals were working at cross purposes. One therapist was trying to get Paul to be more organized and controlled, while the other was seeking less control. (For an adolescent boy, talking to a grown woman about his sexual fantasies requires a conscious lessening of control.) An umbrella organization is essential to pick up these clinical contradictions.

Peter Reder (1986) in England notes that difficulties arise in multiagency relationships with the family, between family members, and among the members of the professional networks. In his view, "pressures on the family and professional workers can create a locked system which prevents natural development of the family" and obstructs effective problem solving (p. 139). His answer is a broader systems approach, and these efforts have been most promising.

The institution of the family in the United States, however, is in severe disarray—even profoundly disturbed, some would say. More new programs and more *intense* programs are needed to provide long-term remedies. Clinicians need to develop programs that can work more intimately with the deep-seated dysfunctions in the family and community systems.

General Principles

Using the IST model, I have found certain principles to be extremely effective. The case example to be presented applies this model to severely troubled families—the kind that social service systems tend to handle. Like all the principles in this book, they are meant to be rules of thumb only. We must always address the specifics of the context to determine exactly how to intervene.

Identify naturalistic networks in the surrounding structures. When a family is working with a social services department, it is vital to consider the impact of other structures on the family and how it might be possible to use resources such as the school, the extended family, and significant people in the family's community to bolster the family's strength and enhance the effectiveness of the social service system. This sociological mapping is the first step in reorganizing the contexts that impinge. In medicine, a "review of systems" is an essential step in recording a patient's history and conducting a physical exam. There is a parallel in Intensive Structural Therapy, but the review is of social systems rather than of bodily organ systems. Indeed, in a case discussed later in this chapter, the community resource person who spent considerable time scanning all of the available networks was as effective as the family therapist in facilitating change.

Plan jointly with social service professionals and other agents, as needed. It is important to ascertain the thinking and the agendas of all participating professionals before including the family in a meeting. This step greatly increases the probability of establishing a coherent context among the professionals and between the professionals and the family unit. I cannot emphasize this enough. There have been times when I have had the hubris to believe that other professionals think as I do. The fact is that they are more likely to have an individual orientation, believing the problem to be firmly placed within one or another of the protagonists in the unfolding drama.

In the case of Paul, for example, there was a major conceptual gap between the family therapist and the therapist in the program for sexual-abuse perpetrators. The latter believed that the problem resided in the boy's psyche and that if he de-repressed his fantasies—that is, talked about them—his behavior would improve. The family therapist believed that transforming the boy's system would ameliorate his behavior. These were two conflicting paradigms, neither reducible into the other.

Learn about and adapt to the family's idiosyncracies. As has been emphasized throughout the book, the clinician must help support and advise the family in achieving a healthy independence and integrity. Nowhere is this principle more important than with social service agencies. As clinicians, we must support and be available to advise and challenge. The fact that the family has a different ethnic culture can sometimes intimidate the clinician and paralyze efforts at change. It is not necessary to be an expert in every culture. On the contrary, it is better to assume what Montalvo (personal communication, 1990) calls a position of "informed one down"—an open-minded stance in which the therapist learns from and respects the family's culture and beliefs, while at the same time being available to counsel the family on the basis of the therapist's expertise in development and systems.

Create a crisis within the structure of social service agencies and then work to maintain and stabilize the new, more functional structure. Just as in working with the family system itself, the clinician can challenge the assumptions of the professionals and attempt to jar the helping system to a new level. This is a difficult task; social service agencies and community alliances frequently have a momentum of their own and have endemic habits of conflict avoidance. For a consultant to try to change the procedures—to generate a different kind of alliance between systems—can be confusing, threatening, and most of all taxing to the agencies. The consultant must respect this fact and proceed respectfully. After the trouble-making crisis has wrought a more viable family structure, the clinician should help consolidate the gain by building reinforcing relationships and subsystems as needed to buttress the family. The stabilized structure is one in which the relationships are comfortable with each other, where there is an absence of stress and tension. The clinician can feel the flow in the room; people are at ease with one another. In the case of Michelle, described in chapter 2, we had the social worker present in the room. We worked to join with her, trying to understand her position and constraints. As I introduced the intervention of shunning, we worked to get her support. By the end of the session, she had become aware of how her agency was part of the problem, having been manipulated by the youngster. In addition, we had gained her cooperation, despite the fact that at the beginning of the meeting she had had a vastly different idea of what should be done.

Work hard to get in the front door and know when to leave. Some families welcome the help of the social service system; many do not. Since many of these organizations work for the state, they must first win a family's trust if they are to join and help. Winning trust is key if we are to meet today's mandate to "save the children" and preserve the family. One viable way is practiced by an organization called Home Builders, begun by Jill Kinney (personal communication, 1992) and her colleagues in Seattle. Home Builders sends a social worker to spend several hours a day with a family in their home for a period of 6 weeks. This approach has wide acceptance and has successfully demonstrated that taking the child out of the home may not be necessary in many problem situations.

Still, working with problem-ridden or resistant families requires the most delicate judgment by the family therapist: when do you give up on the family's resources and its ability to regenerate? How long must you work with the family to determine if a real potential for change exists? The wise family therapist wants to avoid the error of trying to salvage a system that is beyond repair. At times the family is so dysfunctional that a child must be removed or an adult must be institutionalized. Respectable empirical data suggest that sometimes institutions do a better job—hence the necessity for more alternatives for families in these situations. Ideally, once the child is removed, there should be continuing communication between the foster family and the biological family. This then paves the way for the family member's return.

In recent years, many families' ability to regenerate is greatly impaired by the decaying community social network. Community instability and weakness only serve to exacerbate the family's organizational difficulties, compounding the problems of both family and community at large. The weakening of the social fabric is so widespread in certain economically disadvantaged pockets that we have devised a special model to counter-act it.

A Model for
Community Structural Therapy

At the heart of almost every community is its school system. Using the school as a point of entry and contact, we have instituted a new model of family intervention in cases involving children and adolescents. The model is working already in certain portions of New Jersey. It is anchored in the School-Based Youth Services Program, a collection of 22 small social service agencies that provide services to troubled students in high schools throughout the state.

The 22 subagencies provide "one-stop shopping" for social services for children who have psychological problems or difficulties involving either in-school or after-school activities. These subagencies, for example, can even help children whose parents "run away" from home, leaving their children alone. That happened 200 times in a school district last year.

The idea began about 3 years ago when I met with social worker Roberta Knowlton director of the school-based programs. She wanted to institute family therapy into the existing programs. At first I said that I didn't think family therapy worked well with severely troubled families because it lacked the therapeutic depth to transform persistently troubled systems where both the community framework and the family system are so disorganized.

I suggested a hybrid form of therapy, in which family therapy would be augmented by the work of a different kind of practitioner, whom I have termed a community resource person (CRP). This CRP would operate like the old "block captain" of the 1960s—someone who knows all the resources in the community and is intimately connected to the pulse of both the community and the school. This is the model we are now using in New Jersey.

The CRP works in partnership with the structural family therapist. The therapist assesses the system, ascertains the homeostatic maintainer, and thus determines the contextual needs of the system. Then the therapist and the CRP together set out to recontextualize the family, the therapist working at the interior while the CRP finds new resources in the community to stabilize the transformation created in the therapy.

This project was instituted in one rural county and two urban New Jersey cities in 1991. All three counties had a high population of low-income families, many of whom were having profound difficulties with their children. For example, in one high school in one of the crumbling cities, only 46 students out of 2,500 graduated! An evaluation of the first year of the program, using a small sample of 15 random cases, indicated that the program can indeed provide valuable assistance in helping at-risk youths with problems such as substance abuse and poor academic performance (Andes, 1992). Of particular note, the study found the CRP to be of equal importance with the family therapist.

A more rigorous study is proceeding this year with a much larger sample group: a control group of 180 families and an experimental group of 180 families. This, again, is being carried on in three different settings, two urban and one rural.

Our case example comes from a school in the rural county involved in the project. The school system in this county served an area of 158 square miles.

CASE EXAMPLE: LEN

When a family is depleted, disorganized, and alienated from its external community, the therapy must extend beyond the family and introduce a caring external world to complement and support the changes within the family system. Len, a 16-year-old, was referred to family therapy after the death of his father from an accidental drug overdose. His father had had a long history of heroin use, methadone maintenance, prescription drug use, and numerous drug-related incarcerations. Len's mother was concerned about Len's irritability, lack of interest in friends, sleep disturbances, difficulty in concentrating, and severe behavioral problems at home and at school. His younger sister, Kathy, had experienced severe bouts of depression and was socially withdrawn.

Len lived with his mother, Ellen (age 38); her fiancé, Mark (age 37); Kathy (age 14); his maternal aunt, Pat (age 32); and Pat's four daughters (ages 15, 14, 11, and 6). Len's paternal grandmother was alcoholic. Both paternal grandparents lived nearby, but Len had had no relationship with them since his father's death. Len would have liked more contact with them both, but they blamed Ellen for their son's drug problems and death and so refused all contact.

The family was close to the maternal grandmother, who resided in the same town. They limited interaction with the maternal grandfather because he had been prostituting Pat's daughters. The paternal grandfather had sexually abused two of his granddaughters and was sentenced to counseling, probation, and no contact for 2 years.

Ellen, Pat, and their children have lived together on and off for several years. Although Ellen and her husband had been legally separated for many years, Ellen had allowed him to live with the family until he was committed to the state psychiatric hospital after threatening Ellen with a knife.

This family was extremely troubled. Family members seemed estranged from their community and oblivious to the most basic societal moral codes and norms. The goal was to transform existing dysfunctional structural patterns within the family and to reconnect the family to society and to positive role models. Our concept for therapy was first to address the severe structural problems within the family, including Ellen and Len's enmeshment and the conflicts between the sisters, Ellen and Pat, and then to assemble an appropriate mix of outside resources to connect with those of the family, to compensate for the family's insufficient organizing abilities and its estrangement from the community.

The CRP was involved in the therapy from the beginning. Before the first session, she and I (as supervisor) met with the therapist to generate hypotheses regarding the homeostatic maintainer and isomorphic patterns and to decide who to invite to the first session. She attended about half the weekly therapy sessions, and she and the therapist worked closely together in marshalling positive role models and other external resources to bolster the depleted family. The CRP coordinated the enormous task of building cooperation and trust with the child study team, the counseling center, the teachers, and the school-based youth services programs, and bringing together as many as nine people for a meeting. She made many linkages to recontextualize the various family members. Her work ensured that the necessary systems were activated and left the therapist free to concentrate her energies on clinical aspects.

The first session revealed that all family members catered to Len, the only male in his generation. Ellen also expected less of him educationally and behaviorally than she did of his sister Kathy, because Len had been in poor health since birth and was perceptually impaired; he had a total loss of hearing in one ear and related problems, yet he was physically stocky and strong. It was clear that Len had little responsibility. Ellen and Kathy even spoke for him. He tormented his sister and cousins at home but what little discipline he received was inconsistent. Kathy, on the other hand, was interested in music and reading and received As and Bs. Len's grades were poor.

This family was like many others, with an inappropriate closeness between the parent and the adolescent and tension between the two adults (the mother and her sister). The family structure was loose and ineffectual: Ellen and her sister Pat, who were living in the same house, were often in conflict about disciplining the children. The therapist's task was to work on the internal conflicts to firm up the hierarchy. Since Len appeared to be totally and profoundly estranged from social mores, we felt the youngster needed to be better connected to the community as we worked to change the hierarchy. Our commitment was to create positive interplay between the inside and the outside.

The entire household was present at the second session, in which we planned to further develop a parental hierarchy based on Ellen and Pat. At the session were Len, Ellen, Kathy, Pat, Pat's three older daughters, Len's teacher, and Ellen's fiancé, Mark.

Before this session, Len had been suspended from school for threatening to shoot his own teacher and some other teachers. Ten minutes into the session, he stormed out, crying and cursing at the teacher and therapist. His teacher had confronted him, and his mother was pressuring him about the consequences of such behavior, noting that Len's father had been jailed for making terrorist threats. Because the therapist supported the teacher and his mother, Len was furious. Pat tried to rescue him, as did his sister and cousins, by accepting his behavior as grief-related. The youngest cousin went out to the car to console him. Len's behavior at home was regularly dismissed the same way. Pat undermined Ellen's disciplinary attempts, and Ellen frequently capitulated to Len's manipulative apologies.

The third session included Len, Ellen, Kathy, Pat, Pat's two older daughters, and Pat's family therapist. Len was reported to have been well-behaved for the past week. The session focused on helping Ellen and Pat develop a parental alliance, in which they would apply the same rules and consequences consistently. Some proposed consequences for Len would potentially affect his sister and cousins as well.

The team observed notable progress: Ellen had defined her parental role more clearly. Using Len's interest in learning about religion, she reached him with, "You know your friend God? He said to me, 'He's the baby; you're the mommy, and the mommy makes the rules.'" Ellen had become consistent, used good judgment, and refused to ease the consequences. She initiated contact with the school's child study team and was confident enough to tell them what she wanted for Len.

Ellen used the CRP well as a resource for support in the school environment and for information that could not be found easily elsewhere. The CRP helped her to establish a collaborative relationship with the school-based youth program and was invaluable in helping her know which school administrators and teachers to approach, making it easier for the family to work with the school context. The partnership relationship between Ellen and the CRP also resulted in another authoritative relationship for Len.

During the next 6 weeks, Len still had negative impulses and trouble controlling his anger, but his isolation, sleep difficulties, and problems of concentration had been eliminated. He developed an interest in CB radio and through this hobby made new friends. Kathy and their cousins no longer complained about his teasing. In pursuing his religious studies, Len strengthened a grandparent-like relationship with an older couple at church, effectively replacing the wounded grandparental relationships.

Several steps were taken during this period to recontextualize the children. The CRP referred Len to martial arts training to help him channel his impulsive and aggressive behavior. He earned his own money for tuition, and Ellen agreed to supply transportation. The CRP also arranged for his involvement with the school baking program, which improved his socialization, gave him a skill, and guaranteed a 6-week summer job.

At the same time, the CRP introduced Kathy to a self-esteem group in which she flourished. The teenagers in the group, led by an adult, bolster each other's self-esteem, using the concept that reality is confirmation by significant others. The CRP also arranged for a volunteer position to be created for her in a nursing home. Kathy began seeing a new boyfriend and—in a significant first for her—began performing for her drama class and an outside audience at a local church.

The CRP was also effective for Pat's family. Through her intervention, one of Pat's daughters became team manager for the recreation program basketball team. Pat told the therapist and the CRP on several occasions how the girl's position on the team had boosted her daughter's self-esteem.

Although the extended family had been working better under joint parenting, Ellen and Pat's enmeshment hampered their effectiveness. They decided it would be beneficial to all if Pat's family moved into its own home. Since Ellen and Pat were both remarrying soon, they thought it would create stronger family identity if the new mother-father dyads and children could establish themselves in separate households. Len and Kathy were pleased by the decision and anticipated such family activities as home-improvement projects and a regular dinner hour with all four family members. The children began to respect Mark more because Ellen was reinforcing his new role as stepfather.

Making community linkages was critical for both families' success and feelings of growing empowerment. Without the information provided by the CRP, neither the family nor the therapist would have known about most of the programs, groups, and opportunities in which the children participated and from which they benefited. The CRP also created specific opportunities, such as the volunteer work for Kathy. She also served as a role model and buffer for Ellen in dealing with the Child Study Team until Ellen felt sufficiently confident to handle those sessions herself.

While the community resources person worked to reestablish normal, healthy community contact and connection, the therapeutic team worked to fill in the missing pieces of the hierarchy in respect to the parents and the children and the chain of authority. Through the use of dual resources, the children, as well as the family, became tethered to the community, and the family system was gradually transformed.

In a follow-up a year later, the therapist reported that the family was stabilized. The mother, who had felt free to call in daily, had not called in 7 months. Len did well in school that year—in a more restrictive classroom arranged by the CRP.

It is important to note that the community resource person is careful not to supplant the family. The goal is to open the door (through the CRP's expert knowledge and connections with the community) and then to leave the door open for the family to pursue the arrangements whenever possible. For example, in another family, the depressed and isolated mother mentioned that she would love to work in a stable, but she had no connections and felt that nothing could be done. The CRP made calls and visited a friend's daughter who was knowledgeable about horses. They drew up a list of stables to be approached. The mother then came into the office and used the agency's phone. With the encouragement of the staff, the mother—after considerable effort—was successful in getting a position. This self-directed enactment helped catapult the mother from a position of depressed passivity to one of activity. Her depression was considerably abated by the experience of finding the job and then by the actual work at the stable.

These examples underscore how important it is for the CRP to be an integral part of the community, whereas most family therapists and social service agency personnel are not. They also show that it is necessary to deal with problems at the interior of the family, because many social service agents do not. The model shows clearly that it is essential to work with the family at the interfaces. Dealing with only one dimension hampers the work of the practitioners working at either side. The virtue of our model is that it incorporates both the interior and exterior aspects of a living family system.

This method is thus useful for breaking dysfunctional isomorphs that tend to repeat in different aspects of the interacting systems. In our case example, a proper parental hierarchy was restored to the extended family by using the community therapy model to coordinate multiple systems, including the social service system, the school system through the CRP, and the more traditional family therapy framework. As noted in the first-year evaluation report, "the support of school officials, social service providers and community leaders is vital for the success of the program"

(Andes 1992, p. 25). This new, larger system was created by the CRP and incorporated old themes—social work, community organizing, and family therapy—to provide a powerful intervention in the lives of these families.

This may be seen as an extrapolation from the concept of the local mind in individual therapy to that of the nonlocal mind (Dossey, 1989): mind as immanent in contemporary context. Therapeutic intervention has the power to reorganize the nonlocal mind and thus transform the symptoms.

CHAPTER 12

Epilogue: Altruism

The smoke was pouring out of the rowhouse on Penn Street when Jonathan Buie drove by. . . . [He] ran over to the burning house, crawled into the smoke-filled living room while straining to hear a woman's cries, then headed for the porch roof. . . . [T]here was only the notion that . . . there were people who needed help. So without a second thought, Buie . . . was scrambling onto the porch roof, smashing in windows . . . and helping two people out a second-floor window. . . . "It's just that somebody needed help, and I was there to help them."
—Philadelphia Inquirer, December 31, 1992, sec. A, p. 1

AS I REVIEW the contents of this book, I find that altruism may be a common thread running through the fabric of our multiple contexts. When I use this model of therapy, I am always struck by the generosity of spirit exhibited, even by strangers. In many instances, their participation, voluntary sacrifices, and emotional bounty cannot be explained away by simple self-interest, in spite of what the skeptics might say. The very power of IST may be that it taps into this basic human goodness and caring, which creates a new, enlarged community.

In this postmodern, relativistic era, it may sound unsophisticated to talk about something so old-fashioned as altruism. Yet the more scientifically inclined have claimed that altruism is a fundamental human drive (Kohn, 1990). In our case histories, we saw abundant examples of altruism, including the school principal, the judge, the social worker, the wife whose uppermost concern is her husband's physical and emotional well-being, and others. The sacrifices made by family members for the good of other members or for the good of the family are ubiquitous. Indeed, the concept of altruism explains for me a significant amount of behavior between the people highlighted in this book. Particularly compelling for me is unrelated peoples' willingness to go out on a limb (of one sort or another) for others in the therapy process. We saw, for example, adolescents who were willing to violate the universal "fink" taboo and go to adults to inform them about the behaviors of their friends—chiefly because they were worried about them—risking ostracism by their peers in the teenage community.

Another example is the principal of the suburban middle-class school who was willing to risk his own "discomfort factor" in providing treatment for a student with elective mutism. It would have been easier for him to simply transfer the boy out of district, to a specialized school. And then there was the employer who made herself available for her employee's therapy session and, during the course of their therapy, made a conscientious commitment to a behavioral change geared to helping her colleague/friend. In that case, the entire office helped diminish their coworker's symptomatology.

We might argue that altruism is simply expanded self-interest. One tenet of this book is that we now live in different kinds of families, made up of horizontal extended kinships, in which the parties are not necessarily related by birth. Given that perspective, we could be witnessing just another form of people taking care of their families—their newly redefined families. Or perhaps, as I contend, altruism is a basic human drive.

Some authorities dispute the existence of altruism. In Richard Dawkins' (1976) book *The Selfish Gene*, he argues that an enlightened self-interest motivates taking care of the species, and so reduces altruism to a survival instinct. Dawkins sees helping behavior in terms of genetic predisposition to selfishness.

Alfie Kohn (1990), in "The Brighter Side of Human Nature," counters that. He says that although "we raise our children, manage our companies and design our governments on the assumption that people are naturally and primarily selfish and will act otherwise only if they are coerced to do so" (p. 4), he still finds ample and convincing evidence substantiating a humanistic drive toward altruism. He concludes that "it is as natural to help as it is to hurt" (p. 4).

Of course, when we social scientist types start ruminating about basic drives, we find ourselves impaled by the nature-nurture question, although there is some data to support the basic-drive hypothesis. Studies in the last dozen years suggest that of all personality traits, empathy is highly heritable. Karen Matthews, C. Daniel Batson, Joseph Horn, and Ray Rosenman (1981) found that identical twins were more similar in their response to an empathy questionnaire than were fraternal twins.

Evidence about economic self-interest also suggests that people do not seem to act primarily as profit maximizers (Kohn, 1990; Marwell, 1982). Researchers have used various methods to show that people are not primarily driven by economic and personal self-interest. The simplest way to validate this argument, Kohn says, is to ask the person performing the prosocial activity. Nancy Eisenberg-Berg and Cynthia Neal (1979) used this direct approach with subjects likely to be honest—4- and 5-year-olds. Researchers followed the children around preschool and watched for spontaneous acts of sharing and helping. When asked why they helped, the children said simply that the child they helped *needed* help.

In another study, Phillip Hallie (1979) asked the villagers of La Chambon why they agreed to hide Jews, who were complete strangers to them, from the Nazis. This was done at the risk of imperiling their own lives. They replied that they simply did what had to be done: "Well, where else could they go? I had to take them in" (p. 286). Overall, even the most unrepentant egoist would be hard-pressed to deny altruism at work in these instances.

Finally, others argue that prosocial acts are nothing more than an attempt to reduce one's own distress at seeing another person suffer. Without question, witnessing someone in pain often elicits empathy and prosocial behavior, but I think this begs the question. The very discomfort of watching others in distress is innate altruism. This profound discomfort is the very drive that the skeptics are trying to discount! Some interesting research by C. Daniel Batson and his colleagues (1988) made it easy for subjects to avoid helping and to justify why they should not help. This had little effect on the helping behavior of people who felt high empathy for subjects who needed help. If, however people could easily escape this distress without guilt, would they still help? Does genuine altruism really exist? In this and other studies, researchers have shown that people are genuinely altruistic (Batson et al., 1988; Schroeder, Dovidio, Sibicky, Matthews, & Allen, 1988).

All these data point toward prosocial motivation that cannot be explained wholly in terms of self-interest. As David Collard (1978) notes, "it is not that selfish men sometimes appear to behave unselfishly, but that unselfish men sometimes appear to behave selfishly" (p. 69). My belief is that altruism not only exists, but that it is also more often the rule than the exception. Families perform extraordinary acts of altruism in spite of backbreaking adversity, as shown in the following case segment.

CASE EXAMPLE: FATHER WITH THREE SONS

A father, who had adopted three boys, was HIV-positive but was not symptomatic. The family, previously mentioned in chapter 3, was aware that the father had the disease but nothing was spoken. At the session were the father (age 35), a thin, thoughtful-looking man with wire-rim glasses; and his two older sons, James (age 16) and Bob (age 13), both casually dressed, looking like typical petulant adolescents who were convinced that they had much better things to do with their time than be at this session. His 3-year-old son sat on his father's lap during the session.

The session was held in an examination room of a general hospital. The examination table had been pushed to the corner of the room. Doctors and nurses were busily moving about in the hallway outside. I wondered whether the setting heightened the boys' concern for their father. For the first minutes of the session, I was alone with the father.

FISHMAN: Now, Bob knows about your illness?

FATHER: No. I haven't told him because I don't think he's mature enough to handle it. But my other son, James, did mention to him about it. And the next day it was all over the school.

FISHMAN: But I guess you never openly discussed it with Bob.

FATHER: He wasn't mature enough to handle it.

FISHMAN: I think at this point you don't really have a choice.

FATHER: After I brought him to the hospital today, I know that now. But I still don't feel comfortable talking to him.

FISHMAN: The fact is, though, since he knows, if you don't tell him, he's going to blow it way out of proportion 'cause there's fantastic ignorance about this problem.

FATHER: I'll get around to it. The fact is that he knows about my medicine and he makes me take it.

FISHMAN: Seriously?

FATHER: He constantly says, "Dad, will you take your medicine?" I get upset sometimes because he keeps badgering.

FISHMAN: Why don't we invite them in and discuss how he cares for you? And what are some of their concerns. And tell them as much as you want about the disease, because this is probably something that's on his mind. *(To sons Bob and James, who have joined the session)* Your dad tells me, Bob, that you make sure he takes his medicine every day.

BOB: Yes.

FISHMAN: What do you think about that?

BOB: I just make sure he takes them every day. I'm just worried.

FISHMAN: What kind of worries do you have?

FATHER: Worried about what?

BOB: He might go on us.

FATHER: I'm worried you might go on me, too. Where am I going?

BOB: I don't know.

FATHER: What's the medication for?

BOB: I don't know.

FATHER: You don't know, that's truthful. You have no idea. What do you think I take the medication for? Son, you don't even have any thoughts; you don't know what your thoughts are.

BOB: I just make sure you take it.

FATHER: Give me a guess: What do you think I take the medicine for?

BOB: You're sick.

FATHER: Sick how?

BOB: Like you said, you throw up.

FATHER: When do you see me doing that?

BOB: Your stomach . . . when you don't eat, you get dehydrated, I guess.

FATHER: I said that one time. That was seven years ago.

FATHER: (*To James*) You probably know, but what do you think I take the medicine for?

JAMES: I forget.

FATHER: You didn't go to the doctor's with me? What did the doctor say—that I was HIV-positive.

JAMES: Yeah.

FATHER: What's that? What did I tell you?

JAMES: You told me you were going to take the medicine and you'd be all right.

FATHER: What did I say was wrong? I said I had the AIDS virus, you don't remember that?

Some time later, we talked about how the boys might ease his burden.

FISHMAN: Have you thought about how the boys can help you? (*To boys*) Have you thought about that? (*To father*) How can the boys help you? You help them a lot, right?

BOB: I know how I can help. I can help him take his medicine.

FATHER: I can do that on my own. That's not one of the ways you can help me. I think you can help relieve some of the stress by doing some of the things you're supposed to do. But you do things bad in school; it adds a lot of stress and anger to me. The biggest way you can help me and help yourself is in school.

In a later session, the discussion turned to the concerns and fear the boys felt about their father's illness.

FISHMAN: Bob, do you keep your eyes on your dad? In the corner of your eyes, you try to see how he's doing? When he's asleep or taking a nap, do you listen to see if he's still breathing?

BOB: One time I did that. (*To father*) I stayed home from school, tried to call your name but you wouldn't answer. I went in there and shook you and shook you, and you wouldn't turn over or nuthin'. And you didn't say anything till the last minute; then you got up.

FATHER: Yes, he does keep his eye on me. Bob doesn't even want me to sleep. 'Cause it's like if I'm trying to sleep, Bob will walk up and down the steps, do anything to keep me awake, to stop me from sleeping.

FISHMAN: Bob, do you think if you keep your dad awake, you keep him alive? Ever think of that?

BOB AND JAMES: Not really. (*James nods his head yes, as he says "Not really."*)

FISHMAN: (*To James*) Because you worry about him a lot. What do you think? You have a sad smile on your face, I can't tell.

JAMES: (*After a long silence*) Remember that time you came home sick? I was telling Bob that we gotta stop bothering Dad and do good, otherwise we'll make it worse; we just gotta keep quiet. (*As James says this, Bob closely watches his dad's reaction and stands vigilant over him.*)

On this childish, magical level, I believe we see altruism. It is paradoxical and subtle, but it is real. The son was intentionally attempting to keep his father awake—to keep him alive.

This family lived under extremely difficult socioeconomic conditions. The father was raising three boys on little income, in a poor section of Philadelphia, and there was the extra expense of child care. In many ways, they were disadvantaged; yet we see the love coming through, in the form of true caring—not just survivorship, where the child takes care of the parent for fear of losing the parent, but trying to save the parent out of pure love. Ironically, there's an element of self-sacrifice present, even in their capacity for acting out and getting into trouble.

The younger boy thought that if the father stayed awake, he stayed alive. (After all, if he sleeps he can die, but you can't die with your eyes open). This 13-year-old's logic motivated him to sacrifice himself (he got into trouble for the behavior) to keep his father moving.

Most of us were taught that the basic human drives are procreation, aggression, and curiosity. As clinicians, we need to be strongly aware of the other powerful drive—altruism—and to tap into the altruistic part of people we work with, to create a stronger community of support. I want to make clear that by *altruism* I do not mean a Pollyannaish insouciance. There are times when altruism means making difficult decisions, such as encouraging a family to call the police on a wayward child or saying no to a family and referring them elsewhere if the circumstances call for it. One of the most difficult manifestations of altruism occurs when clinicians create therapeutic crises in the system. It is much easier and more comfortable to join with the system to diffuse the conflict; the gift is to grab our seats and help the crisis unfold.

Altruism represents a true challenge and an opportunity for our field. And here is the challenge. By sensing and respecting the family's strength and underlying motivation, which in many situations is altruistic, we can enhance that strength. The human repertoire for positive behavior is remarkable and well documented; we need simply to recognize it and use it to everyone's advantage.

I conclude with a story that I heard first in Israel. It is a tale with many versions, spanning many cultures and races; even Tolstoy had a version.

A person dies and is given the opportunity to visit both Heaven and Hell. When he enters Hell, he sees a very strange sight. Food is everywhere, yet the residents appear to be starving. Walking up to the devil, the visitor asks, "Why, with so much food everywhere, is everyone starving?"

The devil replies, "The people have no elbows. We cannot eat."

The person then visits Heaven. The situation is similar: Food is plentiful, and the people have no elbows. But there is one striking difference—the people are well fed. The visitor queries an angel: "Why is it that in Hell the people have no elbows and they are starving, but in Heaven, even though the situation is the same, the people are robustly well fed?"

The angel looks the visitor directly in the eye and says, "We feed one another."

Perhaps we can strive to reach this level. We family therapists seem to spend much of our own time mopping up situations, heading off crises, or buffering their impact. Our challenge is to learn to enhance our therapy by working with systems to tap this fine side of human nature, altruism. Mastering this, therapists would be more powerful healers—helping people and their systems to reach a new level of complexity; to emotionally repair, heal, and feed each other; and to enrich and reinvent their systems.

References

ACKERMAN, N. (1958). *Psychodynamics of Family life: Diagnosis and treatment of family relationships.* New York: Basic Books.

ACKERMAN, N. (1962). Adolescent problems: A symptom of family disorder. *Family Process, 1*(2), 202–213.

ANDES, F. (1992). *Evaluation report of family therapy substance abuse program.* Prepared for School-Based Youth Services Program, New Jersey Department of Human Services, Trenton.

ANDREWS, G., TENNANT, C., HEWSON, D. M., & VAILLANT, G. E. (1978). Life event stress, social support, coping style, and risk of psychological impairment. *Journal of Nervous and Mental Disease, 166*(5), 307–316.

APONTE, H. (1976). The family-school interview: An eco-structural approach. *Family Process, 15,* 303–311.

BANK, S., & KAHN, M. D. (1982). *The sibling bond.* New York: Basic Books.

BARTLETT, D. L., & STEELE, J. B. (1992). *America: What went wrong?* Kansas City: Andrews & McMeel.

BATESON, G. (1972). *Steps to an ecology of mind.* New York: Ballantine.

BATESON, G., JACKSON, D., HALEY, J., & WEAKLAND, J. (1956). Toward a theory of schizophrenia. *Behavioral Science, 1*(4), 251–264.

BATSON, C. D., DYCK, J. L., BRANDT, J. R., BATSON, J. G., POWELL, A. L., McMASTER, M. R., & GRIFFITT, C. (1988). Five studies testing two new egoistic alternatives to the empathy-altruism hypothesis. *Journal of Personality and Social Psychology,. 55*(1), 52–77.

BERGER, P. L., & LUCKMANN, T. (1966). *The social construction of reality: A treatise in the sociology of knowledge.* New York: Doubleday.

BOGDAN, J. L. (1984). Family organization as an ecology of ideas: An alternative to the reification of family systems. *Family Process, 23*(3), 375–388.

BRADSHAW, S., & BURTON, P. (1976). Naming: A measure of relationships in a ward milieu. *Bulletin of the Menninger Clinic, 40*(6), 665–670.

BRODEY, W. M. (1968). *Changing the family.* New York: Clarkson M. Potter.

CANNON, W. (1932). *The wisdom of the body.* New York: Norton.

CARTER, E. A., & McGOLDRICK, M. (1980). The family life cycle and family therapy: An overview. In E. A. Carter & M. McGoldrick (Eds.), *The family life cycle: A framework for family therapy* (pp. 3–20). New York: Gardner Press.

CASTANEDA, C. (1968). *The teachings of Don Juan: A Yaqui way of knowledge.* New York: Washington Square Press.

Children's Defense Fund Staff. (1989). *A vision for America's future: An agenda for the 1990s.* Washington, D.C.: Author.

COLLARD, D. (1978). *Altruism and economy: A study in non-selfish economics.* New York: Oxford University Press.

COLLIER, J. L. (1991). *The rise of selfishness in America.* New York: Oxford University Press.

Committee for Economic Development. (1987). *Work and change: Labor market adjustment policies in a competitive world.* New York: Author.

COMPHER, J. V. (1989). *Family-centered practice: The interactional dance beyond the family system.* New York: Human Sciences Press.

COOPER, H. (1993, March 16). Cost controls impel psychiatric hospitals to establish more outpatient programs. *Wall Street Journal,* p.B1.

COWEN, E. L., PEDERSON, A., BABIGIAN, H., IZZO, L. D., & TROST, M. A. (1973). Long-term follow-up of early detected vulnerable children. *Journal of Consulting and Clinical Psychology, 41*(3), 438–446.

DAWKINS, R. (1976). *The selfish gene.* New York: Oxford University Press.

DELL, P. (1982). Beyond homeostasis toward a concept of coherence. *Family Process, 21,* 21–41.

DOHERTY, W. J., & BURGE, S. K. (1987). Attending to the context of family treatment: Pitfalls and prospects. *Journal of Marital and Family Therapy, 13*(1), 37–47.

DOROSH, M. (1986). Thistletown interface programme. *Ontario Psychologist, 18*(4), 8–9.

DOSSEY, L. (1989). *Recovering the soul: A scientific and spiritual search.* New York: Bantam.

EBERT, B. (1978). Homeostasis. *Family Therapy, 5*(2), 171–175.

EISENBERG-BERG, N., & NEAL, C. (1979). Children's moral reasoning about their own spontaneous prosocial behavior. *Developmental Psychology, 15*(2), 228–229.

ELIZUR, J., & MINUCHIN, S. (1989). *Institutionalizing madness: Families, therapy, and society.* New York: Basic Books.

ENO, M. (1985). Sibling relationships in families of divorce. *Journal of Psychotherapy and the Family, 1*(3), 139–156.

ERIKSON, E. (1950). *Childhood and society.* New York: Norton.

FALLOON, I., BOYD, J., & McGILL, C. (1984). *Family care of schizophrenia: A problem-solving approach to the treatment of the mentally ill.* New York: Guilford Press.

FISHMAN, H. C. (1988). *Treating troubled adolescents.* New York: Basic Books.

FRIEDMAN, D. E. (1987). Work vs. family: War of the worlds. *Personnel Administrator, 32*(8), 36–39.

GERMAIN, C. B., & GITTERMAN, A. (1980). *The life model of social work practice.* New York: Columbia University Press.

GLANSDORFF, P., & PRIGOGINE, I. (1971). *Thermodynamic theory of structure, stability and fluctuations.* New York: Wiley.

GOLDNER, V. (1985). Feminism and family therapy. *Family Process, 24*, 31–47.

HABER, R. (1987). Friends in family therapy: Use of a neglected resource. *Family Process, 26*, 269–281.

HABER, R. (1990). Family and social network members as lay consultants. *Journal of Strategic and Systemic Therapies, 9*(1), 21–31.

HALEY, J. (1962). Family experiments: A new type of experimentation. *Family Process, 1*(2), 265–293.

HALEY, J. (1973). *Uncommon therapy: The psychiatric techniques of Milton H. Erickson.* New York: Norton.

HALLIE, P. (1979). *Lest innocent blood be shed.* New York: Harper & Row.

HANDY, C. (1989). *The age of unreason.* Boston: Harvard Business School Press.

HARTUP, W. W. (1983). Peer relations. In P. H. Mussen (Ed.), *Handbook of child psychology* (Vol. IV, edited by E. Mavis Hetherington) (pp. 103–196). New York: Wiley.

HOCHHAUS, C., & SOUSA, F. (1987–1988). Why children belong to gangs: A comparison of expectations and reality. *Los Angeles Unified School District High School Journal, 71*(2), 74–77.

HOFFMAN, L. (1980). The family life cycle and discontinuous change. In E. Carter & M. McGoldrick (Eds.), *The family life cycle: A framework for family therapy* (pp. 53–68). New York: Gardner Press.

HOGARTY, G. E., ANDERSON, C. M., REISS, D. J., KORNBLITH, S., GREENWALD, D., JAVNA, C. B., & MADONIA, M. J. (1986). Family psychoeducation, social skills training, and maintenance chemotherapy in the after-care treatment of schizophrenia. *Archives of General Psychiatry, 43*, 633–642.

HOLMES, T., & RAHE, R. (1967). The social readjustment rating scale. *Journal of Psychosomatic Research, 11*, 213–218.

ILGEN, D. R. (1990). Health issues at work: Opportunities for industrial/organizational psychology. *American Psychologist, 45*, 252–261.

IMBER-BLACK, E. (1990). Multiple embedded systems. In M. F. Mirkin (Ed.), *The social and political contexts of family therapy* (pp. 3–18). Boston: Allyn & Bacon.

JACKSON, D. (1957). The question of family homeostasis. *The Psychiatric Quarterly Supplement, 31*, (Part 1), 79–90.

JACKSON, D. (1965). The study of the family. *Family Process, 4*(1), 1–20.

JACKSON, D. (1967). The individual and the larger contexts. *Family Process, 6*(2), 139–154.

JAMES, K., & MCINTYRE, D. (1983). The reproduction of families: The social role of family therapy? *Journal of Marital and Family Therapy, 9*(2), 119–129.

JOHNSON, D. W. (1980). Constructive peer relationships, social development, and cooperative learning experiences: Implications for the prevention of drug abuse. *Journal of Drug Education, 10*(1), 7–23.

JOHNSTON, J. C., & ZEMITZSCH, A. (1988). Intervention beyond the classroom. *Behavioral Disorders, 14*(1), 69–79.

JONES, M. (1987). Having friends and influencing people: Family approaches to peer problems in children and adolescents. *Australian and New Zealand Journal of Family Therapy, 8*(3), 131–136.

KAHN, M. D. (1988). Intense sibling relationships: A self-psychological view. In M. D. Kahn & K. G. Lewis (Eds.), *Siblings in therapy: Life span and clinical issues* (pp. 3–24). New York: Norton.

KANDEL, D. B., & LESSER, G. S. (1972). *Youth in two worlds*. San Francisco: Jossey-Bass.

KEITA, G. P., & JONES, J. M. (1990). Reducing adverse reaction to stress in the workplace: Psychology's expanding role. *American Psychologist, 45*(10), 1137–1141.

KOHN, A. (1990). *The brighter side of human nature*. New York: Basic Books.

LANGSLEY, D. G., & KAPLAN, D. M. (1968). *The treatment of families in crisis*. New York: Grune & Stratton.

LEVI, L. (1990). Occupational stress: Spice of life or kiss of death. *American Psychologist, 45*(10), 1142–1145.

LEVINSON, D. J., ET AL. (1978). *Seasons of a man's life*. New York: Ballantine.

LEWIS, K. G. (1988). Young siblings in brief therapy. In J. D. Kahn & K. G. Lewis (Eds.), *Siblings in therapy: Life span and clinical issues* (pp. 93–114). New York: Norton.

LUOV, R. (1990). *Childhood's future*. Boston: Houghton Mifflin.

LUSTERMAN, D. E. (1985). An ecosystemic approach to family school problems. *American Journal of Family Therapy, 13*(1), 22–30.

MACKINNON, L. K., & MILLER, D. (1987). The new epistemology and the Milan approach: Feminist and sociopolitical considerations. *Journal of Marital and Family Therapy, 13*(2), 139–155.

MAGID, R. Y. (1986). When mothers and fathers work: How employers can help their personnel. *Personnel, 63*(12), 50–56.

MARWELL, G. (1982). Altruism and the problem of collective action. In V. J. Derlega & J. Grzelak (Eds.), *Cooperation and helping behavior: Theories and research* (pp. 207–226). New York: Academic Press.

MATTHEWS, K. A., BATSON, C. D., HORN, J., & ROSENMAN, R. H. (1981). "Principles in his nature which interest him in the fortune of others. . . . The heritability of empathic concern for others." *Journal of Personality, 49*(3), 237–247.

McCANNELL, K. (1986). Family politics, family policy, and family practice: a feminist perspective. *Canadian Journal of Community Mental Health, 5*(2), 61–71.

McGREGOR, R., RITCHIE, D., & SERRANO, A. (1964). *Multiple impact therapy*. New York: Grune & Stratton.

McGUIRE, D. E., MANGHI, E. R., & TOLAN, P. H. (1990). *The family school system: The critical focus for structural/strategic therapy with school behavior problems*. New York: Haworth Press.

McGUIRE, D. E., & TOLAN, P. (1988). Clinical interventions with large family systems: Balancing interests through siblings. In M. D. KAHN & K. G. LEWIS (Eds.), *Siblings in therapy: Life span and clinical issues* (pp. 115–134). New York: Norton.

MEAD, G. H. (1934). In E. W. Morris (Ed.), *Mind, self and society: From the standpoint of a social behaviorist.* Chicago: University of Chicago Press.

MILLER, N. E. (1983). Behavioral medicine: Symbiosis between laboratory and clinic. *Annual Review of Psychology, 34,* 1–31.

MINUCHIN, S. (1974). *Families and family therapy.* Cambridge, Mass.: Harvard University Press.

MINUCHIN, S., & FISHMAN, H. C. (1979). The psychosomatic family in child psychiatry. *Journal of the American Academy of Child Psychiatry, 18,* 76–90.

MINUCHIN, S., & FISHMAN, H. C. (1981). *Family therapy techniques.* Cambridge, Mass.: Harvard University Press.

MINUCHIN, S., ROSMAN, B., & BAKER, L. (1978). *Psychosomatic families: Anorexia nervosa in context.* Cambridge, Mass.: Harvard University Press.

MONTALVO, B. (1986). Family strengths: obstacles and facilitators. In M. A. Karpel (Ed.), *Family resources: The hidden partner in family therapy* (pp. 93–115). New York: Guilford Press.

MONTALVO, B., & GUTIERREZ, M. (1983). A perspective for the use of the cultural dimension in family therapy. In J. C. Hansen & C. J. Falicov (Eds.), *Cultural perspectives in family therapy* (pp. 15–32). Rockville, Md.: Aspen Systems Corp.

MORTIMER, J. T., LORENCE, J., & KUMKA, D. S. (1986). *Work, family, and personality: Transition to adulthood.* Norwood, N.J.: Ablex.

NICHOLS, W. C. (1986). Sibling subsystem therapy in family system reorganization. *Journal of Divorce, 9*(3), 13–31.

OETTING, E. R., & BEAUVAIS, F. (1986, September). Peer cluster theory: Drugs and the adolescent. *Journal of Counseling and Development, 65,* 17–22.

ORBACH, S. (1978). *Fat is a feminist issue: A self-help guide for compulsive eaters.* New York: Berkley Books.

PARKER, S. R. (1967). Industry and the family. In S. R. Parker, R. K. Brown, J. Child, & M. A. Smith (Eds.), *The sociology of industry* (pp. 42–53). London: Allen & Unwin.

PFOUTS, J. (1976). The sibling relationship: A forgotten dimension. *Social Work, 21*(3), 200–204.

PIAGET, J. (1950). *The psychology of intelligence.* New York: Harcourt, Brace & Co.

PIOTRKOWSKI, C. S. (1978). *Work and the family system: A naturalistic study of working-class and lower-middle class families.* New York: Free Press.

POLAK, P. (1970). Patterns of discord: goals of patients, therapists and community members. *Archives of General Psychiatry, 23*(3), 277–283.

POOL, I. de S. (1973). Communications systems. In I. de S. Pool, F. W. Frey, W. Schramm, N. Maccoby, & E. B. Parker (Eds.), *Handbook of communication* (pp. 3–26). Chicago: Rand MCNALLY.

POWER, T. J., & BARTHOLOMEW, K. L. (1987). Family school relationship patterns: An ecological assessment. *School Psychology Review, 16*(4), 498–512.

230   *References*

POZNANSKI, E. (1969). Psychiatric difficulties in siblings of handicapped children. *Clinical Pediatrics, 8*(4), 232–234.

QUINN, W. H. (1991). Review of *Family-centered practice: The interactional dance beyond the family system,* by J. V. COMPHER. *Journal of Marital and Family Therapy, 17,* 203.

RANIERI, R. F., & PRATT, T. C. (1978). Sibling therapy. *Social Work, 23*(5), 418–419.

RAPOPORT, R., & RAPOPORT, R. (1966). Work and family in contemporary society. *American Sociological Review, 30,* 381–394.

REDER, P. (1986). Multi-agency family systems. *Journal of Family Therapy, 8*(2), 139–152.

ROFF, M., SELLS, S., & GOLEN, M. (1972). *Social adjustment and personality development in children.* Minneapolis: University of Minnesota Press.

ROSENBERG, E. B. (1982). Therapy with siblings in reorganizing families. *International Journal of Family Therapy, 2*(3), 139–150.

ROSENHAN, D. L. (1973). On being sane in insane places. *Science, 179*(19), 250–258.

ROSENTHAL, R., & JACOBSON, L. (1968). *Pygmalion in the classroom: Teacher expectation and pupils' intellectual development.* New York: Holt, Rinehart & Winston.

SATIR, V. (1967). *Conjoint family therapy: A guide to theory and technique* (rev. ed.). Palo Alto, Calif.: Science and Behavior Books.

SCHIBUK, M. (1989). Treating the sibling subsystem: An adjunct of divorce therapy. *American Journal of Orthopsychiatry, 59*(2), 226–237.

SCHOR, J. B. (1991). *The overworked American: The unexpected decline of leisure.* New York: Basic Books.

SCHROEDER, D. A., DOVIDIO, J. F., SIBICKY, M. E., MATTHEWS, L. L., & ALLEN, J. L. (1988). Empathic concern and helping behavior: egoism or altruism? *Journal of Experimental Social Psychology, 24,* 333–353.

SCHWARTZMAN, J. (1985). Macrosystemic approaches to family therapy: An overview. In J. Schwartzman (Ed.), *Families and other systems: The macrosystemic context of family therapy* (pp. 1–24). New York: Guilford Press.

SELIGMAN, M. (1988). Psychotherapy with siblings of disabled children. In M. D. Kahn & K. G. Lewis (Eds.), *Siblings in therapy: Life span and clinical issues* (pp. 167–189). New York: Norton.

SHAPIRO, J. (1980). Changing dysfunctional relationships between family and hospital. *Journal of Operational Psychiatry, 11*(1), 18–26.

SLUZKI, C. (1985). Foreword to J. Schwartzmann (Ed.), *Families and other systems: The macrosystemic context of family therapy.* New York: Guilford Press.

SPECK, R. V., & ATTNEAVE, C. L. (1973). *Family networks.* New York: Pantheon Books.

SPEER, D. C. (1970). Family systems: Morphostasis and morphogenesis, or "Is homeostasis enough?" *Family Process, 9,* 259–278.

STAINES, G. L. (1980). Spillover versus compensation: A review of the literature on the relationship between work and non-work. *Human Relations, 33,* 111–129.

STEIN, H. D. (1960). The concept of the social environment in social work practice. In H. J. Parad & R. R. Miller (Eds.), *Ego-oriented casework: Problems and perspectives, Papers from the Smith College School for Social Work* (Vol. XXX[3], pp. 65–88). New York: Family Service Association of America.

SULLIVAN, H. S. (1953). *The interpersonal theory of psychiatry.* New York: Norton.

TAGGART, M. (1985). The feminist critique in epistemological perspective: Questions of context in family therapy. *Journal of Marital and Family Therapy, 11*(2), 113–126.

TUCKER, B. Z., & DYSON, E. (1976). The family and the school: Utilizing human resources to promote learning. *Family Process, 15*(1), 125–141.

VAUGHN, C., & LEFF, J. (1976). The influence of family and social factors on the course of psychiatric illness. *British Journal of Psychiatry, 129,* 125–137.

VIGIL, J. D. (1988). Group processes and street identity: Adolescent Chicano gang members. *Ethos, 16*(4), 421–445.

WHITTAKER, J. (1985). Family matters: An emergent agenda for youth care practice. *Journal of Child Care, 2*(4), 11–26.

WOODCOCK, A., & DAVIS, M. (1978). *Catastrophe theory.* New York: Avon.

WYNNE, L. (1988). Editor's comments. In L. Wynne (Ed.), *The state of the art in family therapy research: Controversies and recommendations* (pp. 267–280). New York: Family Process Press.

YOUNISS, J., & SMOLLAR, J. (1985). *Adolescent relations with mothers, fathers, and friends.* Chicago: University of Chicago Press.

ZEDECK, S., & MOSIER, K. L. (1990). Work in the family and employing organization. *American Psychologist, 45*(2), 240–251.

ZEEMAN, E. C. (1976, April). Catastrophe theory. *Scientific American,* pp. 65–82.

Index

AA (Alcoholics Anonymous), 90
Abandonment, 52
Ackerman, Nathan, 1, 14, 15
AIDS, 70, 113, 219
Alcohol abuse, 154; and Alcoholics
  Anonymous, 90; and Billy (case
  study), 151–54; and Chuck (case
  study), 122–32, 137; and Melissa
  (case study), 84; and Tony (case
  study), 20, 21, 160, 161–68
Allen, Woody, 138
Altruism, 81, 132, 217–23
Anderson, Carol, 194
Andy (case study), 168
Anima, 23
Animus, 23
Anorexia. *See* Eating disorders
Archetypes, 23
Arlene (case study), 152, 153
Assessment, 33–34; and developmen-
  tal pressures, 33–36, 37–38, 46; of
  family history, 33–34, 38–41, 46; of
  family structure, 33–34, 36–38; and
  the five-step model of treatment

(IST), 80–82; and the 4-D model
(IST), 33–56, 128; and generating
  goals and planning treatment,
  80–81; and identifying the homeostatic maintainer, 41–42; and identifying transactional patterns,
  42–56; and isomorphic patterns,
  33, 39, 46, 48, 51, 52, 56–59, 62, 63,
  64, 69, 70, 74; of processes in the
  family system, 33–34, 40-41; and
  rigidity, 43, 44, 70; and the school
  context, 181–82; and the "science"
  of hunchiology, 65–70, 80, 82
Attneave, Carolyn, 6, 27
Autonomy: and assessing structure in
  the family, 37; loss of, and cotherapists, 82; and overprotectiveness,
  44; and rigid families, 43

Bank, Stephen, 105, 106
Bartholomew, Karlotta L., 178
Basic-drive hypothesis, 218
Bateson, Gregory, 15, 43
Batson, C. Daniel, 218, 219

"Best interest" concept, 160
Beth (case study), 108–16, 120–22, 137
Betsy (case study), 91–92
Bible, 105
Big Sister programs, 85
Bilaterality, 19
Billy (case study), 151–54
Biology, 23
Blame allocation, 73–74
Bob (case study), 70–73, 219–23
Body, 23, 39
Bonnie (case study), 29–31, 89
Boundaries, 43, 156–57, 206–7; and
    eating disorders, 135; loss of, and
    cotherapists, 81–82; and the school
    context, 178, 182–83; and the work
    context, 139, 142, 148, 149, 150,
    151, 152, 153
Boyd, Jeffrey, 194
"Brighter Side of Human Nature"
    (article), 218
Bulemia. *See* Eating disorders
Burge, Sandra, 205

Cain (biblical figure), 105
Cannon, Walter, 23–24
Carter, Elizabeth, 35
Case study participants: Arlene, 152,
    153; Beth, 108–16, 120–22, 137;
    Betsy, 91–92; Billy, 151–54; Bob,
    70–73, 219-23; Bonnie, 29–31, 89;
    Chuck, 122–32, 137; Darryl, 85–86;
    Debbie, 160, 168–76; Dorothy,
    16–18, 43; Edward, 199–203; Ellen,
    211–14; George, 37–38, 145–50;
    Heather, 59–64; James, 70–73,
    219–23; Jason, 93–104; Jim, 82–83;
    Joe, 87; Joshua, 59–64; Joy, 161–68;
    Joyce, 134-37; Kate, 78, 109–10,
    113, 120–22; Kathy, 134–37,
    211–14; Keith, 151–52; Lauren,
    108–14; Len, 211–16; Lillith, 7–9;
    Linda, 168; Luis, 9–10, 175; Marcia,
    151–54; Mark, 211–14; Martin,
    199–203; Mary Lou, 65–70, 79;
    Melissa, 83–85; Michelle, 18, 44–56,
    202, 209; Neils, 7-9; in the Olson
    family, 86–87; Pat, 211-14; Paul,
    206–7, 208; Paula, 82–83, 142-45;
    Ralph, 59–64; Ray, 70–73; Ruth,
    200, 201–2; Sally, 185, 186, 188,
    191–92; Sam, 70–73; Seth, 122–23,
    126–27, 129, 131–32; Tiffany,
    45–47, 55, 56; Tony, 20, 21, 160,
    161–68; Vincent, 184–92
Casteneda, Carlos, 171
Catastrophe theory, 28–29
Causality, linear, 80
Child abuse, 159. *See also* Sexual
    abuse
Child custody, 159
Children's Defense Fund, 2
Child Study Team, 214
Chinese language, 27
Choice, 40, 73–74
Chomsky, Noam, 23
Chuck (case study), 122–32, 137
Claustrophobia, 128
Closeness, cultural patterns of, 22
Cognitive development, phases of, 34
Collard, David, 219
College attendance, 118
Collier, James L., 4
Colorado Psychiatric Hospital, 196
Commitment, 157
Compher, John Victor, 5
Complementaries, absence of, 80, 98
Confidence, 141, 145
Confidentiality, 82, 164, 178
Confirmation, 141–42, 182
Conflict avoidance, 21, 44, 57; and
    eating disorders, 135, 145, 154;
    identifying patterns of, 42–43; and
    the legal context, 164, 166; and the
    social service context, 208; and the
    work context, 145, 151–52
Consensus, value of, 157
Corporations, as "shamrock" organi-
    zations, 3
Cotherapists, 81, 106; and peer

groups, 118–19, 132–33; and the school context, 190; and sibling relationships, 116; and the work context, 145
Creativity, 22
Crisis induction, 23; basic description of, 13–14, 27–32; and catastrophe theory, 28–29; and the Missouri factor, 32; as "unbalancing," 88–89
CRPs (community resource persons), 210–16

Darryl (case study), 85–86
Dawkins, Richard, 218
Debbie (case study), 160, 168–76
Dell, Paul, 25
Department of Social Services, 45
Depression, 89, 211, 214; and Melissa (case study), 83–85; and Paula (case study), 82–83, 142–45
Developmental pressures, assessment of, 33–36, 37–38, 46
Diagnosis, 22, 195, 204. *See also* Assessment
Diffusion, 44, 156–57
Disabled children, 106, 107
Distance, emotional, 37, 131, 147
Divorce, 2, 86–87; and developmental pressures, 35, 37–38; and peer groups, 118; and sibling relationships, 105, 106, 108–16
Doherty, William, 205
Dorosh, Marshall, 206
Dorothy (case study), 16–18, 43
Drug abuse, 58, 118, 197, 211; and Beth (case study), 108–16, 120–22, 137; and Darryl (case study), 85–86; and the five-step model of treatment, 78, 85–86; and George (case study), 37–38, 145–50; and Tony (case study), 20, 21, 160, 161–68
Duchamp, Marcel, 34
Dyson, E., 182

EAPs (employee assistance programs), 140, 141
Earthquakes, 28
Eating disorders, 192–93, 197, 198; and Bonnie (case study), 29–31, 89; and conflict avoidance, 135, 145, 154; and the contemporary context, basic concept of, 16–18; and Dorothy (case study), 16-18, 43; and establishing and maintaining a new organization, 90–92; and the five-step model of treatment, 76, 88, 90-92; and Joyce and Kathy (case study), 134–37; and martial arts, 91–92; and Paula (case study), 82–83, 142–45; and recontextualization, 90–91
Ecological perspective, 16, 177
Edward (case study), 199–203
Eisenberg-Berg, Nancy, 218
Elective mutism, 27, 93–104, 218
Elizur, Joel, 195
Ellen (case study), 211–14
Emergency rooms, 196–97, 202
Emerson, Ralph Waldo, 13
Empathy, 39, 218, 219
Empowerment, 17, 27, 45, 49; and eating disorders, 135; and ending therapy, 104; and establishing and maintaining a new system, 101, 103; and feminism, 91; and the hospital context, 195–96, 202–3; and peer groups, 129, 135; and the recruitment process, 77, 95; and the school context, 180, 192; and the social service context, 206, 214
Energy deficit (interface pattern), 140
Enmeshment, 212, 214; and assessment, 43, 44, 57; and ending therapy, 93; and the work context, 143, 145, 147
Eno, Mary, 105
Entropy, 26
Epistemology, 25
Erikson, Erik, 34–35

Ethics, 79, 108. *See also* Morality
Exclusionary rules, "tight," 5

Falloon, Ian, 194
Family: developmental pressures on,
    assessment of, 33–36, 37–38, 46;
    history, assessment of, 33–34,
    38–41, 46; processes in, assessment
    of, 33–34, 40–41; structure, assess-
    ment of, 33–34, 36–38. *See also*
    Nuclear family; Psychosomatic
    family systems; Siblings
Feminism, 5, 91, 92
Fighting, styles of, 133
Fishman, Loren M., 32
Five-step model of treatment (IST),
    11; and addressing the dysfunc-
    tional patterns, 87–89, 98–100; and
    ending therapy, 92–93, 103–4; and
    establishing and maintaining a
    new organization, 89–92, 100–103;
    and gathering the members of the
    system, 76-79, 94–95; and generat-
    ing goals and planning treatment,
    79–87, 95–98; tracking a sample
    case through, 93–104; and triangu-
    lation, 76–77, 79, 86, 87
Freud, Sigmund, 103
Friends, "toxic," 78–79. *See also* Peers

Gangs, 118, 179
Genesis (Bible), 105
George (case study), 37–38, 145–50
Germain, Carel, 16
Gitterman, Alex, 16
Glansdorff, P., 35
Grandiosity, 82
Guilt, 52, 106–7, 186
Gutierrez, Manuel, 22, 153, 154

Haber, Russell, 117, 118
Haley, Jay, 15, 19, 24, 35
Hallie, Phillip, 219
Handicapped children, 106, 107

Handy, Charles, 3, 10
Health insurance, 203
Heather (case study), 59–64
History, family, assessment of, 33–34,
    38-41, 46
"Hit lists," 78
HIV-positive patients, 70, 113, 219
Hogarty, Gerard, 194
Holmes, Thomas, 39
Home Builders, 209
Homeostasis, 11, 14, 75, 199; basic
    description of, 23–27; and catastro-
    phe theory, 28–29; in the human
    body, 23–24; as a value-free term,
    25–26. *See also* Homeostatic main-
    tainer
Homeostatic maintainer, 11, 33,
    41–42, 46, 51, 52; and addressing
    dysfunctional patterns, overview
    of, 87–88; ascertaining, by report,
    70–73; as a basic concept, 13; and
    blame allocation, 73–74; and com-
    munity structural therapy, 210,
    212; and generating goals and
    planning treatment, 82, 83, 84, 85,
    86–88, 98; identification of,
    overview of, 57–74; and the legal
    context, 160, 168; and peer groups,
    137, 129; and personal choice,
    73–74; perturbing the system to
    draw out, 57, 58–64; and the
    school context, 185; and sibling
    relationships, 113; and using
    "hunchiology" to expand the sys-
    tem, 65–70; and the work context,
    145, 146. *See also* Homeostasis
Horn, Joseph, 218
Hospital context, 143, 150, 158,
    184–85, 194–204; and assessment,
    39; and Billy (case study), 151; and
    discharge parameters, 198–99;
    general principles regarding,
    197–99; and the medical model,
    194, 195–96; and Michelle (case
    study), 45, 51, 52, 56; and reorga-

nizing the patient's home context, 199; as a safe, positive place for short-term therapy, 197–99

Hunchiology, "science" of, 65–70, 80, 82

Identity: and joblessness, 153–54; and peer groups, 118; and the work context, 138, 141–42. *See also* Self

Intensive Structural Therapy (IST): basic description of, 6, 13–32; and the five-step model of treatment; and the 4-D model, 33–56, 128; and working with the contemporary context, overview of, 14–23. *See also* Five-step model of treatment (IST)

Imaging procedures, 77, 95

Impulse disorders, 206–7

Incomes, 2, 3

Induction process, 22

"Informed one-down" meetings, 76

Insurance, health, 203

Intelligence tests, 181

Interact (social program), 206

Interface (social program), 206

Interface patterns, 140

Isomorphic patterns, 11; and assessment, 33, 39, 46, 48, 51, 52, 56–59, 62, 63, 64, 69, 70, 74; basic description of, 13, 19–23; and counterisomorphs, 98; and generating goals and planning treatment, 83, 84, 85–86, 87, 97, 98; and the homeostatic maintainer, 57–59, 62, 63, 64, 69, 70, 74; and the hospital context, 199, 200, 202; and the legal context, 156, 167, 168; and peer groups, 128, 129; and the school context, 191; and the social service context, 212; and the work context, 140, 141, 145, 147, 151–52, 153, 154, 155

Isolation, 194, 195, 200, 204

Jackson, Don, 1, 15, 24

James (case study), 70–73, 219–23

Jason (case study), 93–104

Jews, 90, 219

Jim (case study), 82–83

Joblessness, 153–54

Joe (case study), 87

Johnston, J. C., 182

"Joining" techniques, 76

Jones, Margaret, 117, 118

Joshua (case study), 59–64

Joy (case study), 161–68

Joyce (case study), 134–37

Judaism, 90, 219

Judicial system. *See also* Legal context

Jung, Carl, 23

Kahn, Michael, 105, 106

Kaplan, Daniel M., 15

Kaplan, David, 196

Kate (case study), 78, 109–10, 113, 120–22

Kathy (case study), 134–37, 211–14

Keith (case study), 151–52

Kinney, Jill, 209

Knowlton, Roberta, 210

Kohn, Alfie, 218

La Chambon (village), 219

Langsley, Donald G., 15, 196

Lauren (case study), 108–14

Lévi-Strauss, Claude, 23

Leff, Julian, 194

Legal context, 11, 156–76; and the "best interest" concept, 160; and broadening the focus to include the family context, 159–60; general principles regarding, 158–60; and winning over "hanging judges," 158–59

Leibniz, B., 28

Len (case study), 211–16

Levi, Lennart, 139

Lewis, Karen G., 108

Lillith (case study), 7–9

Linda (case study), 168

Love, 142, 222
Luis (case study), 9–10, 175
Lunch sessions, 29–30
Luov, Richard, 2

McCannell, Kathryn, 206
McGill, Christine, 194
McGoldrick, Monica, 35
MacGregor, Robert, 6
Marcia (case study), 151–54
Mark (case study), 211–14
Martial arts, 91–92, 214
Martin (case study), 199–203
Mary Lou (case study), 65–70, 79
Mathematics, 10, 28, 34
Matthews, Karen, 218
Maturana, Humberto, 142
Mead, George Herbert, 14
Melissa (case study), 83–85
Mellaril, 94
Memory problems, 39
Mensa, 84
Michelle (case study), 18, 44–56, 202, 209
Miller, Neal, 140
Mind-body split, 39
Minuchin, Salvador, 14–15, 21, 43, 123, 195
Missouri Factor, 32
Moiré patterns, 35
Montalvo, Braulio, 6, 22, 76, 153, 154, 208
Morality, 4; and deep structures of the self, 175; and peer groups, 118
Mosier, Kathleen, 139
Motivational groundwork, 157
Mourning rituals, 90
Multiple personality disorder, 16
Mutism, elective, 27, 93–104, 218

Narcissism, 4, 168
Nature-nurture question, 218
Nazis, 219
Negative carryover (interface pattern), 140

Neil, Cynthia, 218
Neils (case study), 7–9
Network therapy, 6
New Jersey, 206, 210
Newton, Isaac, 28
New York, 2
Nichols, William, 105, 108
Normality, notion of, 22
Nuclear family: and assessment, 33, 37; and establishing and maintaining a new organization, 89–90; and homeostasis, 25; and isomorphic patterns, 19; and sex roles, 5
Nurturance, 79–80

Oaktree School experiment, 181
Objectivity, 11
Olson family (case study), 86–87
Overprotectiveness, 21, 22, 57, 69; basic description of, 43–44; and Darryl (case study), 85–86; and the five-step model of treatment, 85–86, 98; and Michelle (case study), 52

Paradigms, 1, 19, 178, 194, 208
Paranoia, 62
Pat (case study), 211–14
Paul (case study), 206–7, 208
Paula (case study), 82–83, 142–45
Peers, 117–37; of adults, general principles regarding, 132–34; of children, general principles regarding, 117–20; as cotherapists, 118–19; and different styles of friendship, 133–34; "good" and "bad," 120, 133; parents of, recruitment of, 119–20
Personas, 141
Pfouts, Jane, 105
Philadelphia (Pennsylvania), 160, 217
Philadelphia Inquirer, 217
Piaget, Jean, 34
Piotrkowski, Chaya, 139, 140
Pittsburgh (Pennsylvania), 2

Planning treatment, 79–87, 95–98
Positive carryover (interface pattern), 140
Post-traumatic stress disorder, 16
Pottash, Robert, 31
Power, Thomas, 178
"Power of the third," 76–77, 119
Poznanski, Elva, 106
Pratt, Theodore, 105
Prigogine, Ilya, 35
Priority Management Company, 2
Processes, family system, assessment of, 33–34, 40–41
Psychosis, 199–203
Psychosocial development, stages of, 34–35
Psychosomatic family systems, 16–18; and the hospital context, 204; and transactional patterns, identification of, 43, 44; and the work context, 155
Puerto Rico, 6

Rahe, Richard, 39
Ralph (case study), 59–64
Ranieri, Ralph, 105
Rapoport, Rhona, 140
Rapoport, Robert, 140
Ray (case study), 70–73
Reason, ability to, 34
Recontextualization, 9, 199; basic description of, 18; and community structural therapy, 210; and ending therapy, 93; and establishing and maintaining a new organization, 90–91; and the legal context, 157–58, 174
Recruitment process, 76–79, 94–95
Reder, Peter, 207
"Reframing" concept, 175
Reiss, Douglas, 194
Rejection, fear of, 70
Religion, 90, 150, 213, 214
Research Council, 2
Responsibility, 42, 202; and the legal

context, 159, 168; and the school context, 182, 183; and working with siblings, 105, 106, 107, 115
Retardation, 181
Rigidity, 84, 85, 87, 156–57; and assessment, 43, 44, 70; and the homeostatic maintainer, 70; and peer groups, 126; and suicidal patients, 199; and the work context, 145
Ritchie, Agnes, 6
Rituals, 35, 90
Rosenberg, E., 105
Rosenman, Ray, 218
Ruth (case study), 200, 201–2

Sally (case study), 185, 186, 188, 191–92
Sam (case study), 70–73
Satir, Virginia, 1, 15, 24
Schibuk, Margaret, 116
Schizogenesis, 43
Schizophrenia: and assessing family history, 39; and isomorphic patterns, 19; and sensitivity to context, 194–95
School-Based Youth Services Program, 179, 210
School context, 2, 9–10, 47, 158, 177–93; and assuming the child is strong, 180–81; and clarifying boundaries and roles, 182–83; and determining the agenda for therapy, 180; and encouraging attitudes of shared responsibility and involvement, 182; and establishing alliances between parent and school, 183-84; and exploring parents' attitudes, 180–81; and the five-step model of treatment, 75, 93–104; general principles regarding, 180–84; and searching for conflicting loyalties and hidden agendas, 181–82; and the work context, 141

Schor, Juliet, 2
Schwartzman, John, 5
Seattle (Washington), 209
Self: and the ability to make choices, 40; and assessment, 37; -confidence, 91, 92; and the contemporary context, concept of, 14, 15–16; deep structures of, and morality, 175; diamond metaphor for, 15-16; -esteem, 85, 153–54, 214; -interest, and altruism, 218–19; and the work context, 138, 141–42. *See also* Identity
Selfish Gene, The (Dawkins), 218
Selfishness, 4, 218–29
Seligman, Milton, 106
Sensorimotor stage, 34
Serrano, Alberto, 6
Seth (case study), 122–23, 126–27, 129, 131–32
Sex roles, 5, 118
Sexual abuse, 71, 78, 175; and the hospital context, 198; and the social service context, 206–7, 208
Sexuality, 109, 132
Shivah, 90
"Shunning" intervention, 52, 55, 56
Siblings, 105–116; general principles for, 106–8; and looking at rivalries, 108; and "quasi-adult" roles, 106–7; and reestablishing parents as strong executive units, 107–8
Sluzki, Carlos, 5 Smoking, 140
Socialization, 94, 107, 118, 181
Social service context, 11, 57, 71–73, 205–16; and altruism, 217; and assessment, 45, 46, 49, 51, 53; and community structural therapy, 210–16; and the contemporary context, concept of, 16, 18; and creating a crisis and working toward more functional structures, 208-9; general principles regarding, 207–9; and the hospital context, 199–202; and identifying naturalis-

tic networks, 207; and learning about and adapting to the family's idiosyncracies, 208; and the legal context, 158, 159; and masculine orientation, 206; and planning with social service professionals and other agents, 207–8; and winning the trust of family members, 209
Space-time perspective, 11, 34
Speck, Ross, 6, 27
Stein, Herman, 16
Structure, family, assessment of, 33–34, 36–38
Suicide, 44, 83–85, 198, 199
Sullivan, Harry Stack, 14
"Sunburn crisis," 31
Sweden, 6, 156, 177

Termination, 92–93, 103–4
Theater, concept of, 168
Therapists: as "arms of social control" vs. confidential helpers, 164; paranoia on the part of, 62; subjective responses of, 41. *See also* Cotherapists
Thermotactic system, 24
Thom, René, 28
Tiffany (case study), 45–47, 55, 56
Time, space-, perspective, 11, 34
Tolstoy, Leo, 223
Tony (case study), 20, 21, 160, 161–68
Toronto (Canada), 206
"Toward a Theory of Schizophrenia" (paper), 15
"Toxic friends," 78–79
Tranquilizers, 94
Transactional patterns, identifying, 42–56
Transference, 21, 151
Treadway, David, 160
Treatment markers, 86 Triangulation, 63–64, 69; and the five-step model of treatment, 76–77, 79, 86, 87; and generating goals and planning

treatment, 83, 86, 87; and the legal context, 156; and the "power of the third," 76–77; and the school context, 179, 180; and sibling relationships, 108
Trust, 209, 212
Tuberculosis, 194
Tucker, B. Z., 182

Ulwan, Olof, 156, 177
Unbalancing tactic, 88–89
Unemployment, 153–54

Vaughn, Christine, 194
Videotaping, 77, 159
Vilayat Khan, Pir, 33
Vincent (case study), 184–92

Walter (case study), 135

Weakland, John, 15
Weddings, ritual of, 35
Whitaker, Carl, 133, 195
Whittaker, James, 206
William of Occam, 75
Women, in the work force, 2, 139
Work context, 11, 134, 138–55; and altruism, 218; different meanings of, for women and men, 139; and menial jobs and joblessness, 153–54
World War I, 10
Wynne, Lyman, 19, 25

Yeats, W. B., 1

Zedeck, Sheldon, 139
Zemitzsch, A., 182

Made in the USA
Las Vegas, NV
03 January 2024

83814310R00144